THE SECRETS OF DOCTOR JOHN DEE

Being his Alchemical, Astrological,
Qabalistic, and Rosicrucian Arcana

*Together with Symbolic Illustrations
of the Trees of the Planets*

Introduction and Commentary
by
Gordon James

HOLMES PUBLISHING GROUP

ISBN # 1-55818-317-5

Gordon James has been a student of the
Western Tradition for over thirty years and
offers lectures and classes in Alchemy
and Qabalah. To arrange a presentation
in your area, forward all inquiries to:
Mr. Gordon James
c/o Holmes Publishing Group
Postal Box 623
Edmonds WA 98020 USA

For a Complete List of Publications,
Please address:
Holmes Publishing Group
Postal Box 623
Edmonds WA 98020 USA

Contents

INTRODUCTION

While researching Dr. John Dee and Enochian Magic in the British Library in the Spring of 1979, I found *The Rosie Crucian Secrets*. The catalogue attributed this book to the Elizabethan magus. The voluminous work (more than a thousand pages) was bound in boards not contemporary with Doctor Dee and on closer examination the contents revealed a date of March 12, 1713. I did not have the time to read the whole book even with repeated visits. I made arrangements to have the entire MS. microfilmed and sent to me in the United States.

It was months before I had the MS. reproduced on paper from the microfilm. I spent several years reading portions of it, shelving it, perusing it, re-shelving it, and reading it again. My first impression remains my feeling—it was wonderfully strange!

Essentially, this hand-copied work can be divided into four main segments. The first is the main body text of *The Rosie Crucian Secrets* which investigates the Astrological, Geomantic, Qabalistic and Alchemical secrets—all processes for the unfoldment and expansion of consciousness and the confection of the Philosophers' Stone. This portion is faithfully reproduced in its entirety in modern language that delivers a clarity more desirable than the ponderous Elizabethan style of the original. The symbolic diagrams of the Trees of the Planets are reproduced in this volume. This is the first appearance for these important alchemical tools in modern times.

The second part may be considered a continuation of the first in that it has no separate chapter or separate heading. The writing continues as a new paragraph in the copied manuscript. However, this portion has been reprinted by various publishers. It contains two letters supposedly written by Dr. John Frederick Helvetius to Dr. John Dee. This is curious in that the dates do not support the events. John Dee died in 1608 while John Helvetius is reputed born in 1625, perhaps under the name Schweitzer. The events described in the letters were to have taken place in 1666-67. To add to the mystery I quote the manuscript: "To conclude these Secrets I shall here insert Dr. John Frederick Helvetius' letter to Dr. John Dee." The voice reveals that "I" to be neither Helvetius nor Dee, but perhaps that of the 1713 copyist or his employer. This leads me to suspect the entire manuscript was not homogenous. It may be the copyist, for himself or under someone's employ, merely gathered or was given various works to copy, the which, all came to be bound under one cover. All four segments appear to be by the same hand, though I do not pretend to be expert in these matters. The letters in question contain transmutations to have been performed by one Elias Artista. To those interested, the personalities of Artista and Helvetius are examined by Mr. Manly P. Hall in *Orders of the Great Work - Alchemy* where portions of the above letters are included. Both letters are reprinted in their entirety (with ever so slight variations) in John Frederick Helvetius' *Golden Calf*. It has had several publishers, the most recent being the Holmes Publishing Group, P.O.Box 623, Edmonds, WA 98020 U.S.A.

The third segment of the manuscript is titled: "*Clavis Chymicus*, or, An Explanation of Certain Chymical Hard Words, Used in Dr. Dee's Works—Alphabetically Digested." Few of the words on this list are used in The Rosie Crucian Secrets. This may have been a small dictionary that Dr. Dee composed and copied or one that was passed among certain "brethren." Those terms which do appear in this work are duly commented upon. My commentary throughout the manuscript is enclosed within { } brackets. I have chosen to omit the dictionary for two reasons. First, the often one-line explanation for the particular term is as enigmatic as the original term itself. The second reason for exclusion is that A.E. Waite appears to have attempted this very project. Some of these words with their short definitions are included in Waite's, "A Short Lexicon of Alchemy," also available through Holmes Publishing Group. Waite gathered various terms and listed what others have said concerning them from other source works and little seems to be of his own invention. Most of what others have said, especially if they were True Alchemists, is also enigmatic. This leaves the reader with the greater burden of understanding what is actually meant by the term. In any event, Dee's alleged list would require extensive commentary to be of real value.

The fourth and final segment of Harley MS. #6485 is titled "Of the Laws and Mysteries of The Rosie Crucians." This work has been reprinted several times in different languages. The attributed author or editor is Michael Maier and the usual title is *Laws of the Fraternity of the Rosie Crosse: Themis Aurea*. The first German edition appeared in 1618 and subsequent English editions are verbatim with the Harley MS. The language is straightforward. There does not seem to be a coded agenda or hidden subtext, at least, not enough to warrant any commentary with another complete edition, even though the Elizabethan style may prove a bit cumbersome for today's reader. The six Laws therein were also investigated succinctly by Dr. Paul Foster Case in *The True and Invisible Rosicrucian Order* within four pages of text. Another copy of this segment of the MS. would foster little value in terms of new knowledge or insight.

The main body of *The Rosie Crucian Secrets* is not without its reprints, at least, in parts. Portions of the MS. do appear in Thomas Vaughan's *Lumen De Lumine*. There was some commentary added by A.E. Waite in *The Collected Works Of*

Thomas Vaughan (1919). *Elharvareuna, or Rosicrucian Medicines of Metals* by John Heydon, which first appeared in 1665, contains large sections of the Harley MS. #6485 as well.

I do not have access to the vast manuscript libraries of Great Britain or the Continent. It is and would be difficult to trace down the notable authors, their works and their reputations in any period. So I cannot say, for certain, whether these authors borrowed from the original of this copy, described as Harley #6485, or this copy was made from others' efforts, or even if this truly is a copy of an original Dee manuscript. On some pages, in the upper left corner, are notes indicating: "The seventh sheet of Dr. Dee," and so on, numerically. Dee may have copied it, or had it copied, from someone or something that may have circulated earlier, perhaps even in a foreign language. Finally, signature forgeries are certainly not out of the question. Whether "D" copied from "C", or both copied from "B", who forged a name from "A" is not my ultimate concern—for the content is genuine! The person(s) first responsible for putting these thoughts on paper is, in my opinion, a genuine alchemical master who was far ahead of the mass consciousness in whatever period it was written. The original could have been copied, plagiarized or the signature even forged, but its content could not have been fabricated. How can I conclude this? Because the thought and consciousness in between the lines of Harley MS. #6485 agree with all world esoteric traditions. Its Alchemy agrees with the *Turba Philosophorum*, *The Book of Lambspring* and *Splendor Solis*. The original author(s) teaches the same as Roger Bacon, Paracelsus, Geber, Jacob Boehme and other Masters in the Art. Its tenets agree with esoteric principles and processes of Yoga in the East and that of the Bible in the West and it corroborates the essence of the *Koran* and Sufism. The manuscript corresponds, almost exactly, with the secret Yaqui Indian knowledge and teachings rooted in early Central America. It portrays how the One, All-Consciousness unfolds in each of us, from the East or West, from above or below the Equator.

This endeavor, like all true Wisdom, was written by one or more persons already enlightened. It was written for those others who are so, or who are about to become so, through the Sole Grace of the One-Source, Almighty. Fourth Dimensional Awareness cannot be fabricated. Those who have been given a full measure or even a glimpse of the vision of the Blessed Substance cannot be duped by charlatans hawking fool's gold. One can "see" and feel the texture and quality of the writings from the Source. This knowledge and awareness is through us, not from or by us. True Alchemists always allude to this fact and humbly give due thanks accordingly.

Alchemy has found a new vitality in a generation hungry for a clear Road of Return. One problem with many alchemical commentaries, whether with the following manuscript or other genuine writings, is the concept of a necessity for some Alchemy to be performed in a physical laboratory. Despite warnings from the original authors that Alchemy is not chemistry, the absurd myth persists.

Some writers conclude these cautions to be blinds, and believing so, continue with "a new insight" that spurs laboratory experimentation. In this question, believe the Forty-Eighth Dictum in *Turba Philosophorum*: "It must be known for certain that nothing of the work can be bought, and that the science of this Art is nothing else than vapour and the sublimation of Water."

There is a school of thought that implies that pursuing Alchemy in a physical lab and the inner work simultaneously will bring certain victory. Nothing could be further from the truth. Alchemy is the way of union in the West and is equivalent to Yoga in the East. It would make as much sense to approach Alchemy in a laboratory as it would to try to achieve "union" by modification of the diet alone. If your intention is to use Alchemy to achieve perfect health or "to enhance dreams where one meets master guides," then don't feed your delusion any longer as it would be a waste of time and expense. Homeopathy and Natureopathy (the only true descendents of Paracelsian physical alchemy) can presently offer over the counter what one requires to balance one's state of health.

Alchemy is a Chemistry of Consciousness—One Consciousness. The content of the Harley MS. #6485 is almost entirely Qabalistic and Alchemical. Its aims (some of them repeated in a different manner for emphasis) are designed toward one end—merging the separated, personal consciousness with the One-All. Cryptic and metaphorical, the manuscript is not for the beginning seeker but those on the Road of Return to the King. It assumes one has some familiarity with Alchemical and Qabalistic ideas. It does not explain fundamentals. Like the study of literature in a foreign language, the foundation work of learning vocabulary, declensions and conjugations is the preface to understanding.

This is not a writing that can be read just once if you expect to reap the harvest. It is a text to be read repeatedly and used as a sound reference against other alchemical writings as your studies progress. As *The Rosicrucian Secrets* (spelling modernized in this book) is Qabalistic, it is not sufficient merely to know the Qabalistic Tree of Life, its spheres, paths and attributions. We must use the tools of the Literal Qabalah, the Magical Language. We must gather pictorial imagery suggested by the use of Hebrew, Greek or Latin words or phrases, reduced to number. Comparing a number root with words and phrases of equal value broadens the field of imagery in our consciousness. This important procedure is not just an intellectual exercise. True Alchemy is not an intellectual ideal. Since True Wisdom writings delve into fourth dimensional awareness, universal pictorial imagery is the only real language of that level. Where an author scatters text with one of the ancient tongues, we are obligated to find its *gematria*, as it is an example of the presence of the Magical Language. Some times there are terms in English that must be converted back into the other tongues to retrieve the number. Where do we find these terms? They hide in phrases or sentences that are repeated frequently throughout the text, and in passages that clearly make no common sense in context. Look up the word in common Latin, Hebrew and Greek dictionaries. One need not be a scholar in these languages to retrieve its number, but one must have compiled some sort of *gematria* reference number catalogue. English terms disguising *gematria* may suggest the original MS. might have been copied from a Hebrew or Latin version, but this is speculation on my part. I have no grounds to prove this conjecture. Latin was widespread throughout Europe in the "alchemical" centuries. Odd terms and phrases put into English, German, French, Italian or whatever, would have been pointers to the erudite Qabalists in that period. Knowledgeable readers would have had finger-tip awareness or looked up the term in Latin at least. In this way, the secret information was passed on and preserved. Some *gematria* has been done for the reader in my commentary. Most foreign terms have been examined and their number symbolism illustrated and compared with other ideas of equal value. Some English terms and phrases are also offered and their Latin equivalents investigated. Since commentary is merely a remark or note, space prohibits a full explanation of each term. Full development of some *gematria*, using all three languages, would take paragraphs, even pages. It is hoped that my commentary offers the reader suggestions and examples to perform these procedures. Please take the time and effort to develop this. The joy of discovery remains intensely personal, and it is genuine. A *Satori* coupled with an actual physical effect may be your reward. *Gematria* is only one tool of the Magical Language. The presence of *Notariqon* and *Temurah* are a bit more difficult to detect in English, but they are here. Also consider Theosophical Extension, Theosophical Reduction and Theosophical Articulation with respect to using *gematria*. The crux of fourth dimensional awareness lies hidden in procedures such as these. If one believes that the hidden symbolism of words is a petty mind trap, then most of this MS. and most genuine alchemical writings will be inaccessible. The genuine writers showed the way. They did not lie to us. They force us, with diverse puzzles, to use our minds and creative imagination in our meditations. We must stretch our desire and abilities to meet them. This is what brings on Light.

When Alchemists compared mineral substances with aspects of the Universal and Personal Consciousness, they were nothing short of brilliant. Superconsciousness is like Mercury as it glitters, reflects; it is changeable, quick, and fluid. The letters of *Mercurius* add up to 115. This is equal to the letters in *Aqua Fortis*, the Strong or Resolute Water that alchemists are always advising us to use as our solution. Superconsciousness is the strongest Water in all creation. On the other hand, Arsenic is like an aspect of our personal consciousness. The Latin form is *Arsenicum*, which letters sum to 93. This equals *Vas Naturae*, the Vase, Belly or Womb of Nature, our own subconscious mentation. *Ars Nummae*, The Art of Coins, also sums to 93. Coins are physical, tangible results and manifestations of previously formed images. Creative imagery is a function of the subconscious mind. "Our Arsenic" is an intrinsic process within us. It is *like* a poison when it manifests horrible, hellish conditions in our lives. It is *like* the white powder in that when "seen" in fourth dimensional awareness, our astral body (the body of the subconscious mind) is whitish, powdery or smoky. Arsenic is the collective, subconscious power of three force-centers or chakras. The Moon center gathers memory substance which is formed by creative imagery under the awesome power of the Venus center. The image and the "mind-matter" are then coalesced or fixed into tighter compaction under the regimen of the Saturn center. Together all three of these functions are those of subconsciousness, called *Arsenicum* by the alchemical writers.

When True Alchemists advise us, "to take equal amounts of Mercury and Arsenic, or as much as you please," you must employ *gematria* as a beginning. *Mercurius* (115) *et* (23) *Arsenicum* (93) = 231—this is the number of *hals* (Greek for Salt). Salt is another symbol for material coagulation. It is also the number of *Spiritus Corporalis*, Embodied Spirit, which is all anything is! When "Our Arsenic" is imbued or "tinctured" with the aid of Superconsciouness, the "Aid of Mercury," its stringent poison is purified and our manifested images are in rhythm with Universal Principles which result in harmonious conditions and circumstances. This is the *Aurum Philosophorum* (231), the Gold of Philosophers. Such a consciousness will not lack sufficient health or wealth to carry one through any life-mission our Soul has been assigned by the One-Life to complete. And that mission will be our heart's desire here on Earth and beyond our wildest dreams.

It took all this writing to explore a simple phrase. Yet, an ardent Miner would do it all again in Hebrew, and then in Greek. Then one would attack it again with *Argentum Vivum et Arsenicum.*

This is the way an Alchemist works. The only laboratory is within the limits of Our Glass Vessel. Mixing, boiling, blending or baking the actual, physical elements of Mercury and Arsenic or whatever in a basement or attic laboratory will not help, not even remotely. I do not doubt that if one were to do so in a physical laboratory, that one would concoct something. However, I fear the poor chemist would die by inhalation of mercury, arsenic, lead or sulphur fumes, or choke to death drinking down some magical elixir, long before he saw any expected fruits of his handiwork.

One True Artist said it succinctly: "The best thing one can do, I think, is to stay in one's own laboratory, work and pray, and wait for God's blessing." Dr. John Dee, or the real author, had this idea in mind when he wrote *The Rosie Crucian Secrets.* May the fullest extension of God's Living, Loving Light be bestowed upon you who take up this Great Work. Your Crowned Success is an aid unto us all.

Gordon James

THE ROSICRUCIAN SECRETS
Their excellent Method of making Medicines of Metals.
Also their Laws and Mysteries.

The Preface

The contemplative order of the Rose Cross has presented to the world Angels, Spirits, Planets and Metals with the times in Astromancy and Geomancy to prepare and unite them Telesmatically. {Note the adjective "contemplative." What are to follow are all inner processes. We, mankind, are the talismans.} The Water is not extracted by the hands of men but it is made by nature a spermatic, viscous, composition of water, earth, air and fire; all those four natures united in one crystalline, coagulated mass. By Mercury I understand not quicksilver but Philosophical Saturn, which devours the Moon and keeps her always in his belly. {Qabalistically the third sphere on the Tree is Saturn, the Divine Soul, Neshamah, while the Moon and the ninth sphere is the Vital Soul, Nephesh, held within the Divine.} By Gold I mean the spermatlc Green Gold, not the adored lump which is dead and ineffectual. {The First Matter of the Universe is the Substance of the Universal Subconscious Mind, most frequently called Water. The "spermatic Green Gold" is the Universal Matter in its raw, greenish stage before Art cleanses the impure thought forms saturating the fluid Substance. The Yaqui Indian tradition of Mexico describes this Substance as a green, crystalline fog.} This is the substance which at present in our study is the child of the Sun and Moon, placed between two fires, and in the darkest night receives a light from the stars and retains

{The Child is regenerated personality of the Christ Consciousness, filling self-consciousness, a product of Sun and Moon or Super and Subconsciousness. It lies within, between the Virgin Sulphur at our center and the Universal Virgin Sulphur of Masloth, the Sphere of Fixed Stars. There is also an inner point between two, physical fires to be noted later.} Angels or Intelligences are attracted by a horrible emptiness and attend the Astrolasme forever. {Astrolasme is the star-stuff plasma, Virgin Sulphur within AIN SUPh AUR.} He has in him a thick fire by which he captivates the thin Genii. At first a Telesme is neither metal nor matter, neither solid nor fluid, but a substance without all form but what is universal. He is visible and a fume of Mercury not crude but decocted. This fume utterly destroys the first form of Gold, introducing a second and a more noble one. He has no certain color, for chameleon like, he puts on all colors, and there is nothing in the world that has the same figure with him when he is purged from his accidents. He is a water colored with fire, deep to the sight and, as it were, hollow and he has something in him that resembles a commotion. In a vaporous heat, be opens his belly and discovers and airy heaven tinged with a milky white light; within this Caelum he bides a little Sun, a most powerful red fire, sparkling like a Carbuncle which is the red Gold of the Rosicrucians.

That you may know the Rosicrucian Philosophy, endeavor to know God Himself, the worker of all things, and to pass into by a whole image of likeness (as by an official contract and bond) whereby we may be transformed and made as God as the Lord spoke concerning Moses, saying, I have made thee the God of Pharaoh. This is the true Rosicrucian Philosophy of wonderful works, that they understood not, the Key whereof is Intellect, for by how much the higher things we understand, with so much the sublime virtues are we endowed, and so much greater things do we work, and more easily and efficaciously. But our Intellect being included in the corruptible flesh, unless it shall exceed the way of the flesh and obtain a proper nature, cannot be united to these virtues (for like to like) and is searching into the Rosicrucian Secrets of God and Nature altogether inefficacious. {Our Mercury is the Self-conscious mode of mentation which aids the Operation of Sun and Moon. Our Intellect aids or fails in the effort. As we evolve more God-like it becomes absorbed by Universal Mercury which completes the Work.} For it is no easy thing for us to ascend to the heavens, for how shall he that has lost himself in mortal dust and ashes find God? How shall he apprehend spiritual things that is swallowed up in flesh and blood? Can man see God and live? What fruit shall a grain of corn bear if it be not first dead? For we must die to the world, to the flesh and all senses and to the whole man animal, who could enter into these closest of secrets not because the body is separate from the Soul, but because the Soul leaves the body, of which death St. Paul wrote to the Colossians, Ye are dead and your life is hid with Christ. And elsewhere he speaks more clearly of himself, I know a man whether in the body or out of the body, I cannot tell, God knows, caught up into the third Heaven {This is a paraphrase of II Cor. 12:2} and I say by this death, precious in the sight of God, we must die, which happens to few, and not always, for very few whom God loves, and are virtuous are made so happy, and first those that are born not of flesh and blood but of God. Secondly those that are dignified by the blessed assistance of Angels and Genii, the power of Nature, influences of the planets and the heavens and virtues of the figures and ideas at their birth.

BEHOLD THE ROSICRUCIAN CROWN

This Crown is set with Seven Angels, Seven Planets, Twelve Signs, Seven Rulers, Twelve Ideas and Sixteen Figures. Observe this harmony. The Seven Angels guide the Seven Planets, the Seven Planets move continually in the Signs, the Seven Rulers run in the Twelve Ideas {Astrological Houses}, over the face of the Earth and with the Elements project Sixteen {Geomantic} Figures. These have their Influence upon the Seven Metals which you must prepare for the diseases of mankind {The Metals are force centers or Chakras on the surface of the Glass Vessel (human aura) and which terminate as points in the spine and brain.}. As for example, if Mars cause the disease, Venus and Kedemel will cure it, and you must make the Medicine of Copper.

If Saturn and Zazel cause the disease, Jupiter and Hismael in prepared Tin will lend you their Influence to cure the party. If Saturn cause the disease, the Sun and prepared Gold will cure the disease.

Now I will demonstrate in what thing, of what thing, or by what thing is your Medicine or Multiplication of Metals to be made. It is even in the Nature, of the Nature, and by the Nature of Metals, for it is a principle of all philosophers that Nature cannot be bettered but in his own Nature.

Trevisan says: Every substance has his own proper and principal seed of which it is made. A pear tree brings forth a pear and an apple tree an apple, and God said in the beginning, let everything bring forth his fruit, and let the seed be multiplied in itself. And Arnoldus de Villa Nova says: Every seed is correspondent to its seed, and every shrub brings forth his proper fruit, according to his kind, for nothing but man is engendered of man, nor of the *Animals* but their like. Whereupon Paracelsus concludes thus: True Alchemy, which only alone teaches the Art to make Sol and Luna of five Metals, will not admit any other receipt because that which is thus (and it is truly spoken) perfect metals are made only of metals, in metals, by metals and with metals, for in some metals is Luna and in others is Sol. If this be true that in Metals are their seed whereby they may be multiplied, how is it then that the philosophers say their Gold and Silver are not common gold and silver, for common gold and silver are dead but their Gold and Silver lives. To this I answer, common gold and silver are dead except they be revived by Art, i.e., except their seeds which are naturally included in them, be projected into their natural Earth, by which means they are mortified and revived like as the grain of wheat that is dead and unapt to increase, except by art and industry of man it is in due season sown in his kindly Earth and there putrefied and again revived and multiplied. For which cause Trevisan has written that the vulgar bodies that nature only has perfected in the mine are dead, and cannot perfect these imperfect bodies. But if we take them and reiterate perfection upon them 7, 10 or 12 times, {Here the author considers meditations by Planets, the Sephirotic Tree and the Zodiac.} then will they tinct infinitely, for then are they entering, tincting and more than perfect and quick in regard of that they were before.

Paracelsus likewise affirms metallic spirits are dead and lie still so that they cannot work, unless by art they be revived which thing Arnoldus verifies. Gold and Silver, therefore, simple and absolute in their bodily and metallic form are dead, but by art they are revived and made Gold and Silver of the Philosophers. And they are revived and brought to yield their seed by reducing them into their first matter which is called *Prima Materia Metallorum*, for it is impossible for the species or forms of Metals to be transmuted but by reducing them into their First Matter.

Now the First Matter of Metals is *Argent Vive*, i.e. Quicksilver, as all Philosophers verify. For the First Matter of anything is the self same thing into which it is resolved as snow and ice are resolved into water which is the proper and first matter. And so metals are dissolved into *Argent Vive*, therefore, *Argent Vive* or Mercury is the First Matter of Metals. Therefore, Metals of necessity must be reduced into Mercury and not into cloud water as the Philosophers affirm, but into a viscous water which is the First Matter of Metals, for it is the opinion of Paracelsus, Arnoldus and Trevisan that labor is lost which is spent in the separation of the elements for Nature will not be reversed by human distinction but has her own separation in itself. Therefore metal should not be reduced into cloud water but into a viscous water. {It is clear here that physical steam is not to be derived from actual physical minerals. The viscous water is Universal Mind Matter, also called Universal Mercury, Living Silver or even Quicksilver, described by all who have seen it as an oily, slimy fatness, yet living. This is the Mind Substance of which all creation is comprised and therefore may again be reduced, in profound meditation, when we are given the actual inner vision of this Living, Loving, Light-Substance. We "see" and realize all form-objects separated from their light-energy essence.}

Albertus Magnus said the First Matter of Metals is *Argent Vive* which is a viscous, incombustible moisture, co-mixed in a strong and wonderful mixture with a subtle earthliness in the mineral caves of the Earth which continually move and flow because successively one part has rule over another; as the cause of flowing and moving is by moisture bearing the chief rule, and terrestrial dryness bearing chief rule over the action of moisture is the cause it will not stick to that which it touches or moistens.

Trevisan says that is the nearest matter of metals whose viscous moisture is mixed with his subtle earthliness. {Here Magnus, Trevisan, and Geber below, are referring to the First Matter within us, in the laboratory of Assiah. This is *Chylus*, an oily, milky substance conveyed by the lacteals at the upper portion of the small intestines, "between two fires" of the stomach and intestinal digestive processes within *Terra Adamica*. This is the "nearest matter" to us in the "bowels of the Earth." It is just like the Universal First Matter but in different form. Both are "oily, milky, viscous" substances.}

And Geber says, we could never yet find anything permanent in the fire; but this viscous matter or moisture, which is the self same note of all metals, and all the other moistness do easily fly from the fire by evaporation and separation of one element from another, as water by fire. One part goes into smoke, another into water, another into earth remaining in the bottom of the vessel; but the viscous moistness, that is to say Mercury, is never consumed in it nor separated from its earth nor from any other element, for either they remain altogether or vanish altogether, so that no part of the weight may perish.

Geber thus describes the nature of Quicksilver: *Argent Vive*, which the Alchemists call Mercury is nothing else but a viscous water in the bowels of the Earth, of a moist subtle substance of which Earth, united together by a moist temperature by the least parts until the moist be tempered by the dry and the dry by the moist, so that being thus both equally united and mixed, neither of them may be separated nor taken from one another by the fire." And in this *Argent Vive*, the Mother of all Metals, is the whole perfection, for it has in its composition Sulphurous parts dry, the which tincts and colors whiteness in action, and redness in power, and therefore this is the True Sulphur which perfects, forms, coagulates, colors and fixes by his action. But this incombustible hidden and unknown Sulphur, which is in power in *Argent Vive*, cannot bring itself forth into action but by due decoction {continuous, persistent meditation}, wherefore you may now perceive that neither nature in the veins of the earth, nor we above ground have no other matter to work upon but only pure Mercurial form wherein Sulphur is included, that is to say, fire and air, which indeed is the internal and essential part of the Mercury itself, {This is consistent with all the sages who tell us that their nature, matter, means and results are the operation of just One Thing and that all we could ever need or want is already intrinsic within Itself.} but it does not dominate therein, but by the means of heat, the which is caused by the reflection of the fiery sphere which encloses the air, and also proceeding of continual and equal motion of the heavenly bodies, which do stir so lent an heat as that it can hardly be perceived or imagined. And thus by most perfect decoction, and also by continual proportional digestion in long success of time introduced in Art and made manifest in the end of the operation of nature, that aforesaid unknown and incombustible Sulphur which is the true form or ferment of Gold. And thus may you see that metalline form take their original only of pure Mercurial Substance, the which is the Mother of all Metals and couples and is united with her male, that is with the said Sulphur, the Father of Metals, the which causes the diversity of Metals according to different degrees of decoction and alteration caused in Mercury by his own natural heat of inward Sulphur. {Sulphur and Mercury, Red and White, Pingala and Ida are the Right and Left nerve currents within the Sympathetic Nervous System which comprise Kundalini. It is eventually raised by Decoction (meditation) and Digestion (*Chylus* with sensible elements, i.e., light, water, breath and food) under guidance from the Universal Mind, or Universal Mercury, via astrological timing, "the continual and equal motion of heavenly bodies".}

The Philosophers do agree that there {are} in the nature and original of Metals two sperms or seeds, the one Masculine and Agent, which they call Sulphur, the other Feminine and Patient, which they name Mercury; and these two have the natural conjunction and operation one with another in the womb of the Earth whereby they engender Metals of diverse form and quality according to the difference and diversity of their degree of digestion and concoction.

Now I will briefly discourse the difference between Sulphur and Mercury; and the beginning and natural generation of them and then show how they have their natural operation, the one with the other in the bowels of the Earth to be made Metals perfect and imperfect. {See the "Tree of Our Mercury" on page 93.}

Sulphur is double in every Metal but only in Gold, that is to say external burning, and internal not-burning, {Mercury, Sulphur and Salt are equivalent to the Three Gunas in the Bhagavad-Gita. Sulphur, or Rajas Guna, is frequently translated as Passion or Desire. It works in two directions, internally and externally, from all the force centers or chakras. See Chapter 2 of Boehme's *Three Principles of the Divine Essence*. He separates the word into SUL and PHUR to illustrate its dual, inward (upward) action from the outward (downward) expression. The three gunas are in the Universal AIN SUPh AUR (as above) and in all the metals or chakras (so below).} which is of the substantial composition of *Argent Vive*, the Mercury or Quicksilver spoken of is engendered or compounded in the bowels of the Earth of clear viscous water by a most temperate heat, united by the least parts indissoluble with an earthly substance incombustible white sulphur, most subtle in art, without the which the substance of *Argent Vive* cannot subsist, which colors it naturally with a white color, but in our Magistery it makes it white and red as we will by governing the nature of it; wherefore only *Argent Vive* is the total material cause and total substance of the Philosophers' Medicine containing in itself that internal Sulphur, being a simple fire, lively, quickening, the which indeed is the true Masculine Agent that before we spoke of, the which, by perfect and due digestion and proportional decoction, conglutes, colors, forms and fixes his own *Argent Vive* into Gold according to nature and to Art in the Philosophers' Medicine, but when that *Argent Vive* is by Nature thus fixed and made perfect by most high digestion into Gold only by its own proper and inward Sulphur, which is the true ferment, then the external combustible sulphurs cannot enter in nor be mixed with him but it is parted clear away as the corruptible from the permanent, wherefore it enters not into Gold and therefore cannot be the matter or form or any part of the matter or form of the Philosophers' Medicine. And thus you may understand the difference between the true Sulphur and Mercury, for when it appears simple it is flowing and is called Mercury and is volatile, carrying or holding its proper incombustible Sulphur or ferment hidden in power. But when in the end of the aforesaid Decoction that hidden Sulphur is brought wholly into Action, whereby the whole is manifest does show the nature of Sulphur, then is it called Sulphur which does coagulate, reduce and fix his *Argent Vive* to its proper nature which is to be made Gold. Wherefore this is the only tincting Sulphur of the Philosophers, the which is unknown to the common people. {*Argent Vive*, Universal Mercury, is the whole Matter. Within is Sulphur, artificially excited by the "decocting" meditation process. Our raw desires are Red Sulphur, but turned inward, and aspiring, it becomes White Sulphur, which attracts Universal Mercury in its raw stage. Our White Sulphur conglutes, forms and fixes the impure First Matter into its own Gold. Corruptible, combustible sulphurs (outward desires which burn up quickly) are cleared by the permanent attraction to Universal Mercury, AIN SUPh AUR.} But the compound of them is called the mixed medicine, perfect and sound, and in the co-mixing they are made all one as wax. And so in truth you may now see that these two Spermatic matters are of one root substance and essence, that is to say, of the only essence of pure *Argent Vive*. But the diversity of the sundry shapes, forms and bodies of metals the which is the cause of the perfection or imperfection of them is according to the diverse and several degrees of alteration caused by their decoction and digestion. For the Mercury is *Argent Vive* running in the veins of the Earth, conjoined and mixed with this aforesaid external Sulphur, and being so mingled and conjoined together by the sundry and different degrees of the decoctions of the internal Sulphur caused by the motion of the Heavenly Bodies there is engendered the sundry shapes, forms and bodies of the Metals in the entrails of the Earth. {Raw *Argent Vive* running in our blood, mixed with our raw desires, shape the energies expressed through the force centers (metals). Primitive man reacts adversely to stellar vibrations in this state until we consciously cooperate with the evolutionary process. Meditation hones our sulphurous energies which alter to align us harmoniously with the cosmic ebb and flow.} For first, in the first degrees of natural operation and digestion, the heat of the internal sulphur, working and somewhat prevailing in the humidity of his Mercury begins somewhat to fix and coagulate the Mercurial humor, and gives it the form of Lead. And by further digestion and decoction the Sulphur yet somewhat more prevailing over his Mercury, the Mercury is somewhat more fixed and receives the form of Tin. Then does the heat dominate more and make Copper, and then Iron and further proceeding in their digestion the internal Sulphur yet more subduing the moist and cold of his Mercury by a temperate heat and attaining by his concoction, purity and perfection of whiteness it more firmly fixes his body and gives it the form of fixation and tincture of Silver. And now the essence that was in power is brought forth into action, whereby the external, Earthly Sulphur, which gave a transitional form to the undigested Metals is almost utterly expoliated and separated by reason of his perfect form introduced by the mean of due digestion and proportional decoction. {The original author has explained the various mixtures of Mercury (sattva guna) with Sulphur (rajas guna) within the chakras. When Sulphur turns external and earthly the chakras gather, or take on, more Salt (tamas guna), which fixes. The most dense fixation of Salt is in Mars.}

And yet in the Silver there are some small parts of external Sulphur, the which are by the last and most temperate, complete digestion of nature wholly and thoroughly expoliated, {*expolio, -ire*; to polish, to refine} and then by nature is accomplished the most perfect, simple and pure substantial form of Gold, which Gold in the perfection of his Metalline nature is pure fire, digested by the said Sulphur existing in Mercury, whereby his Mercury, that is to say his whole substance, is converted into the nature of his pure Sulphur and made permanent and triumphant in the force and violence of the fire. And by the separation of the external Sulphur, the Metals are made perfect according to their diverse degrees of their decoction, digestion and alteration, wherein they separate themselves from the Earthly and combustible Sulphur, and attain their true, complete, pure form and fixation. {Turn the sulphurous desires of the metals inward, through meditation, to perfect their energies.}

But whereas the Philosophers do seem to set down by degrees, first Saturn then Jupiter then Luna, then Venus, then Mars and then Sol, they had a further meaning therein which is not to be understood according to the letter, for indeed Venus and Mars are planets after Luna, not that it should be believed that Luna does turn or go into an imperfect body as Venus and Mars, but in truth they are placed after Luna for two causes. First because of the over great and excessive burning of their filthy and fixed, earthly, external Sulphur which is joined with their Mercury and is outwardly by too much intemperate and over great, superfluous drying, combustible heat, coagulated and decocted with the *Argent Vive* to a corruptible body; the other cause is philosophically to be understood in the order and degrees of the colors in the working of the philosophers Medicine which is a similitude and analogy, and this over great quantity of burning, gross, earthly, external Sulphur is the cause of the hard melting of Mars. {The author is suggesting the purification of some centers before the Mars center because of their less intense "fixedness" or Salt content. Mars, or Iron, is most difficult to melt because of its preponderance of Salt to Sulphur and Mercury. Mars' external Sulphur is encrusted with Salt making it difficult to turn.} But so soon as nature by a temperate, complete digestion has introduced into Art the internal, pure Sulphur, then are separated all those external Sulphurs from the Mercury, and a perfect form is introduced. Example; in the projection of the Philosophers' Medicine, which, being cast upon imperfect metals molten, does only by virtue of the most pure, temperate, high and mighty digestion fix and give a true, natural form to the Mercury of the bodies {the sattva guna in the chakras} whereby is expoliated away all external Sulphur and they are perfected into fine Gold. And you must also know that Nature does not always of these degrees in passing through the dispositions and paths of the metals, or any one of them, but does oftentimes engender perfect Sol, as the aforesaid beginning, by a most temperate and due decoction in the bowels of the Earth, the reason hereof the knowledge of the countries and mines will make manifest unto you. {Some are drawn to this Art quickly by way of Satori or an enlightenment from the Heart (Sun) Center. The natural human evolves more slowly and steadily through the other centers.}

And thus I have made plain the very Operation and works of Nature in the Earth as all the philosophers deciphered it. And this operation of Nature are we to imitate and follow as near as possible in our Art according to the earnest precepts and prescriptions of all the philosophers in this behalf.

Now I shall show how and in what manner our Art must imitate the operation of Nature; but first I will resolve, wherefore do the philosophers call Mercury or Quicksilver the First Matter of Metals, when there is another matter or sperm as we have declared which must be joined with it before Metals can be engendered.

The Philosophers do truly call Mercury the First Matter of Metals, being so indeed, for the Sulphur which is the masculine sperm, is of her, and she is the root of him and his coagulation, as Hermes said. And also the same man says, this Water congeals when it is congealed, and running water is the Mother of that which is congealed and coagulated and so it was ever. For which cause the Philosophers call the feminine sperm the Patient, or matter which suffers the action of her Agent, and takes the impression of his forms in her substance, and therefore the Philosophers said truly that Sulphur gives the form and beginning of being more than matter, when as that it is his action and matter, power, and form; for according to the truth of forms, they are named the substances of things; but matter may after another sort be called more the substance in as much as it is the beginning of everything, and from it are extracted all forms. {The Universal Sulphur (Universal Desire) in the AIN SUPh AUR gives the running-water form to the First Matter. Desire gives permanency to the Fluid Intelligence, the Universal Mercury. This congealed Matter is Patient to the Sulphurous Agent. Then, the Permanent, Liquid, *Prima Materia* is the substance Agent for all congealed, created manifestations in the Assiah universe, the Patient. "This water congeals when it is congealed."}

If therefore any man would know the form of Gold, he must of necessity know the matter of Gold, the which is *Argent Vive*, and springs flowing, liquid, flying, bright and suffers coagulation, and is therefore truly called the First Matter of Metals because all Metals have their first matter or substance from her, their mother. The forms of the Metals being affected by the moving of the active elements, fiery and airy of Mercury, that is to say, Sulphur, the which moves *Argent Vive* as this proper matter for generation into Metals according to the degrees of his motions.

Now we proceed to apply the operation of our Art to the operation of Nature, and show what is the first work of Art. Learn to know the first work of Art by the first work of Nature, always provided that it be that first work of Nature that Art is able to perform. But because the first work of Nature was to make the Sperms of Nature, which Art cannot do, therefore the second work of Nature, which is the conjunction of the two Sperms in one, must of necessity be the first work of Art, and the creation or making of the two Sperms must be only referred to Nature, who has provided and prepared to Art the matter that Art is to work upon. According to the saying of the Philosophers, Art of itself cannot create the Sperms, but when Nature has created them, then does Art, joined with that natural heat which is in the Sperms already created, mix them as the instrument of Nature, for it is plain that Art does add neither form, nor matter, nor virtue but only aiding the thing existing to bring it to perfection. And again, Nature has created a matter unto Art, unto which Art neither adds anything nor takes anything away, but removes such things as are superfluous. Likewise Nature has prepared for us one Stone and Matter and one Medicine, unto the which we by our Art add no foreign thing, nor in any point diminish it, but in removing that which is superfluous in the preparation; and this is done in the purification which is effected by solution. {Sages of all times agree on this point. Meditation is the Solution by which we come to discover the First Matter, which contains all that is necessary to complete the Art.} By these words it plainly appears that Nature has prepared the matter wherein Art is to work, and Art by no means can make the same matter; but the only work of Art is to cleanse and purify that which Nature has left impure, and make that perfect which Nature has left imperfect, as is verified by this last saying of Arnoldus, and that first of Trevisan.

Now therefore it follows, that the first work of Art wherein Art does imitate nature, must of necessity be that which is the second work of Nature (viz:) as the second work of nature after she had created the sperm, was to join those two Sperms of Nature together, whereby to make the First Matter of Metals, so the first work of Art must be to conjoin the Sperms of Metals together, whereby

22

we must make the first matter of one pure medicine, that may bring the impure and imperfect metals into the purity and perfection of Nature, and this can be no otherwise done but by reduction of them into their first matter, as is before said, by which means we may have (as Arnoldus says) the same Sperms of the Metals about the Earth that Nature did work in under the Earth. And this reduction is nothing else but the dissolution in which they are dissolved into the Natural Mercury and Sulphur again, but more pure than they were before by reason that they are in their dissolution, separated and purified from the fex and impurity of their nature, and made more pure and perfect, whereby to engender a more pure and perfect matter than Nature could do, and for this cause has the Philosopher written this conference in the lamentation of Nature between Nature and Art: Without me which do yield the matter, thou shalt never effect anything, and without thee also which does minister unto me, I cannot alone finish this work. {Nature unaided, fails. Through persistent, patient meditation, we turn the Sulphur in each of the Metals to its Mercury. If successful, an influx of Superconscious energy completes the purification process of all the Metals. The result is union of the Red and the White, Sol with Luna, Sulphur with Mercury, the masculine Sperm with the feminine Sperm and Pingala with Ida within Kundalini. If we do not aspire by study, prayer and meditation, in effect, if we do not *desire* it, this influx will not be forthcoming.}

It is the chief and highest secret of the Philosophers to know out of which of the Metals must we have these sperms. I ought not to disclose the same in plain terms but in dark speeches and figures as they have done. Notwithstanding, mark that {which} shall follow, and I will discover to you the secrets of the philosophers, in hope that you will hide them in your heart, and commit the papers to the fire. Now first and chiefly you must call to remembrance the words of the philosophers before named who say that in some Metals is Sol, and in some Metals is Luna, that is to say, in some of the Metals is the Masculine Sperm, and in some is the Feminine Sperm. In some of the Metals is the tincture of Gold, and in some of the Metals is the tincture of Silver. Some of them are masculine and some of them are feminine. For that these words are true in their expositions, the words of Hermes do very well prove, who says Red Sol is his Father and White Luna his Mother. If, therefore, Sol be the Father and Luna the Mother, and in some of the Metals be Sol, and in some of them be Luna, what is this but to say that some of the Metals are masculine and some of them feminine, or in some of them is the Masculine Sperm, and in some of them is the Feminine Sperm. Now therefore consider which of them are the masculine bodies, and out of the which the Masculine Sperms are to be had, and then shall we the more perfectly discern the feminine bodies whence the feminine sperms are to be fetched.

Note that the Philosophers do diversely name these two Sperms. The Masculine they call the Agent, the Sulphur or rennet, the body or ferment, the poison or Flower of Gold, the Tincture or inward Fire, and the Form. The Feminine Sperm they call the Patient, Mercury, the Spirit Volatile, *Argent Vive*, *Menstruum*, Water, Azoth and the Matter, and by many other names they name them both. But this Caveat in discerning of them, I give you for three causes especially. The one is because you should in reading of the philosophers not mistake any one of them for the other. The second cause, that you should by these names know which of the Metals are masculine by the quality of their names. And the third cause is that you should thereby gather and understand, that the two sperms, being of two several natures and qualities, can by no means be fetched from one body, as diverse have misconstrued, no more than both the Sperms of man and woman are in man alone, or in the woman alone. But they are to be had of two substances of one root, as Trevisan and Arnoldus and the rest of Philosophers affirm. But I will give you this secret note, that the two sperms must be had out of two, several bodies. {This is the Mercury and Sulphur in each of the Metals or Chakras. Jean d'Espagnet says in *Hermetic Arcanum* that the Philosophers extract their Stone out of seven stones.} Yea, two bodies in one only root, which is the same Hermaphrodite of the Philosophers which they often write of, or their Adam, as in due place shall be disclosed, but in all the reading of the Philosophers keep well this Caveat in your mind, of the several names, and natures of these two sperms. {The Masculine Sperm and Feminine Sperm, from one root, are wedded in the Alchemical Marriage by the influx from Superconscious, Universal Mercury, AIN SUPh AUR.}

But now I shall proceed to prove by the Philosophers which are the Masculine bodies. And here a question will arise whether that which gives the Form or Tincture is the Masculine Sperm or the Feminine. You need not to doubt that among the Metals Sol and Luna are both Agents and Masculine Sperms, for they both give form and tincture severally, the one to the White Work, the other to the Red Work, according to the sayings of the Philosophers.

For Arnoldus in his *Rosary* says Gold is more precious than all other metals, and is the tincture of redness tincting and transforming every body. But Silver is the tincture of whiteness tincting all other bodies with a perfect whiteness. {The Red Work is the work of Superconsciousness, Sun, Sol or Gold. The White Work is that of Subconsciousness, Moon, Luna or Silver.} And therefore he who knows to tinct *Argent Vive*, with Sol and Luna, comes into the secret. Likewise in another place he says thus: The first work is to sublime Mercury and to dissolve it that it may return into the First Matter; then let the clean bodies be put into this clean Mercury, but mix not the white body with the red, nor the red with the white, but dissolve every one, severally, apart, because the white water is to whiten, and the red water to make red, therefore mix not the water of the one medicine with the water of the other because you will greatly err, and be blinded if you do otherwise. {Sublime Self-consciousness with studies, prayers and meditation until the First Matter is revealed. Then cleanse the White

Waters of Subconsciousness with this clean water. The Red Water, Superconsciousness, cleans the deeper elements of the Subconscious. When the First Matter is revealed to us, we are shown how the three levels of the All Consciousness work separately, yet together.} By these two sentences of Arnoldus it appears not only that Sol and Luna are Agents, the one giving form to the Red Work, the other to the White, but also there is another body that is to be dissolved into Mercury, which is the Patient of these two, for as much as these two are to be put into the same, yet is it not the Patient to them both together, but each of them severally and asunder, which proves them plainly to be both Masculine and Agent, and none of them Patient to any other, nor by any means to be mixed one with another, but a third thing to be Patient to them both. That is to say, the same Mercury or *Argent Vive* that they before spoke of, where they said, that he who knows how to tinct *Argent Vive* with Sol and Luna comes to a secret. Likewise the noble Trevisan says: Our Medicine is made of two things being of one essence, to wit, of the Union, Mercurially fixed and not fixed, spiritual and corporal, cold and moist, hot and dry, and of no other thing can {it} be made. By these words it is manifest that the two Mercuries whereof our Medicine is to be made, are both of one root but of contrary qualities, that is to say, the one is a Mercury fixed, the other not fixed, the one Corporeal, the other Spiritual, the one hot and dry, the other cold and moist, which several mercuries are contrary, and contrary matters cannot be included in Sol and Luna. For they, as Agents, are only hot and dry, corporeal and fixed, but they are not, as Patients, cold and moist, volatile and spiritual, and unfixed, and therefore in them may be the masculine sperm, but in no wise the feminine. And therefore says *Turba Philosophorum*, a Tincture proceeding from the fountain of Sol and Luna gives perfection to imperfect metals, upon which considerations they have also set down this most excellent Cannon and Principle, (viz.): The secret of all secrets is to know that Mercury is the Matter and *Menstruum*, and the Matter of perfect bodies is the form; what is this but as who should say, seeing the Mercury drawn from the perfect bodies is the form, or Agent Sperm of Our Medicine, then Mercury of an imperfect body must needs be the Matter, or Feminine Sperm; to the confirmation whereof Paracelsus says thus: Philosophical Mercury that is of Sol, is in the conjunction compared unto the corporeal spirit of Mercury, as is the husband to his wife when as they are both one and the self same root, and original, although the body of Sol remains fixed in the fire, but the metallic woman unfixed. Notwithstanding that, compared to this, is no otherwise, than seeds to the field or earth. By these words of Paracelsus it is evident that the difference between the Metallic Man and the Metallic Woman is that the Metallic Man is fixed, and the Metallic Woman unfixed, by which means it is plain that this Metallic Woman cannot be Silver or the spirit of Silver, as some do fondly surmise, and as the most do take it, but of some imperfect body that is unfixed. For who is so simple but knows that Luna is fixed and permanent in the fire and inseparably united with his pure white Sulphur.

Thus it is proved the two perfect bodies are the Agents, giving the forms and tinctures, and so consequently to be the Masculine Sperm, and no less proving that the Feminine Sperm is to be had from an unfixed body, of which nature neither of them is, and therefore we must yield to the apparent reasons and authority of the Philosophers.

I shall now expound by some other philosophers the saying of Hermes, that his Father is Sol and Luna is Mother. These words of Hermes though they be full of truth and have no deceit in them, yet a great number have been deceived thereby. The cause of their error is because they do not consider the nature of Luna, when they take to be meant of Hermes to be the mother of our matter. For if they did either consider the Masculine property of Silver or perused the philosophers touching their construction of this point, they should well perceive that Luna is not the Silver that Hermes means but a certain unfixed matter or Mercury, of the nature and quality of the Celestial Luna, as in the *Canons of the Philosophers* appear, and in *Turba Philosophorum* by these words: It is a thing worthy to be noted that Luna or Silver is not the Mother of common Silver; but it is a certain Mercury endued with the nature and quality of the Celestial Moon, which is the same Mercury or Woman before spoken of that is not fixed as Silver is, but is of the nature of the Celestial Moon in respect of her moist, unmixed and watery quality, having her fixation, form and tincture of her Sulphur, as the Celestial Moon takes light of the Sun. Therefore out of doubt it must be drawn from a body of the same nature, and not from a body of a contrary quality; for what can be more absurd than to think that an unfixed matter can be in a fixed metal, or a fixed nature in an unfixed body. Consequently what can be more evident, and manifest, seeing the Philosophers do all affirm, that the Metallic Man is fixed and his Metallic Woman unfixed, than that the fixed sperm must be had out of a fixed metal, and the unfixed and volatile nature out of an unfixed substance; and therefore, by no means had from Luna, because of her fixed and masculine nature, which all the Philosophers in plain terms confirm to be true as in their *Canons* by a question demanded and answered in this manner. The question among wise men is, whether the Mercury of Luna joined with the Mercury of Sol may be had instead of the Philosophical *Menstruum*. They answer, Mercury of Luna does hold the nature of the Male or Masculine, but two males cannot engender no more than two females. Likewise in another place, Thus the Sulphurs Sol and Luna are the two Sperms or Masculine seeds of the Medicine, and in the *Turba* thus: Metallic Lunes are of a Masculine nature. Thus I have proved that the two perfect Metals are the two masculine bodies, from which we are to fetch our two Masculine Sperms, forms or tinctures, i.e., both of the red and of the white, which, seeing they are fixed and perfect bodies, the form and tincture and agents of our matter, they have sufficient reason of themselves to persuade that they can be no other than the Masculine Sperms, except we will contrary all rule of reason and nature, have One Thing both the Agent and the Patient.

Now I will demonstrate which are the Feminine Bodies, and out of which the feminine sperms of out matter is to be fetched.

This secret of both these secrets is the greatest, and requires of itself to be kept as secretly in the hearts of all wise men hereafter as it has been of all ancient philosophers heretofore.

Understand this secret by this figure 3, which number indeed it does contain in itself, and is the very figure of the Trinity in the Deity.

First I will show the reasons as the marks and tokens whereby you shall understand and know that this 3 is the same feminine body where is the feminine sperm of our blessed matter, which I will prove by the authority of the Philosophers in this manner.

First the Philosophers do all agree, that the Metallic Man in our matter is fixed and the Metallic Woman unfixed. If, therefore, I prove our matter 3 to be unfixed, it is a great argument and probability that our 3 is the same woman.

The second mark and token whereby she is known is that the Philosophers likewise agree, that their Mercury or Water which reduces their Gold or Sulphur into its First Matter is the same that abides and is permanent with it as Trevisan declares. There is required in our natural solution the permanency of both, viz., of water dissolving and of the dissolved body; and in another place, no water dissolves the metalline essence with a natural reduction but that water which is abiding therein in matter and form, which water also the metals themselves being dissolved are able to congeal. And Arnoldus says: The nature of the dissolved body, and the dissolving water is all one, but only that the nature of the body is complete, digested and fixed, but the nature of the water is incomplete, undignified and volatile, until it be fixed by the body. And in Paracelsus our woman dissolves her man, and the man fixes the woman. By these words it is plain that the water which dissolves the body is the same that is permanent with them; that is to say, the woman or feminine sperm that is to .be joined with the man or masculine. {The AIN SUPh AUR or Limitless Sea of Awareness is comprised, principally, of Three Modes which alchemists call Mercury, Sulphur and Salt. These are also, Intelligence, Desire and Substance, or Sattva, Rajas and Tamas. The Limitless Light, or Water, is Permanent due to its Sulphur. If it were not for the Desire of the Universal Mind to make a substantial universe, all would be naught, or "incomplete, undigested and volatile." The Universal Desire maintains it by fixing its own Substance Nature into forms. Our world of objects is but frozen, universal "mind-matter" which can be dissolved again into its primal nature if the Desire were to retract itself, as if in a dream, which again, is what our physical world and lives are really.}

Paracelsus says plainly, speaking in the person of the figure 3: My spirit is the Water, dissolving the congealed bodies of my brethren. And Raymond Lullius says in his *Epistle to the King*: Our Water, you know, is extracted from a certain stinking *Menstruum*, which is compounded of four things, and is stronger than all the Water of the world and it is mortal, whose spirit multiplies the tincture of the ferment. And in another place he says: All Alchemical Gold is made of corrosives, and of an incorruptible quintessence, which is fixed with ferment, but such quintessence is a certain spirit reviving and mortifying the mineral medicine. And *Turba Philosophorum* says: Take the black spirit, and with it dissolve bodies and divide them. Now consider the nature of our figure 3 and judge if this be that Water or no. It must needs be the same, for the words fits the nature. Consider yet another note or mark whereby she is known, as the ancient and modern philosophers do affirm. That their Gold must be sown in his own proper earth; as also in the *Turba*: Let our Gold be sown in his own proper earth. Arnoldus, in his *New Light* says: With my own hands, my eyes being witnesses, I made the Elixir that converted Saturn into Sol, which matter truly I have now named, and it is the Philosophers' *Magnesia*, out of which they did draw Gold out of the bottom of his body, and which they found quicksilver of quicksilver, and Sulphur of Sulphur. To construe these words rightly, what is our Figure 3 but Mercury of Mercury, and what is our Gold but Sulphur of Sulphur. I will yet impart a greater secret.

It is written by good philosophers and found true infallibly by daily experience that the figure 3 is never found simple or pure by itself in the mine, but ever is mixed with Gold or Silver, whole grains or seeds in him are plainly to be seen to the eyes by which means it appears that there is no mine of himself, but he is the mine of them, and so their very natural Earth. {The grains or seeds are the glinting, shimmering flecks or filaments of Light Essence due to Its Mercurial Omniscience within the viscous matter. Each fleck is supremely *aware*! This whole slimy substance is the Alchemical Earth, formless and void. Within it are the Alchemical Air, Mercury, Intelligence; Alchemical Fire, Sulphur, Desire; and Alchemical Water, Salt, Substance.}

Consider these words following of Flamellus and you will yet hear a greater secret than these. Mercury being never so little congealed in the veins of the earth there is straightaways fixed in it the grain of Gold, which of the two sperms do bring forth true springs and a branch of Mercury as we may see in the Caves of Saturn, wherein there is no mine in any in which the true grain of the fixed may not be contained manifestly, that is the grain of Gold of Silver. For the first congelation of Mercury is the mine of Saturn in which it is put by nature. This may truly be multiplied into his perfections without fail or error; being, notwithstanding, in his Mercury not separated from his mine. For Metal consisting in his mine is Mercury, from which if the grain be separated, it will be as an unripe apple plucked from its tree, which is altogether destroyed. The fixed grain is the apple, and Mercury is the tree; therefore the fruit is not to be separated from the tree, because it cannot elsewhere receive nourishment than from his Mercury. It is as great a folly to put Gold or Silver into Mercury as to fasten an apple again to the tree from whence it was taken. Therefore, that this business might be duly accomplished, the tree together with the fruit must be taken, that again it might be planted, without taking away the fruit, into a more fertile and new soil, which will give more nourishment in one day than the first field would have yielded in an hundred years, for the continual agitation of the winds. Go up, therefore, into the Mountain that you may see the vegetable, Saturnian, Royal and mineral herb; for let the juice be taken pure, the feces being cast away, for thereof you may effect the greatest part of your work. This is the true Mercury of the Philosophers.

Trevisan confirms this matter thus: Our work is made of one root and two substances Mercurial, taken crude, drawn out of the mine clean and pure, conjoined by fire of amity as the matter requires it, cocted continually until that of two be made one; and in this one, when the two are mixed, the body is made spirit, and the spirit is made body. Paracelsus, likewise speaking plainly in the name of our figure 3 says: It would be profitable to the lesser world if he did know or at the least believe what lay hid within me, and what I could effect, for he that does discourse upon the Art of Alchemy would more profitably understand that which I can do, if he would use that only that which is within me, and that which by me may be done. {The Caves or Mines of Saturn may rightly be alluded to as the stomach and intestines of the human body. Flammel is correct when he states "the first congelation of Mercury is the mine of Saturn in which it is put by nature." Juice, in the previous paragraph, is from the Latin, *Chylus*, referred to in a previous note. Paracelsus offered to show a group of nobles the First Matter, but was ridiculed out of the chamber when he presented to them a sack of human excrement. Roger Bacon records in his *Root of the World*: "This Stone is no stone that can generate a living creature. It is cast upon the dunghill as a vile thing, and is hidden from the eyes or understandings of ignorant men." Excess *chyle* is excreted with the waste or Ash. An Alchemist employs this extra portion into the blood stream at the lacteals, within the body, "not separated from the mine," by suggestion from Our Mercury, self-consciousness. This "true Mercury of the Philosophers," in Assiah, is what charges body cell tissues to induce optimum health. The Juice must "be taken pure, the feces being cast away." It most certainly could be "profitable to the lesser world (man, the Microcosm) if he did know or at least believe what lay hid within." This is done by an alchemist, effortlessly, and at no cost.} And in another place, under an enigma, he notably discovers this our blessed matter where he says: Whatsoever stains into a white color has the nature of life and the power and property of light which casually effects life; and contrary, whatsoever stains into blackness or makes black has the nature common with death and the property of darkness, and the strong power of death. The coagulation and fixation of such manner of corruption is the earth with her coldness. The House is always dead but the Inhabitant (The Christ Consciousness) of the same lives; and if you can find from the example thereof, you have prevailed.

By these words it appears that as the tincture of whiteness is the cause of Life, which is the spirit of generation; so the blackness, which is the spirit of corruption is death; and these two tinctures are in our blessed herb. The natural blackness whereof, that is to say our figure 3, is the spirit of the corruption or mortification which is the same Earth that he here notes with his coldness. The same dead house within the artificial digestion is death and mortification and putrefaction of the matter; and our Silver and Gold, which is naturally included in the same, is the tincture in his first artificial operation according to the philosophers, who say there is no Gold, but first was Silver before it was Gold. This Tincture of Whiteness is the same Inhabitant which lives in the same dead house according to the saying before the House is dead but they live who inhabit it. By which means it is plain, that this is the same example which he speaks of when he says: The example whereof if you are able to find out, you have your purpose.

Arnoldus notes in his *Rosary*: This we see, that in the calculation of our figure 3, that first is converted into black powder, next into white, then into a more yellow or red. Which words very well discover his enigma written of this matter. Elsewhere he says this: The thing that has a red head, white feet and black eyes is the masterie. Likewise it appears by the enigma of Hermes: The Falcon is always on the top of the Mountain crying I am the white of the black, and the red of the Cytren {*sic*}.

Now I will show how there is in our figure 3, the number of 3 that I before spoke of, {and} the other thing {is} to show how it is the Hermaphrodite or Adam of the Philosophers.

In our Mineral Herb is the number of 3 thus. First therein is our Figure 3. Secondly there is our Sulphur, i.e., our Gold or Silver which is naturally mixed with him. Thirdly the root of these two, that is to say Mercury or Quicksilver, whereof they were engendered, and whereunto they must be reduced, in respect of which Trinity in unity it represents the Figure of the Deity. Now of our Hermaphrodite or Adam therein. What else is our Mercurial Herb, but one root of two substances, wherein is both our man or woman, that is to say, our Gold is our man, our Sperm Masculine or Silver, according to his natural mine, which is also the Sulphur, the Tincture, the Ferment and form before spoken of, having the perfect and fixed nature of the man, and the two Agent Elements of fire and air in them; and our Woman is our figure 3, i.e., which is the Feminine Sperm, the Patient, the Aqua, the *Menstruum*, the Matter, the Spirit Volatile and the condigested {*sic*.—This is curious. The MS. appears to be correctly written as 'undigested,' then the prefix is scratched out with 'con' written above it.} or unfixed body, having in her the two Patient Elements of water and earth.

Thus you see that Sol and Luna are the Masculine Sperms in our matter, or Figure 3 is the natural woman, water and earth of them both, where, by nature, they are planted and spring, that is to say the matter of our red work is our Figure 3 joined with Sol, and the matter of our white work in our Figure 3 joined with Luna, which matter are first to be had for more surety and security of art even in nature itself, called *fex plumbi* {"maker of Lead." This totals 96 in Latin Gematria, that of *Tinctura*, or Tincture}, or *Quehaeli Hispanica*. And thus do you see in our blessed matter 4, 3, 2 and 1, {and 5!} yea, in one only thing, according to the words of all Philosophers, that you may not in the least doubt of the truth hereof I have truly laid it open. The rest of the operation of Art in this matter shall hereafter be at large declared. {The AIN SUPh AUR is Triune in nature. This with Sol, superconsciousness, tincts Red. With Luna, or subconsciousness, it tincts White. They are both coagulators, or Lead makers, in that they congeal Light Energy into form.} of our figure 3 and no other of the imperfect bodies but her, for all the Philosophers agree, that she is earthly, dark, cold and stinking; and Paracelsus names her plainly, the water dissolving her brethren. {The Universal Black Light or Spirit has a most peculiar dissolving nature or characteristic. It is all Loving and forgiving. It relieves the happy recipient of all guilts, cares and worries whatever, while It revives and revitalizes the object of Its Love with an entirely new direction and purpose for being. It is four in that It contains all the Elements, yet It is five because of Its fifth principle of Spirit. One ALL encompasses it all in a glittery, unctuous soup...*Menstruum* is as good as any other description.}

Commending, for this great and gracious Mystery and secret of Nature, to the Godhead all eternal glory, to Whom it is due.

The Lord illuminate my heart with His Light and Truth, so long as my Spirit remains in me, for His Light is very delightful and good for the Eye of my Soul to see by; for so shall the night be enlightened to me as the day, neither shall the clouds shadow it; it shall not be like the light of the sun by day, because it shall not be clouded, nor like the light of the Moon, because it shall never be diminished as her light is.

The Sun was made to rule the Day, and not to give light to it only, as appears {in} Gen:1. And the Moon was made to rule the Night, not to give light to it only, because she has no light to give. Also God made the whole Host of Heaven, the fixed stars and planets, and gave them virtues together with the Luminaries, but their virtues are not so great as the virtues of the Luminaries. Neither is the Moon so great as the virtue of the Sun because she borrows her light from the Sun. Also the whole host of Heaven, that is the fixed stars, move all in the same sphere {Qabalists call this sphere, Chokmah Assiah, the sphere of the fixed stars, Masloth, and Virgin Sulphur.}, and therefore their distance is always the same, but it is not so with the planets, for their course is various, and so is their distance the one from the other, and so is their latitude. For sometimes they are upon the ecliptic, sometimes North from it, sometimes South, sometimes retrograde, sometimes direct, sometimes in conjunction one with another, sometimes in opposition, sometimes in other aspects. The reason of this is because the sphere of one is lower than the sphere of the other, and the lower the sphere is, the sooner they make their revolution.

The nearest to the Earth of all the planets is the Moon, and therefore her course is swiftest; and besides her difference in longitude and latitude, there happen other accidents to her which are not visible to other planets. For sometimes she increases, sometimes decreases, and sometimes she is invisible or fails in light. The reason why the planets are not seen horned as the Moon is, because their distance is greater from us. All planets seem biggest when they are at their greatest distance from the Sun or when they are nearest to the Earth, according to Copernicus. Also sometimes the Moon is eclipsed but not in the same manner as the Sun; for the Sun never loses his light but is only shadowed from a particular people or place by the body of the Moon. But the Moon, eclipsed totally, loses her light, and the reason is, the Sun's light is his own, but the Moon is a borrowed light. This being premised, I consider that all things under the Moon universally, whether men, beasts or plants are changed and never remain in the same state, neither are their thoughts and deeds the same. Take council of your head and it will certify you of the truth hereof, and they are varied according to the various course and disposition of the planets. Look upon your own Genesis, and you shall find your thoughts moved to choler so often as the Moon transits the place where the body or aspect of Mars was in your Genesis; and to melancholy when she does the like to Saturn. The reason is because the Moon is assimilated to the body of man, whose virtue, as well as her light, increases and diminishes, for she brings down the virtue of the other planets to the creatures and to man if he lives upon Earth.

The Sun causes heat and cold, day and night, summer and winter. When he arrives to the house of his honor or exaltation, to wit Aries, then the trees spring, living creatures are comforted, the birds sing, the whole creation rejoices, and sicknesses in the body show themselves in their colors. Also when he arrives at his fall, to wit Libra, the leaves of trees fall, all creatures are lumpish, and mourn like the trees in October. Another notable Rosicrucian experiment. Usually sick people are something {somewhat} eased from midnight to noon, because then the Sun is in the Ascending part of the heaven, but they are most troubled when the Sun descends, that is from noon to midnight.

The course of the Moon is to be observed in many operations both in the sea and rivers, vegetables, minerals, shellfish, as also in the bones and marrow of men and of all creatures. Also seed sown in the wane of the Moon grows either not at all or to no purpose.

The Rosicrucians have experiences of many virtues of the Stars and have left them to posterity; and have found the changes and terminations of diseases by the course of the Moon. Wherefore the 7, 14, 20 or 21, 27, 28 or 29 days of the sickness are called Critical Days, which cannot be known but by the Course of the Moon. But rest not in the number of days, because the Moon is sometimes swifter, sometimes slower. As for such diseases as do not terminate in a month (I mean a Lunar month) the time when the Moon moves round the Zodiac, which is in 27 days and some odd hours and minutes, you must judge of those by the course of the Sun.

The day is called critical because the Moon comes to the quartile of the place she was in at the Decumbiture, sometimes a day sooner or later.

When she comes to the opposition of the place she was in at the day of the Decumbiture, she makes a second Crisis, the third, when she comes to the second quartile, and the fourth when she comes to the place she was in at the Decumbiture, and then is the danger.

The reason of the difference of the Moon's motion is the difference of her distance from the Earth; for when the Center of her Circle is nearest to the Center of the Earth, she is swift in motion. And hence it comes to pass that sometimes she moves more than 15 degrees in 24 hours, sometimes less than 12. Therefore if she be swift in motion she comes to her own quartile in six days, if slow, not in seven, therefore must you judge according to the motion of the Moon, and not according to the number of days.

Upon a critical day, if the Moon be well aspected with good planets, it goes well with the sick, if by ill planets it goes ill. You must be resolved in one particular, which is, if the Crisis depend upon the motion of the Moon, and her aspect to the planets, what is the reason if two men be taken sick at one and the same time, that yet the crisis of the one falls out well, and not so in the other. I answer, the virtue working is changed according to the diversity of the virtue receiving. For you all know the Sun makes the clay hard, and the wax soft. It makes the cloth white, and the face black; so then if one be a child, whose nature is hot and moist, the other a young man, and the third an old man, the Crisis works diversely in them all because their ages are different.

Secondly the time of the year carries a great stroke in this business; if it be in the springtime diseases are most obnoxious to a child because his nature is hot and moist. A disease works most violently with a choleric man in summer; with a phlegmatic man by reason of age or complexion in winter.

If the Moon be strong when she comes to the quartile of the place she was in at the Decumbiture, viz., in her House or Exaltation, the sick recovers if she be aspected to no planets.

Judge the like of the Sun in chronic diseases, but judge the contrary if either of them be in the Detriment or Fall. If the Moon be void of course at the beginning of a disease the sign is neither good or bad. Look then to the sign Ascending at the beginning of a disease, and let the Moon alone for a time.

Observe the following directions how to prepare all the seven Metals. If

33

Mars cause the disease, Venus helps more than Jupiter, that is a medicine of Venus cures. If Saturn, then Jupiter more than Venus, prepared Jupiter {medicine} cures. Whatsoever is said of the Moon in acute diseases will hold as true of the Sun in chronic diseases.

What diseases every Planet signifies and the diseases that are under the Twelve Signs, with the parts of the body every Planet rules, the cure of those diseases by Rosicrucian physic, by the seven metallic preparations, shall in its proper place be handled at large.

To unlock this Grand Rosicrucian Mystery of the Astrobolismes of Metals, the Miraculous Saphiric Medicines of the Sun and Moon, the Astrolasmes of Saturn, Jupiter Mars, Venus and Mercury. {Mr. A.E. Waite added a footnote in Vaughan's *Lumen de Lumine* which is worthy to repeat here: "*Astrobolismus* is an equivalent in late Latin for the classical *sideratio*, meaning primarily the withering or blasting of trees through wind or drought; but it stood also for a seizure of human beings, known otherwise as planet-struck, a benumbed condition, one of temporary paralysis."}

Seriously consider the system or fabric of the world. {From here to the section "On Mercury" is presented by Thomas Vaughan in *Lumen de Lumine*. He begins his section with "When I seriously consider...etc.} It is a certain series *a non gradu ad non gradium*, from that which is beneath all apprehension, to that which is above all apprehension. That which is beneath all degrees of sense is a certain horrible, inexpressible darkness, the magicians call it *Tenebrae Activa* {active darkness}, and the effect of it is cold, etc. For Darkness is *Vultus Frigoris* {an appearance of cold}, the Complexion, Body and Matrix of Cold, as Light is the Face, Principle and Fountain of Heat. That which is above all degrees of intelligence, is a certain Infinite, Inaccessible Fire or Light. Dionysius calls it *Caligo Divina* {divine darkness}, because it is invisible and incomprehensible. The Jews style it EIN {the AIN; Aleph, Yod, Nun, gematria = 61. AIN is the exact equivalent to the Hindu "Night of Brahma," the Vedic "Pralaya," the Egyptian "Black Osiris," the "TAO" of Lao-Tze, and the "Night" of Genesis.} that is *Nihil* or Nothing; but in a Relative sense, or as the schoolmen express it, *Quoad nos* {relative (as far as) to us}. In plain terms it is *Deitas nuda sine indumento* {naked Deity, from any envelopment}, the Middle Substances or chain between these two, is that which we commonly call Nature. This is the Scala of the Great Chaldee which does reach a *Tartaro ad primum ignem* {from lower Hades to the primal fire}, from the Supernatural Darkness to the Supernatural Fire. These middle natures came out of a certain Water which was the Sperm of First Matter of the Great World, and now we will begin to describe it. *Capiat qui capere potest* {Let him receive it who can}. It is in plain terms {a dissolved and flowing water—Greek omitted}, or rather it is {something melted— Greek omitted}, that is {a solution of earth and a certain plasticity of earth—Greek omitted}, an exceeding soft, moist, fusible, flowing Earth; an Earth of Wax, that is, capable of all forms and impressions. It is *terrae filius aqua mixtus* {Son of earth mixed with water}, and to speak as the nature of the thing requires, {mixed earth and marriage of earth—Greek omitted}. The learned Alchemist defines it {Divine and Living Silver, an union of spirit in matter—Greek omitted}. It is a Divine, *Animated* mass, of complexion somewhat like Silver, the union of Masculine and Feminine Spirits.

The Quintessence of Four, the Ternary of Two, and the Tetract of One. These are His Generations physical and metaphysical. The thing itself is a world without form, neither mere power, nor perfect action, but a weak Virgin Substance, a certain soft, prolific Venus, the very Love and Seed, the mixture and moisture of Heaven and Earth.

Now the Rosicrucians, who without controversy were the wisest of Nations, when they discourse of the generation of Metals, tell us it is performed in this manner. The Mercury or Mineral Liquor, they say, is altogether cold and passive, and it lies in certain earthly subterraneous caverns: But when the Sun ascends in the East, his beams and heat, falling on this hemisphere, stir up and fortify the inward heat of the Earth. {The subterranean caverns is accessible by deep meditation. Again, this is the notion, "between two fires," touched upon previously.} Thus we see in winter weather that the outward heat of the Sun excites the inward natural warmth of our bodies and cherishes the blood when it is almost cold and frozen. Now then the central heat of the Earth, being stirred and seconded by the circumferential heat of the Sun, works upon the Mercury and sublimes it in a thin vapor to the top of its cell or cavern. But towards night, when the Sun sets in the west, the heat of the Earth, because of the absence of that great luminary, grows weak and the cold prevails, so that the vapors of the Mercury, which were formerly sublimed, are now condensed, and distill in drops to the bottom of their cavern. But the night being spent, the Sun again comes about to the East, and sublimes the moisture as formerly.

This Sublimation and Condensation continue so long till the Mercury takes up the subtle, Sulphurous parts of the Earth, and is incorporated therewith, so that this Sulphur coagulates the Mercury, and fixes him at last what he will not sublime, but lies still in a ponderous lump and is concocted to a perfect metal. {Bear in mind that these are all internal processes.}

Take notice then that our Mercury cannot be coagulated without our Sulphur, for: *Draco non moritur sine suo compare,* {The Dragon dies not without his companion.} It is Water that dissolves and putrefies Earth, and Earth that thickens and putrefies Water. You must therefore take two principles to produce a third Agent, according to that dark receipt of Hali the Arabian: {Following are several quotes on the First Matter from different Philosophers. In the MS. they are all in Latin, and immediately repeated in English. I have omitted the Latin portions.} "Take," says he, "the Corascen Dog and the bitch of Armenia, put them both together, and they will bring you a sky colored whelp." This sky colored whelp is that sovereign, admired and famous Mercury, known by the name of the

Philosophers' Mercury. Now for my part I advise you to take two living Mercuries, plant them in a purified Mineral Saturn, wash them and feed them with Water of Salt Vegetable, and you will see that speech of the Adept verified: "The Mother will bring forth a budding flower, which she will nurture at her own milky breast, and being helped by the Father, will turn herself into food for it utterly." But the process or receipt is no part of my design, wherefore I will return to the First Matter, and I say it is no kind of water whatsoever. If you will attain to the truth, rely upon my words, for I speak the truth. The Mother or First Matter of Metals is a certain watery substance, neither very water, nor very earth, but a third thing compounded of both and retaining the complexion of neither. To this agrees the learned Valentine in his apposite and genuine description of our Sperm: "The First Matter," says he, "is a waterish substance found dry, or of such a complexion that wets not the hand, and nothing like to any other matter whatsoever."

Know then for certain that this slimy, moist Sperm or Earth must be dissolved into water, and this is the water of the philosophers, not any common water whatsoever. This is the grand secret of the Art, and Lully discovered it, with a great deal of honesty and charity. "Our Mercury," says he, "is not common mercury or quicksilver, but our Mercury is a water which cannot be found upon Earth, for it is not made or manifested by the ordinary course of nature, but by the Art and manual operations of men." Look not then for that in nature which is an effect beyond her ordinary process; you must help her that she may exceed her common course or all is to no purpose. In a word you must make this water before you can find it. {We make this Water by sincere, ardent, persistent meditation, backed by desire. The First Matter is not revealed to us, that is by Nature, unless we force her hand by desirous quest. Studies, prayers, meditations and visualizations are the methods of Art and Manual Operations.} In the interim you must permit the philosophers to call their Subject or Chaos a Water, for there is no proper name for it, unless we call it Sperm which is a watery substance, but certainly no water. {Roger Bacon called this Sperm *semen solare*, Seed of the Sun, which has lead many alchemists down some degrading paths. *Semen solare* totals 112 by Latin Gematria, which equals *Prima Materia*.} Let it suffice that you are not cheated, for they tell you what it is and what it is not, which is all that man can do. If I ask you by what name you call the sperm of a chick, you will tell me it is the white of an egg, and truly so is the shell as well as the sperm that is within it; but if you call it Earth or Water, you know well enough it is neither, and yet you cannot find a third name. I judge then as you would be judged, for this is the very case of the philosophers. Certainly you must be very unreasonable, if you expect that language from men which God has not given them.

Now that we may confirm this our theory and discourse of the Sperm not only by experience but by reason, it is necessary that we consider the qualities and temperament of the sperm. It is then a slimy, slippery, diffusive moisture.

But if we consider any perfect products they are firm, compacted, figurated bodies; and hence it follows they must be made of something that is not firm, nor compacted, nor figurated, but a weak, quivering, altering substance. Questionless thus it must be, unless we make the sperm to be of the same complexion with the body, and then it must follow that generation is no alteration. Again it is evident to all the world that nothing is so passive as moisture. The least heat turns water to a vapor, and the least cold turns that vapor to water. Now let us consider what degree of heat it is that acts in all generations, for by the Agent we may guess at the nature of the Patient. We know the Sun is so remote from us, that the heat of it (as daily experience tells us) is very faint and remiss. I desire then to know, what subject is there in all nature, that can be altered with such a weak heat, but moisture? Certainly none at all; for all hard bodies as salts, stones and metals preserve and retain their complexions in the most violent excessive fires. How then can we expect they should be altered by a gentle, and almost insensible warmth? It is plain then, and that by infallible inference from the proportion and power of the Agent, that moisture must needs be the Patient. For that degree of heat, which nature makes use of in his generations, is so remiss and weak it is impossible for it to alter anything but what is moist and waterish. This truth appears in the *Animal* family, where we know well enough the sperms are moist. Indeed in vegetables the seeds are dry, but then Nature generates nothing out of them till they are first macerated or moistened with water. And here the Peripatetic Philosophers are quite gone with their *pura potentia* {pure power}, that fanatic Chaos of the Son of Nichomachus. But I must advise my chemists to beware of any common moisture, for that will never be altered otherwise than to a vapor. See therefore that your moisture be well tempered with Earth, otherwise you have nothing to dissolve and nothing to coagulate. Remember the practise and magic of the Almighty God in His creation, as it is manifested to you by Moses. "*In principio,*" says he, "*creavit Deus Coelum et Terrum.*" But the original, if it be truly and rationally handled, speaks thus: "*In principio Deus miscuit Rarum et Densum*—In the beginning God mingled or tempered together the thin and the thick." For Heaven and Earth in this text signify the Virgin Mercury and the Virgin Sulphur. This I will prove out of the text itself, and that by the vulgar, received translation which runs thus: "In the beginning God created the Heaven and the Earth, and Earth was without form and void, and there was darkness upon the face of the abyss, and the spirit of God moved upon the face of the waters." In the first part of this text Moses mentions two created principles, not a perfect world, as we shall prove hereafter, and this he does in these general terms, Heaven and Earth. In the latter part of it he describes each of these principles by itself in more particular terms, and he begins with the Earth. "And the Earth," says he, "was without form and void." {The "formless and void" is the Alchemical Earth, AIN SUPh AUR. Once more, "void" in Genesis is BHV (bohu), which letters sum to

13 in gematria, that of AChD (Achad), Unity. This hints the Limitless Light as one homogeneous Substance prior to any separation of Itself.} Hence I infer that the Earth he speaks of, was a mere rudiment or principle of this Earth which I now see, for this present Earth is neither void or without form. {This physical Earth is frozen or coagulated AIN SUPh AUR, Alchemical Earth.} I continue then that the Mosaical Earth was the Virgin Sulphur, which is an Earth without form, for it has no determined figure. {Virgin Sulphur lies within AIN SUPh AUR.} It is a laxative unstable, uncomposed substance, of a porous empty crasis, like sponge or soot. In a word I have seen it, but it is impossible to describe it. {This is the problem for all who have seen the First Matter, first hand, through the inner vision. There simply are no words, in this plane, that adequately describe it. It can only be alluded to by metaphors.} After this he proceeds to the description of his Heaven, or second principle, in these subsequent words: "And there was Darkness upon the face of the abyss, and the Spirit of God moved upon the face of the Waters." Here he calls that an abyss and Waters, which he formerly called Heaven. It was indeed the Heavenly moisture or water of the Chaos, out of which He separated Heaven, or habitation of the stars was afterwards made. {Separated here is curiously accurate. The Hebrew, BRA (bera), is frequently translated as "created" in Genesis 1:1. But an outdated expression is "cut, separated, divided" which implies something pre-existent that was divided. The Black Water, Ain SUPh AUR, swirls and rotates about a point, becoming more compact and dense until, by a twisting motion, it "bursts" into the "day" of manifestation as a center of a Crab Nebula, creating a physical universe of suns and stars.} This is clear out of the original, for HMIM {Ha-Maim}, and HShMIM {Ha- Shmaim} are the same words, like *aqua*, and *ibi aqua*, and they signify one and the same substance, namely, Water. {HMIM is the Waters, while HShMIM is the Heavenly Waters or Fiery Waters.} The text, then being rendered according to the primitive natural truth and the undoubted sense of the author, speaks thus: "In the beginning," or according to the Jerusalem Thargum or Tradition, "in Wisdom God made the Water and the Earth. And the Earth was without form and void, and there was darkness upon the face of the deep, and the Spirit of God moved upon the face of the Waters." Here you should observe that God created two principles, Earth and Water, and of these two He compounded a third, namely, the Sperm or Chaos. Upon the water or moist part of this Sperm, the Spirit of God did move, and, says the Scriptures, there was darkness upon the face of the deep. This is a very great secret, neither is it lawful to publish it expressly, and as the nature if the thing requires, but in the Magical work it is to be seen, and I have been an eye witness of it myself.

To conclude, remember, that subject is no common water, but a thick, slimy, fat Earth. This earth must be dissolved into water, and that water must be coagulated again into Earth. This is done by a certain Natural Agent, which the philosophers call their Secret Fire. For if you work with common fire it will dry your sperm, and bring it to an unprofitable red dust, of the color of wild poppy. Their Fire then is the Key to the Art, for it is a natural Agent but acts not naturally without the Sun. I must confess it is a knotty mystery but we shall make it plain. It requires indeed a quick, clear apprehension.

On the Fire

Behold our 7 BRAMAAH, {This is a curious term, unless it is the early English spelling for Brahma of the Hindus. This might make some sense since the Hebrew term AIN is exactly equivalent to the Hindu "Night of Brahma." Then, the 7 Brahmas would be equal to the "7 Days" in Genesis. The seven interior planets also have their Sulphurous Fires, which, if turned towards their Mercury eventually confects The Stone. However, further on in this work our author comes up with "DRAMAAH." Vaughan omits both terms in *Lumen de Lumine*. Maybe he didn't know either.} and their wonderful Mysteries, for by them you may cure all diseases young or old, but know first our *fire* and *USE* it in the work.

Fire, notwithstanding the diversities of it in this Sub-lunary Kitchen of the Elements {subconsciousness}, is but one thing from one root. The effects of it are various according to the Distance and Nature of the Subject wherein it resides, for that makes it vital, or violent. It sleeps in most things as in flints where it is silent and invisible. It is a kind of perdue; lies close like a spider in the cabinet of his web to surprise all that come within his lines. He never appears without his prey in his foot, where he finds ought that is combustible there he discovers himself, for if we speak properly he is not generated but manifested. Some men are of opinion that he breeds nothing, but devours all things, and is therefore called *Ignis quasi ingignens* {A fire, as it were, inbreeding}. This is a grammatical whim, for there is nothing in the world generated without fire.

What a fine Philosopher then was Aristotle, {who} tells us this Agent breeds nothing but his *Pyrausta*, a certain fly which he found in his candle, but could never be seen afterwards. Indeed too much heat burns and destroys, and if we descend to other natures, too much water drowns, too much earth buries and chokes the seed that it cannot come up. And veritably at this rate there is nothing in the world that generates. What an owl was he then that could not distinguish with all his logic, between excess and measure, between violent and vital degrees of heat, but concluded the fire did breed nothing, because it consumed something? But let the mule pass, for so Plato called him, and let us prosecute our secret fire. This fire is at the root, and about the root (I mean about the center) of all things both visible and invisible. It is in Water, Earth and Air. It is in minerals, herbs and beasts. It is in men, stars, angels, but originally it is in God Himself, for He is the Fountain of heat and fire, and from Him it is derived to the rest of the creatures in a certain stream or sunshine.

Now the Rosicrucians afford us but two notions, whereby we may know their fire. It is as they describe it moist and invisible. Hence have they called it *Ventor Equis* {horse's belly}, and *Fimus Equinus* {horse's dung}, but this only by way of analogy. {Horse Dung has been used by many other writers and prompted many a physical alchemist to gather some for the lab. The Qabalist, however, would not have missed the metaphor as *fimus equinus* totals 158 in Latin Gematria, that of MIM ChIIM, Living Waters, another name for the Ocean of Awareness, AIN SUPh AUR.} For there is in horse dung a moist heat, but no fire that is visible. Now then let us compare the common Vulcan with this Philosophical Vesta, that we may see wherein they are different. First then the philosophers' fire is moist, and truly so is that of the kitchen too. We see that flames contract and extend themselves, now they are short, now they are long, which cannot be without moisture to maintain the flux and continuity of their parts. I know Aristotle makes the fire to be simply dry, perhaps because the effects of it are so. He did not indeed consider that in all complexions there are other qualities besides the predominant one. Sure then this dry stuff is that element of his, wherein he found his *pyrausta*. But if our natural fire were simply dry the flames of it could not flow, and diffuse themselves as they do. They would rather fall to dust, or turn like their fuel, to ashes. The common fire is excessively hot, but moist in a far inferior degree, and therefore destructive, for it preys on the moisture of other things. On the contrary, the warmth and moisture of the Magical Agent are equal, the one temperates and satisfies the other. It is a humid, tepid fire, or as we commonly express ourselves, blood-warm. This is the first and greatest difference in relation to our decided effect, we will now consider their second. The kitchen fire, as we all know, is visible, but the Philosophers' Fire is invisible, and therefore no kitchen fire. This Almadir expressly tells us in these words: "Our work," says he, "can be performed by nothing but by the invisible beams of our fire." And again: "Our fire is a corrosive fire, which brings a cloud about our Glass, or Vessel, in which cloud the beams of our fire are hidden." To be short the philosophers call this Agent their Bath, because it is moist as baths are, but in very truth it is no kind of bath, neither *Maris* {of the sea} nor *Roris* {of dew} but a most subtle fire and purely natural, but the excitation of it is artificial. {The artificial excitation is performed by meditation and a redeployment of the sex energy. Total chastity is not warranted, but a certain continence rechannels energy to cloud the human aura with a vapor "seen" in fourth dimensional awareness. Hence we read many sages give instruction to set an operation in *Balneo*. This Latin phrase sums to 64, that of *sperma*.} This excitation or preparation is a very trivial, slight, ridiculous thing, nevertheless all the Secrets of Corruption and generation are therein contained. {The energy from the Mars (Iron) Chakra is the force that breaks down or corrupts tissue-cell structure in humans. Rechanneled, it is the same force that reproduces, or generates, new and stronger cells able to contain more Light-Substance. This is the Iron Key referred to by some writers.}

Lastly, I think it just to inform you that many authors have falsely described this fire, and that of purpose to seduce their readers. For my own part, I have neither added nor diminished, you have here the true entire secret, and in which all eastern sages agree; Alfid, Almadir, Belen, Gieberim, Hali, Salmanazar and Zadich, with three famous Jews; Abraham, Artefius and Kalid. Now I will teach you how to use it.

Take our two serpents, {Pingala and Ida of Kundalini} which are to be found everywhere on the face of the Earth. They are a living male and a living female. Tie them up both in a Love Knot and shut them up in the Arabian *caraha* {The Glass Vessel or Human Aura}. This is your first labor, but your next is more difficult. You must encamp against them with the fire of nature, and be sure you do bring your line round about. Circle them in, and stop all avenues, that they find no relief. Continue this siege patiently {persistent attempt to gain control}; and they will turn to an ugly, slabby, venomous, black toad, which will be transformed to a horrible devouring Dragon, creeping and weltering in the bottom of her cave without wings. Touch her not by any means, not so much as with your hands, for there is not upon Earth such a violent, transcendent poison. As you have begun, so proceed, and this Dragon will turn into a Swan, but more white than the hovering virgin snow when it is not yet sullied with the Earth. Hence forth I will allow you to fortify your fire till the Phoenix appears. It is a red bird of a most deep color with a shining, fiery hue. Feed this bird with the fire of his father and the aether of his mother, for the first is meat, the second is drink, and without this past he attains not to his full glory. Be sure to understand this secret, for fire feeds not well unless it be first fed. It is of itself dry and choleric, but a proper moisture tempers it, gives it a heavenly complexion and brings it to the desired exaltation. Feed your bird then as I have told you, and he will move in his nest and rise like a star of the firmament. Do this, and you have placed Nature in *horizonte aeternitatis* {in the horizon of eternity}. You have performed that command of the Cabalist: "Unite the end to the beginning, like a flame to a coal: for God," says he, "is Superlatively One and He has no second." Consider then what you seek, a miraculous, indissoluble, transmuting, uniting union. But such a tie cannot be without the first unity: "To create and transmute," one says, "essentially, and naturally or without any violence, is the only proper office of the first Power, the first Wisdom and the first Love." Without this Love the elements will never be married, they will never inwardly and essentially unite, which is the end and perfection of Magic. Study then to understand this, and when you have performed, I will allow you that test of the Mekkubalim: "Thou hast understood in wisdom, and thou hast been wise in understanding; thou hast established this subject upon the pure elements thereof, and thou hast posited the Creator on His throne." {This Latin sentence was not translated in the MS., but done by Waite or Vaughan in *Lumen de Lumine.*}

To close this section, I say it is impossible to generate in the Patient, without a vital generating Agent. This Agent is the Philosophical Fire, a certain moist, heavenly, invisible heat. But let us hear Raymond Lully describe it: "When we say the Stone is generated by fire, men neither see, neither do they believe there is any other fire but the common fire; nor any other Sulphur or Mercury but the common sulphur and mercury. Thus are they deceived by their own opinions, saying that we are the cause of their errors, having made them to mistake one thing for another. But by their leave it is not so as we shall prove by the Doctrine of the Philosophers. For we call the Sun a fire, and the natural heat we call his Substitute, or Deputy; for that which the heat of the Sun performs in a thousand years in the mines, the heat of Nature performs it above the Earth in one hour. But we and many other Philosophers have called this heat, "The Child of the Sun, for at first it was generated naturally by the influence of the Sun without the help of our Art or Knowledge." Thus saith Lully.

But one thing I must tell you, and be sure you remember it. This very natural heat must be applied in the just degree, and not too much fortified, for the Sun itself does not generate but burn and scorch where it is too hot. "If you shall work with too strong a fire," says Lully, "the propriety of our spirit, which is indifferent as yet to life or death, will separate itself from the body, and the Soul will depart to the region of her own Sphere."

Take therefore along with you this wholesome though short advice of Lully: "My son," says he, "let the heavenly power or Agent be such in the place of generation or mutation that it may alter the Spermatic Humidity from its earthly complexion, to a most fine, transparent form or species." See here how the solution of the slimy, fat earth to a transparent, glorious Mercury! This Mercury is the Water which we look after; but not any common water whatever. There is nothing now behind but that which the Philosophers call *Secretum Artis* {Secret of the Art}; a thing that was never published, and without which you will never perform, though you know both Fire and Matter. An instance here we have in Flammel, who knew the Matter well enough and had both Fire and Furnace painted to him by Abraham the Jew; but notwithstanding he erred for three years, because he knew not the third secret. Henry Madathan, a most noble Philosopher, practiced upon the Subject for five years together, but knew not the right method, and therefore found nothing. At last, he says: "After the sixth year, I was entrusted with the Key of Power by Secret Revelation from Almighty God." This Key of Power or Third Secret was never put to paper by any philosopher whatever. Paracelsus indeed had touched upon it, but so obscurely, it is no more the purpose than if he had said nothing. And now I have done enough for the discovery and regiment of the Fire, and more than any one author has performed. Search it then, for he that finds this Fire, will attain to the true temperament, he will make a noble, deserving Philosopher, and to speak in the phrase of our Spaniard: "He will be worthy to sit at the table of twelve peers." {On the Secret Fire—in Proverbs 1:2,3 we are advised: "to know Wisdom and instruction...to receive the discipline of Wisdom." Solomon's highest aspiration was to "Above all, get Wisdom." Paracelsus instructs us that first, and chiefly, the principle subject of this Art is *Fire*. And in *The New Chemical Light*: "Among the three principles the Sages have justly assigned the first place to Sulphur, as the whole Art is concerned with the manner of its preparation." Whether we seek Wisdom, Fire, Sulphur or *Desire*, these are all attributed to the second sephirah, Chokmah, and is all the very same instruction.}

And now I will teach you how to make the DRAMAAH {At the beginning of this section DRAMAAH was spelled BRAMAAH} into Medicines mixed with the Metals, and first:

Of Mercury

The Rosicrucians describe unto us the Mount of God and His Mystical, Philosophical Geomancy, which is nothing else but the highest and purest part of the Earth; for from Tetragrammaton He shines upon the Orders and they carry His Power to the Planets, so you see the superior secret portion of this element is holy ground; it is the seed plot of the eternal nature. {Light-Energy, from the AIN to tangible substance, comes to us in gradations or layers of shimmering hues, which waver. The most dense light energy, furthest from the Center, far below the sphere of human sensation as AIN is above, Qabalists term Qliphoth.} And the Chaos was divided into eight parts. The eighth was deadly; but first of the seven; the matter was the body of the Lapsed Angels. After light began to appear, the Center was red, an ash color bluish, the circumference blue. The second Division green, fiery red and purple. In the third Division the center was fiery, the inferior waters purple, and the superior white. The fourth Division was azure bluish, the Sun and Moon then appearing pale bluish. In the fifth Division the Earth was red, and the Center fiery, the waters bluish azure, the Sun and Moon ash color. The sixth Division of the Earth was a red bluish, and Center fiery. The seventh Apparition is the immediate vessel and recipient of heaven whence all Minerals have their life, and by which the *Animal* Monarchy is maintained. {Perception of the gradations or separations of Light-Energy are extremely subjective, depending on the degree of Adeptship. Our original author claims to have experienced eight. Other world disciplines vary. The Mexican, Yaqui Tradition first separates three major layers into whitish, chartreuse and amber, with further bands of color within and between these.}

This Philosophical, black Saturn mortifies and coagulates the invisible Mercury of the Stars and on the contrary the Mercury kills and dissolves the Saturn, and out of the corruption of both, the Central and Circumferential Suns disgenerate new bodies; the Green Lion in a bluish circle; the Green Lion swallowed to the hinderparts; the virtues in a purple vessel of Nature, half Moon made; the vegetable, *Animal* Mineral in a bluish, calcination of fiery and blue Earth; sublimation, fiery, airy and azure; solution black, white and azure; the spirit descends. {These color gradations will make little to no sense for those of us unable to explore fourth dimensional awareness in our energy, vital, astral or subconscious light-bodies (these are all the same). When we can redeploy enough energy to reach our light-body, we may grow sufficiently adept to isolate dozens of hues. There are endless numbers of them. Qabalistically illustrated, they are the King, Queen, Emperor and Empress color-scales on the Tree in Four Worlds. They are not to be considered firm as the light-bands scintillate and waver. The aura of our living Earth, for example, changes like our personal auras.} The masculine and feminine Mercury generated, there will appear azure purple, ash color yellow and red, in putrefaction our matter is black and azure; the Spirit descends. In conception our *Astrum Solis*, the mineral spiritual Sun, is a bloody, fiery, spirited Earth, the Spirit descends and the superfinals, azure in impregnation; the *Astrum Solis* ascends from a muddy water, and the spirit with it. In fermentation the black, slabby toad lies sweltering in the vessel and the spirit in azure descending appears, in separation of fire, air, water and earth. The Toad lies in the earth black, the Earth ash color, the water green, the air blue, the fire blood-red, and the aether a liquid white fire; the Spirit ascends.

In Conjunction of Elements the fire is red, air blue, water green and earth dark ash, and the Spirit descends in a clear sky. In Separation of earth, fire, air and water, the earth lies in the bottom dark, the fire flaming upon it, breaking through the air to the water and disperses itself. {This and the following three paragraphs were broken up from the solid MS. text. Hopefully it eases otherwise tedious and difficult reading.}

In Conjunction of Water in air the Spirit descends in a clear sky, to that blue composition, the air in the water is green, the fire red and earth ashen. In the Separation of fire, water, air in water, earth, the earth is dark, muddy, the air in water blue, the water transparent, and the fire flaming red and white, and the Spirit ascends in an azure sky.

In Conjunction of Air in fire, fire in water, water in air, earth, the earth is dark and heavy, the water in air blue, the fire in water green, the air in fire a blushed red, the Spirit descends in a clear sky. In Separation of air water, fire in air earth, the earth is ash color, fire in air blood red flaming through the azure water and air, the spirit ascends.

In Conjunction Fire in air, water in fire, air in water, earth, the earth is black, the air in water is green, the water in fire is like the sunbeams in a mist, the fire above all lies in the air blue, flaming, the Spirit descends. The next Separation is flames of fire breaking out in all the Elements, the Earth only lies of a darker color, the unnatural fire stands thus, air water, fire earth; the earth covered with a blue flame, the fire ascending to the central color, water and air, the Spirit descends.

The rising of the Rosicrucian Medicines the earth *cineri coloris* {colored ashes}, a white star and moon, appearing in a star, the power and Spirit ascends in a clear sky. In Fermentation a dark star lies in the earth, and the Spirit descends to it in a clear sky. In Purgation the earth is black, and the Spirit descends clear. In this Separation there appears water in air, fire in water turned upwards, below is a blue space, then the earth in fire is red, air in earth ash color.

This conjunction of air in fire, water in earth, fire in air, earth in water; the earth in water in dark, the fire in air red but not violent, the water in earth green, the air in fire blue, the Spirit descends. And this Conjunction of earth in air, water in fire, and fire in earth; here in the bottom the earth is *Animated* with a secret fore, invisible, occult, the water shadows a mild fire, the air in water above these is green and glorious, the earth in air is a bluish white, the Spirit descends.

In this Exaltation of the Quintessence the Pelican is in the bottom, next above is azure; then two circles, of the first the upper is blue, the lower a white fire; The next is a green and red sea of fire environing the white matter; and this Exaltation of the Quintessence is azure, a Globe in the bottom, divided in four quarters, from the East to South is blue, from the South to the West green, from the West to the North white, from the North to the East red, and all the upper part of it azure; above this Globe the fire flames upon both sides. {Variations of this globe may be seen in Secret Symbols of the Rosicrucians.} In Fixation the branches of fire spread both ways round the white and azure Globe; this projection is upon a blue and white powder, the perspect in Multiplication runs down the vessel through the azure to the matter in the bottom.

In Imbibition the Serpent lies at the bottom of the matter. In Sublimation a strong fire drives the azure part to the top. In Congelation the azure binds or weighs down the fire to the bottom. In Conjunction the fire star lies in the bottom. In this Exaltation the double circled fire arises; and in the quintessence appears an Angel amidst the ascending Globes of fire, and in Fixation all is circled with purple and red fire; in the middle stands as Angel, in a star doubled with his wings spread and holding the glorious Crown of the Rose Cross in his hands. {This was a vast and detailed array of the AIN SUPh AUR. Whether the original author recorded someone else's experience, or were they his own is unknown. These were accomplished by repeated visits to inner realms, or by one, prolonged Samadhi, as was experienced by St. John or Jacob Boehme. Whatever, we could safely deduce this person an accomplished Adept.}

1. Of the Preparation of the Gold Mercury or *Argent Vive*.
2. Purification.
3. Sublimation.
4. Calcination.
5. Exuberation.
6. Solution.

7. Separation.
8. Conjunction.
9. Putrefaction.
10. Fermentation.
11. Multiplication in Virtue.
12. Multiplication in Quantity.

{"Notwithstanding, the philosophers have subtly delivered themselves, and clouded their instructions with enigmatical and typical phrases and words, to the end that their art might not only be hidden and so continued, but also be had in the greater veneration. Thus they advise to decoct, to commix, and to conjoin; to sublime, to bake, to grind, and to congeal; to make equal, to putrefy, to make white, and to make red; all which things, the order, management, and way of working is all one, which is only to decoct."—Roger Bacon, *The Root of the World*. Decoction, in the meaning of True Alchemists, is Meditation.}

1. He that can make the Medicine of *Argent Vive* or Mercury alone, is the greatest searcher out of Art and Nature because there is all that in Mercury which wise men do seek; for Quicksilver is the Mother and Sperm of all Metals, and their nearest matter; and it is not only a Spirit but a Body, it is also a middle nature, and also a Sulphur. It is a lingering Mercury, it dies and rises again, and is fixed with its own proper Elements: wherefore it is first necessary that it be purged from its impurities. {The First Matter is perceived a greenish color, impure with lower, astral thought forms. Our first regimen is to clear the Substance within our aura from these influences.}

2. The Purgation or Purification is on this wise. Grind it upon a Marble with a Muller, or a wooden pestle in a wooden Mortar with common Salt and a little Vinegar sprinkled thereupon till the Salt be black, then wash it well with Vinegar, and dry it easily at the fire, or at the Sun, then strain it through a double cloth of a new skin of a sheep till it be dry, and the Vinegar clear taken away, and be of a white color and clear. {None of this is to be considered literally. The Vinegar is investigated further on in the text.}

3. Grind it upon Marble with a little Mercury Sublimate, and let it mortify and incorporate with it: then grind it with its equal weight of Saltpeter and Green Copperas till it be like a paste; then put all into a subliming Glass, and in ashes sublime all the Mercury that it be white and clear as snow in the head of the Limbeck, sublime it again three times or oftener, and it will be pure Mercury and Sublimate.

4. Put one pound of this Mercury Sublimate into two pounds of common *Aqua Fortis* {Resolute or Strong Water, gematria = 115. This is the First Matter, cleared with the first step.} by little and little at once as by two at a time till all be dissolved like sugar in wine, then shut the Glass and set it in *Balneo* {Seal the

Aura by sexual continence (Hermetic Seal), in *Balneo* has been explained previously.}
to dissolute the space of ten days, then distill away the *Aqua Fortis* in a lent heat
in *Balneo*, and the Mercury will remain in the bottom like butter of a white
color, and calcined by corrosive water.

5. Put this calcined Mercury into an earthen body with a Limbeck and in
ashes sublime the whole dissolved substance three times which will then be
very white, and then it is called Mercury Exuberate.

When you have three or four pounds of this receive the third part and fix it
by often sublimation till it remain in a hard mass and ascend no more but
remain fixed, which is called the Glue of the Eagle or the prepared body
permanent and the volatile made fixed which is to be reserved for the earth of
the Stone.

6. Dissolve the other two parts in *Balneo* or in a cold cellar or put it in a
bladder and hang it over fuming hot water till it be all come to water. Take this
water, thus made, and digest it in a Circulatory {the human sanguinary system},
well closed, the space of nine days, then put it in a body with a head and
receiver well luted and in ashes or *Balneo*, distill the water of a white color or
milk which is called *Lac Virginis*, dissolving all metals and so you have separated
the spirit of the Stone which is also called the lingering spirit and the White
Tincture of the White Stone of Mercury.

7. Take the third part which before you reserved and fixed called the Glue
of the Eagle, as much of it as you please, and add thereto equal weight of its
spirit or *Lac Virginis* and close up the Glass, and so you have joined the man and
the woman, Mercury with his own Earth, the Spirit with the Body.

8. Set your *Lac Virginis* thus joined with his own, each in *Balneo* to putrefy
150 days and there let it stand unmoved; after 40 days it will be black, and it is
then called the Head of the Crow; then it will be of a green color; after that the
peacock's tail, and many false colors, for between this and white it will appear
red, but at last you shall see it white and then increase your fire and it will stick
to the sides of the Glass like fishes' eyes, then have you each in the nature of
Sulphur.

Take of this Sulphur as much as you please, and weigh it, and add thereto
two parts of the White Tincture or *Lac Virginis* and set it in *Balneo* to dissolve
the space of six days, then distill away the *Lac Virginis* of Tincture, and the
Sulphur will remain in the form of Liquor, for it is the liquor of the White
Sulphur of Mercury which is to be joined with the Liquor of the Sulphur of
Luna or Silver. {*Lac Virginis*, Virgin's Milk, gematria = 112. This is the white, milky
substance, *chyle*, generated from the lacteals at the intestines, the Virgo region within
the body. The gematria equals that of *prima materia* and *semen solare*.}

9. The Sulphur of the White Luminary or Silver or Luna is made as the
other, whereof we shall speak more in the next branch. This Liquor of the
Sulphur is the Soul which is joined with the Spirit and Body which quickens

the whole Stone. The other conjunction before was only the union of the Spirit and the Body; but this is a threefold copulation, viz; the uniting of the Soul, Spirit and Body. Add equal weight of these two Liquors of Sulphur that is to say the Liquor of the Sulphur of Mercury, and of Silver and Luna, and close well the Glass, and set it in ashes till it be white, for it will be of all colors again, and at last white; and then it is the perfect stone converting all metals into Silver.

10. This Medicine or Elixir is thus multiplied in virtue, dissolve it in your *Lac Virginis* and distill it away and dry it and dissolve it again, etc. And let it be so often dissolved and dried till it will dry no more but remain in an incombustible oil. And (it) is then Elixir of the third Order. {"The extremes of the Stone are natural *Argent Vive* and perfect Elixir."—Jean d'Espagnet, *Hermetic Arcanum*. Purify the raw First Matter, incorporate it into the body with *Lac Virginis*. This is the Elixir of Life. There is also an Elixir, an essence, of every perfected Metal.}

11. Take one part of this Elixir and project it upon 100 or 1000 parts of melted Silver (according to the goodness and virtue thereof) and it will turn the Silver into a brittle mass or Substance, which beat to a powder in an iron or brass mortar or upon a marble, and project one part of this powder upon 100 parts of Mercury purged, made hot, and it will be perfect Medicine whereof one part turns 100 or 1000 parts of other bodies into good Silver. And this way is your Medicine multiplied in quantity. Here follows the Mercurial Medicine prepared after we have taught you to make the Medicine of the Moon. {Via the Circulatory System, the purified Matter will imbue the body cell-structure, infecting other cells and organs by a progression. This is done by our subconscious mind, a "Medicine of the Moon."}

12. It remains now that we speak of the Medicine or the Elixir of Life, which is called Potable Silver. But although the Liquor of Silver may be made Potable Silver if it be corroborated before by digestion in *Balneo* 7 days with the Spirit of Wine and then distill away the said spirit of wine, that the oil of the Silver may remain in the bottom which may easily be given for medicine. Yet the philosophers would have us do otherwise for they teach us to bring the metals first into their quintessence before they be taken inwardly, and that there is no other quintessences but those that are of a second nature according to the old saying:

> *Elixir de te est res secunda*
> *De quo sunt facta copora munda.*

{"The Elixir from you is the second thing from which are made perfect bodies."}

That is to say the 4 Elements are destroyed {air, food, water and light}, and by putrefaction a new body created and made into a Stone, which is the Quintessence as Lully would have it, but I do boldly and constantly affirm that there is no true Silver or Potable Silver nor Quintessence unless it be first Elixir and that is done in a quarter of an hour by projection of the Elixir upon Silver or pure Gold molten according as the Elixir was red or white. If therefore you desire after the first composition of the Elixir to make the Arcanum of Argentum or *Aurum Potabile*, project the Elixir or Medicine according to his quality or property upon pure Silver or Gold molten, and then it is made brittle and frangible and grind it to powder, and take thereof so much as you please and dissolve it in distilled Vinegar (or rather in Spirit of Wine) the space of nine days, then distill away the Vinegar or Spirit of Wine, that which remains in the bottom is the true Medicine, Quintessence, Elixir of Life, Ferment of Ferments and Incombustible Oil converting Metals and Man's body into perfect health from all diseases of man's body which proceed from Mercury and Luna. And thus is the true Potable Silver made, curing the Vertigo, Syncope, Epilepsy, Madness, Frenzy, Leprosy, etc. {Wine has always been synonymous with Blood in the Mystery Writings. *Spiritus Vini*, the Spirit of Wine or Essence of Wine, is Blood charged with *Lac Virginis* and other essences extracted from the Metals by Vinegar. *Spiritus Vini* sums to 168 in Latin Gematria, that of *Pater Metallorum*, the Father of Metals. It perfects the Metals. Vinegar, in Hebrew, is ChMTz (chometz), which is the noun "leaven, fermentation," and sums to 138. Distilled Vinegar is Meditation that acts as leaven or fermentation on consciousness which raises the energy flowing through the Chakras. The organs influenced by the Chakras secrete their own "Elixir" that charges blood along with the Virgin's Milk. This makes *Aurum Potabile* (gematria = 138), Drinkable or Potable Gold. This Drinkable Gold charges cells that build new bodies. It is the core of the parable in Mark 2:22. New skin in the Latin of this verse is *uter novus*, gematria = 138. As all this is primarily a process of the subconscious, alchemists may interchange *Aurum* with *Argentum Potabile*, Potable Silver, which sums to 161, that of *corpus novus*, new body. Bodies with such blood cells are naturally free from all the above diseases and very many more.}

And this is the right way of making the Stone of Mercury alone; but the Elixir cannot be made without the addition of Silver to the White and Gold to the Red. {White and Red, Ida and Pingala, are the Lily and Rose in the Song of Solomon. *Lilium et Rosa* sum to 138.}

To teach this work, consider 8 principles:

1. Luna.
2. Pure Silver
3. Calcination
4. Solution
5. Putrefaction
6. The Sulphur
7. The Liquor of the Sulphur
8. White Ferment.

1. Hermes says the Elixir is nothing else but Mercury, Sol and Luna. By

Mercury nothing is understood but the Sulphur of Nature, which is called the true Mercury of the Philosophers, and that Sulphur gotten by putrefaction by the conjunction of the spirit and of the body of imperfect bodies or metals.

By Sol is meant Gold, by Luna Silver; both of them are to be joined to imperfect bodies, that is to say, White Sulphur and Red, whence the same Hermes, in his Seven Treatise of Sol {*Seven Golden Chapters*} says there happens a conjunction of two bodies {Ida and Pingala} and it is necessary in our Magistery {MS. has Maistry?}. And if one of these bodies only were not in our Medicine it would never by any means give any Tincture. Upon which Morienus says: "For the Ferment prepares the imperfect body and converts it to its own nature and there is no Ferment but Sol and Luna, that is Gold and Silver." Of which Rosinus: "Sol and Luna prepared, that is to say their Sulphurs, are the ferments of Metals in color."

But this is made more evident by Raymond in his *Apertory*, where he says there is no ferment except Sol and Luna, for the Ferment of the Medicine to white is Silver, and to the red Gold, as the philosophers do demonstrate because without Ferment there does proceed neither Gold nor Silver nor anything else that is of its kind or nature, therefore join the Ferment with its Sulphur that it may beget its like because the Ferment draws the Sulphur to its own color and nature also, and weight and sound, because every like begets its like. Because the Ferment, even as Sol, tinges and changes his Sulphur into a permanent and piercing Medicine. Therefore the Philosopher says he that knows how to tinge Sulphur and Mercury with Sol and Luna shall attain to the greatest secret. And for this reason it is necessary that Sol and Luna be the Tincture and Ferment thereof.

2. And so also Arnoldus says in his *Rosary*: "There is no body more noble and pure than Sol or his shadow, that is to say Silver, without which no tingeing Mercury is generated. He that endeavors to give color without this Gold or Silver goes blindly to work, like an ass to a harp, for Gold gives a golden and Silver an argentive color; therefore he that knows how to tinge Mercury with Sol and Luna comes {to} or reaches the secret which is called White Sulphur, the best to Silver, which, when it is made red will be Red Sulphur, to Gold best."

3. Take pure Luna, that is to say Silver; that is best which is beaten into leaves, and bring it into Calx with Mercury, and it is then called water Silver, then is the Luna well prepared for Calcination.

4. When you have your Silver thus prepared, take 4 or 6 ounces thereof and put it in double proportions of *Lac Virginis* mixed with equal quantity of corrosive water to dissolve in an egg glass. {This is the human aura compared to an egg due to its oval shape. The Hen's Egg is the body and aura. It is like a glass because it is transparent.} After it has dissolved so much as it can in the cold, set in *Balneo* and there let it stand 9 days till the whole substance of the Silver be dissolved

into a green water, then let the *Balneo* cool and take it out, and put the dissolution into the body, and set thereon a head, and distill off the water from the matter remaining, which is the oil of the Silver calcined not into a Calx but a Liquor, because this *Lac Virginis*, if it be mixed or joined with common *Aqua Fortis* or alone without it (as it pleases the operator) is so strong that the very Diamond cannot resist it but is dissolved. Therefore this Water is called the Water of Hell, and is the only miracle of miracles of the world, because it contains such a fiery nature in itself and propriety of burning of all bodies into Liquor, whereas the elemental fire prevails no further than to reduce Metals into Calx or ashes. But to return from where I digressed, I now come to the third operation.

5. To the end, therefore, that this Liquor or Oil of Silver may be more perfectly dissolved, and that all the imperfection of adustion {*adustio-onis*, burning} may be taken away, which by the ancients is called the corroborating of the best humidity, put this Oil or Liquor into another egg glass like the former, pour thereupon so much Spirit of Wine above it, 4 fingers, then close well the glass and set it in *Balneo* to digest 7 or 10 days and you shall find the Oil or Liquor turned into a thin or rare water-oil. Put this water into a still and in *Balneo*, draw away the Spirit of Wine till none of the Spirit of Wine remain with the Silver dissolved, and thus have you your Silver prepared for Putrefaction.

Observe the power of the Moon, and her Angel over Chasmodai, Muriel, Populus, Via and Silver. Practice and prepare after this manner. This Medicine cures all the diseases of the neck and breast, etc. It must be Silver purely refined. {See the graph: Geomancy: The Harmony in this Preparation on page 104 and the "Tree of the Moon" on page 91.}.

6. This Liquor of Silver is potable, but not the Quintessence. Put this water into a fit putrefying glass and seal it up and set it to putrefy in *Balneo* till the time of putrefaction be past which is about 150 days, {When some alchemists give numbers it may actually be the time it takes to purify an aspect within our nature through meditation, or they may be hinting something by gematria.} and when you see the first sign of putrefaction which is called the Head of the Crow, increase your fire a little till all colors begin to appear and you see it begin to be white.

When you see it white, increase your fire yet more and it will rise up and stick to the sides of the Glass, most transparent, like the eyes of fishes, {This is a glittery effect on the surface of the aura.} which is Sulphur of Nature or Salt, or the putrefied body of the white Luminary, viz., Luna, which yet is not so hard as a body nor so soft as a Spirit, but of a mean hardness between a Spirit and a Body, and is called the Philosophers' Mercury and the Key and mean of joining Tinctures.

7. But to come to the Liquor of the White Luminary. this body being brought into Quintessence is prepared for dissolution like the Sulphur of the imperfect body; but whereas that is done by virtue of the white tincture or *Lac Virginis*, I

rather do it by virtue of the fire natural, which is the Spirit of Wine, and after the drawing away thereof it remains in a Liquor.

Now this Liquor of Luna dissolved is the Quintessence, which then is the liquor of the White Luminary, and the sole (as Exinadius says) quickening the whole medicine without which it is dead and will never give form nor color.

8. Therefore the fourth part of this liquor of the White Luminary is to be joined to three parts of the former liquor of the Sulphur of Mercury, and after to be kept in a lent fire of ashes, well closed, till it passes through all colors, and at last come to its former color of whiteness, and so the medicine is ferment and turned into the White Elixir.

The residue of the aforesaid dissolved Sulphur keep diligently, and therewith ferment the White Sulphur of other imperfect bodies or stones into Elixirs, which, when they are thrice dissolved and again congealed and remain in a liquid substance, then they are called incombustible oils and Elixirs of the third order. {The first order Elixir is AIN SUPh AUR, cleansed. The second order is *Lac Virginis*. The third order is the combined Sulphur-Mercury essence within each Metal. For elucidation read d'Espagnet's *Hermetic Arcanum*, para. 61—64.}

And thus the Medicine is made of Mercury alone as follows by this example. Having spoken of the White Medicine, it now rests that we speak of the making of the Red Elixir, whereof there are two processes, the first whereof is from the Radix, i.e., the long way; the other an accurtation that is much shorter and more excellent. And this way the Elixir may be made in 80 days, and excels all other accurtations, neither is there found therein any diminution of the virtue, but a plentiful and perfect fullness of power and virtue, having all the properties which the Elixir ought to have.

The Operation Under These Heads
1. Vivum
2. Sublimation
3. Calcination
4. Precipitation
5. Solution
6. Fixed Oil
7. Inceration
8. Dessication
9. Contrition
10. Fermentation
11. The Red Elixir
12. The Third Table.

1. Purgation of Mercury I shall omit because it was spoken of before. {*Vivum*,

with gematria of 77, is the Living Silver, AIN SUPh AUR. The first reduction of 77 is 14, that of ZHB (zaheb), Gold; but also that of DI (dee), Sufficient, Enough. The author hints, as other sages, to the discovery of the Gold as being all that is necessary.}

2. The Sublimation is to be done otherwise than in the former work, for that which is called Sublimation here is not done with Vitriol and Saltpeter, but is only the distillation of Mercury in an earthen body with a Limbeck, and that without any additament.

3. When the Mercury is once sublimed in ashes wholly into the head of the Limbeck, having a retainer joined thereto, take off the head and with a feather gather the sublimed matter, and you will find your Mercury of a black color, having lost his fairness, and like a dust or powder sticking to his body.

4. Put it again into the body and sublime it as before, and reiterate this work 7 or 9 times until you have a sufficient quantity of this powder, a pound or more, and this is the Calcination.

5. When you see your Mercury will ascend no more but remains in the bottom of a black color, and that it is dead and brought perfectly into Calx, let it cool and remove your body into sand till it be turned into a red color. And this is the perfect precipitation, {for} proof without the help of any corrosive water, take a little of this powder upon a hot Iron plate; if it fume, dry it longer, if not it is well.

6. Take of this red powder as much as you will, dissolve and put thereupon at least his double weight of *Lac Virginis* and set in *Balneo* till you see your *Lac Virginis* stained a yellow or red color, then filter it from its feces and keep it by itself in a glass well stopped and dry the matter that remains in ashes, and pour thereon new *Lac Virginis*, and do as before till you have drawn out all the Tincture. And so your Mercury is dissolved.

7. Put these solutions into a body, luting to a head and in *Balneo*, distill away the *Lac Virginis*, and red oil precipitate will remain, which is fixed and needs no distillation, but is the tingeing oil of Red Mercury, and the red tincture of the red medicine of Mercury and the Soul and Spirit of the Medicine joined, as for example: "The Tree of Universal Mercury"—{on page 89.}

8. Take part of the White Sulphur reserved in the first Table, and rubify it in ashes till it be red; then imbibe it with equal weight of the oil of the tincture of this Red Mercury and set it to dissolve in *Balneo*, and when you see it is dissolved into a liquid substance, take it out.

9. Then set it in ashes or under the fire to fix till the matter, being dried, remains fusible and fixed, standing in a mean heat, not over-hot, which try upon a hot iron plate, and if it fume not, it is well, if it does, increase your fire till it be totally fixed and dry.

10. If this matter be imbibed again with its oil till it drink up as much as it will, and again dissolved in *Balneo* and then dried in ashes it will show many

colors and lastly appear red. And then it is the Stone, penetrating and fusible, apt for form.

11. Join this imbibed matter (or Medicine) with the fourth part of the Liquor or Oil of the Red Sulphur of Gold or the Red Ferment, and dissolve it in *Balneo*, and dry it again; and again dissolve in a Glass hanged in the fume of hot water or Balneum, and congeal it again till it stand like honey. Then it is the perfect Red Elixir of Mercury.

12. The Multiplication or Augmentation of the virtue and quantity is shown before in the preparation of the White Elixir.

Of Gold—SOL

1. The Preparation of Gold Sol
2. Purged Gold
3. Calcination
4. Solution
5. Putrefaction
6. *Filius Solis Coelestis*
7. *Filia Lunae Coelestis*

1. The Putrefaction or Purgation of Gold is done as the goldsmiths used to do by melting it with Antimony, that the Gold may remain in the bottom pure and clear from other metals, which they call *Regulus*. {*Regulus* sums to 93, that of BNI AL (beni al), Sons of God, and *omnia ab uno*, All from One. *Regulus* means King, Prince or Chief, and refers to the One-Ego, seated in Tiphareth, the True Gold within us after elimination of the separative ego. Those who have purged themselves of the false ego are counted among the Sons of God, from the One.}

2. Take 4 or 5 ounces of this refined Gold leaf or filings and dissolve it in *Lac Virginis* mixed with equal weight of *Aqua Fortis* wherein Salt Armoniac sublimed is dissolved, and when it is dissolved into a red liquor or deep yellow, then it is well calcined. {*Sal Armoniac*, it should be noted, has the same value as VITRIOL, 94. Both have the same metaphorical, burning effect.}

3. The Solution and Putrefaction is done as you did before with Silver in the preparation of the White Ferment.

4. When you have your White Sulphur of Nature (after Putrefaction) sticking to the sides of the Glass, let it cool, and take out the Glass and set it in ashes, and increase your fire, but not too much, lest your matter vitrify, and let your ashes be no hotter than you can hold your hand therein, and so let it stand till the Sulphur be of a perfect deep red color. Then have you the red Sulphur of the Red Luminary; as for example: {See the graph of "Observe the Harmony of Geomancy in the Preparation" on page 104.}

Behold the Power of the Sun and his Angel upon Sorath, Verchiel, Fortuna

Major and Minor in Gold and of his Medicine, which, being thus prepared, has performed incredible, extraordinary cures upon the bodies of the Princes and Poor of Europe. {See the Tree of Sol on page 95.}

5. If you resolve this Red Sulphur in Spirit of Wine or distilled Vinegar into an oil, it is then the Liquor of the Red Luminary and *Aurum Potabile* curing all infirmities if the Spirit of Wine or Vinegar be distilled from it; but for this Work it were better to dissolve it in our red *Lac Virginis*; distill away the Lac from the Sulphur in ashes, and the Sulphur remaining in an oil is the Ferment of all stones to the red.

6. The Augmentation of this Red Elixir in virtue is with his red Tincture as before in the White Tincture. The Augmentation in quantity is by projection upon the body of Gold molten, and that brittle matter of Gold upon Mercury; and if it be powdered and resolved with Spirit of Wine in an oil, as was said before of Silver, then it is the Quintessence of Gold, and the great Elixir of Life, and the spiritual ferment for the transmutation of metals, and the health of man's body.

Although Raymond, writing to the King, was pleased to say that every Accuration diminishes the perfection, because Medicines which are made by accuration have less effect of transmutation, which I also assent to with him for a truth, if the work be begun from the first fountain; yet because this work has its beginning from those things which before were brought to a perfect degree of perfection, therefore in this there is no diminution of the perfection.

"Therefore it ought to be declared unto you, that if they be both well prepared, and that you begin with them, you will do a wonderful work without any great labor sooner than if you should begin with one thing alone. Therefore, my son, begin your work of two things together as I showed you in the greater Medicines when we spoke of the two-fold custody of the actions which are caused by the bodies and Spirits." Thus far Raymond. By that which is caused by the bodies and Spirits he means nothing else but Sulphur, willing that we should begin with Sulphur, to which I do so well agree that I begin this my accurtation with this Sulphur alone, and I add no other body to this Elixir, but only the Sulphur of Mercury, alone created of his own body and Spirit.

Take, therefore, two ounces of the White Sulphur, described at the beginning of this treatise, and set it in ashes to rubify. In thirty days it will be turned into Red Sulphur, which, when you have done, dissolve that Sulphur in the red Tincture of Mercury. When it is dissolved draw away the Tincture; in the bottom remains the Liquor of the Sulphur.

To which, if you add a due proportion of the Liquor of the red Luminary, it will be perfect Ferment, which, if you dissolve and congeal as before is showed, it is then Elixir of very great virtue to the Red Work and no man can make a shorter abbreviation in the world; and when the Sulphur of any body is prepared, it may this way very speedily be converted into Elixir by adding the liquor of the Ferment.

Now I will lay down instructions concerning:

1. The Body.
2. The Spirit.
3. The Lion.
4. The Eagle.
5. The Philosophers' Lead.
6. Antimony.
7. Antimony Mercury.
8. The Glue of the Eagle.
9. Solution of the Red Lion into Blood.
10. Solution of the Glue of the Eagle.
11. Solution of the Blood of the Red Lion.
12. Conjunction.
13. Putrefaction.
14. Fermentation.
15. In the Trinity of the Physical and Alchemical Tincture of the Soul.
16. In the Unity of the Medicine.

1. Take Antimony, calcined, so much as you please and grind it to a subtle powder, then take twice so much *Lac Virginis* and put your powder of Antimony therein and set it in *Balneo* seven days, then out it into a body, and set it in sand or ashes till the *Lac* be turned red, which draw off and pour on more, and so let it stand. When that is colored red, pour it to the other, and thus do till you have drawn out all the tincture. Set all this water in *Balneo* or lent ashes to distill with a Limbeck, and distill it with a lent fire; and first of all the *Lac* will ascend; then you shall see a stupendous miracle because you shall see through the nose of the Limbeck, as it were, a thousand veins of the liquor of this blessed Mineral to descend in red drops, just like blood, which, when you have got, you have a thing where{unto} in all the treasure in the world is not equal. Now you have the Blood of the Lion according to *Rupesissa* {*sic*}. I will now speak of the Glue of the Eagle, of which Paracelsus thus says.

2. Reduce Mercury so far by Sublimation till it be a fixed Crystal. This is his preparation of Mercury, and his way of reducing it into the Glue of the Eagle, but above all I require that way be used which is described by me before or that hereafter set down after this. {"Reduce Mercury so far by Sublimation" is meditation. We enter so far within that AIN SUPh AUR is revealed. This is the Gluten of the Eagle. The Eagle's emanations is a metaphor used consistently in Yaqui teachings. The First Matter is like a glue since it holds all things in solution and suspension, and adheres all parts of the fabric of existence with each other.}

3. Then, says the aforesaid Author, go on to Resolution {To resolute the First Matter is to cleanse it within the limits of our Glass Vessel. *Aqua Fortis* is then Coagulated into the physical body by Solution.} and Coagulation, and I again will give you to observe the same manner of Solution showed at first.

4. Now let us come to Conjunction after the Solution of these two, take equal weight of them and put them in a vessel well shut. {The Hermetic Seal enhances the Eagle's Gluten and the Blood of the Red Lion.}

5. After you have thus joined them together, set your glass in your furnace to putrefy after the space of certain days. Therefore Paracelsus says: "Then at length and presently after your Lily is made hot in your glass, it appears in wonderful manners (or demonstration) blacker than the Crow. After that, in process of time, whiter than the Swan, and then passing by yellow to be more red than blood."

6. This being putrefied and turned into red is to be taken for the Medicine, and then it is time to be fermented.

7. Of which Fermentation Paracelsus thus speaks: "One part thereof is to be projected upon 1000 parts of molten Gold and then the Medicine is prepared, and this is the Fermentation of it." {Fermentation, identified earlier as meditation with Vinegar and the Hebrew term ChMTz (chometz), augments and multiplies *Aqua Fortis* throughout the body cell structure.} But if the half or one part of the Liquor of the Sulphur of Gold before described be added to it, then it would be spiritual Ferment, and would be much more penetrating in fortitude, and fusible, as Paracelsus does testify in his *Aurora*, where he would have us to join the Star of the Sun or the Oil of Sol to this *Pantarva* {This may be another term for the Bath within the Glass Vessel}. And thus the physical, Alchemical tincture is performed in a short time for curing all manner of infirmities and human diseases (which is also the great Elixir for metals so courtly concealed by the ancients.) which Hermes Trismegistus the Egyptian, Osus the Greek, Hali an Arabian, and Albertus Magnus a German, with many others have sought and prosecuted, everyone after their own method, and one in one subject, another in another, so much desired by the philosophers only for prolongation of life.

8. In this composition Mercury is made a fixed and dissolved body, the Blood or Spirit of the Red Lion is the Ferment or Soul, and so of trinity is made unity, which is called the physical and Alchemical tincture, never before, that I know of, collected or written in one work, and I had not done this except that otherwise the Composition of this blessed medicine had been ever forgot. {Here the numbered paragraphs end in the MS.}

A Shorter Way to Make the Glue of the Eagle

If you desire to make the Glue of the Eagle in a more brief way. Take part of the red precipitate prose {sic} as is taught before in Mercury, and dissolve it in distilled Vinegar, and the Vinegar will be colored into a yellow or delightful golden color; and after you have distilled away the Vinegar there will remain in the bottom a white substance of the Mercury, fixed and fair, which is to be joined to the Oil of the Lion; and this work is much shorter and less laborious.

The Calcination of Antimony into the Red Lion

Take Antimony, well ground, so much as you please and melt it in naked fire with Salt Armoniack, {*Sal Armoniac*, gematria = 94} and when it is melted, cast it suddenly into a vessel almost full of distilled Vinegar, wherein Salt Armoniack has been dissolved, and thus melt it and cast it in three times; then pour off the Vinegar from the Calx of the Antimony and dry it well and grind it small and dissolve it as before is taught, and so have you the Red Lion of the Philosophers' Lead or Antimony.

{The Philosophers' Lead or Antimony is our physical body. Within flows blood of the Will-Sex-Urge symbolized as a Lion. When the energy is rechanneled, redeployed, it heightens awareness through perfecting all the Metals, charging the blood further. Eventually increased perceptions reveal the First Matter, the Gluten of the Eagle. "The Blood of the Red Lion and the Gluten of the White Eagle is sufficient for our work."—Paracelsus}

The Rosicrucian Medicine or Elixir of Copper

I will make plain the:
1. The Elixir.
2. Conjunction.
3. Separation.
4. The Medicine.
5. Fermentation.
6. The Earth.
7. Spirit Oil, Blood of the Lamb.
8. Distillation.
9. Resolution.
10. Putrefaction.
11. Solution.
12. Vitriol.
13. Calcination.
14. Copper.

1. Now many have sought the way of the Mineral *Pantarva* in Vitriol or Green Copperas, but they were altogether deceived, which common Vitriol by the Philosophers is called the Green Lion of fools. But this our noble Red Lion takes its original from the metallic body of Copper. {Copper and Venus, attributed

to Netzach on the Tree, is the Desire Nature or Kama Manas of the Hindus. As such it truly is the original impetus of both the Green and Red Lion.}

Although I am not ignorant how to draw an oil out of Roman Vitriol of a more sweet smell and delightful taste than any balsam if the Tincture be taken out of the calcined Vitriol in Spirit of Wine. Yet the philosophers' will is to command that it does consist of a metallic virtue, wherewith the transmutation of metals is to be effected. Therefore they say it is to be made of bodies and not of spirits, as of Vitriol, Sulphur as well and the like. Whence I find it written in the Philosophers' *Turba*, and in the first exercitation: But the Philosophers' Medicine is a Metallic Matter, converting substances and forms of imperfect metals, and it is concluded by all the philosophers that the conversion is not made except by its like, therefore it is necessary that the *Presoria* be made of a metallic matter; yet if any be made of spirits it would be better and much more philosophical, and more near to a metallic nature, to be made of bodies than of spirits. But if by Art the body should be turned into a Spirit, then the same body would be both body and spirit; and not to be doubled, but the medicine might be made of such a body or Spirit. But let us return to our purpose: it being granted that this our Vitriol is such a body according to which Paracelsus testifies in his *Aurora Philosophorum* under this *Aenigura* {enigma} or Secret of the ancient philosophers: *Visicabis Interiora Terrae Rectificando Invenies Occultum Lapidem Veram Medicinam.*

2. Out of the first letter of every word of this *Aenigura* is gathered this word *Vitriolum*, by which is meant that thereof the medicine is made. {The gematria of *Vitriolum* = 124, that of *Magnum Opus*, the Great Work.}

3. Therefore Paracelsus says, the inward parts of the Earth are to be visited; not only the Earth which is *vitriol*, but the inward parts of the Earth, he means the sweetness and redness, because there lies hid in the inward parts of *Vitriol* a subtle noble and fragrant juice and pure oil. {Red Vitriol is burning desire. White Vitriol is that desire absorbed by the One-Ego in Tiphareth. As chemical vitriol is a sulphate of zinc, which forms glassy crystals that reflect light, it was used to represent the inner, True Ego in Tiphareth, which reflects the brilliance of Kether. The juice and oil in us, the Earth, is *Chylus.*}

4. And this is especially to be noted. The production of this Copper into *Vitriol* is not to be done neither by calcination of the fire nor distillation of the matter, lest it be deprived of its greenness, which being lost it wants both power and strength. {Our desire for union should not be burned away nor dissipated but rechanneled, redeployed, toward Tiphareth.}

5. Paracelsus speaks not one word of the preparation of this *Vitriol*, by whose silence many have erred; therefore I determine to leave him here a little, and to prosecute and follow the order of the Table wherefore I begin with the Calcination of the Metal. And note that this Calcination of Copper is made that it may be turned into *Vitriol*, and not the Calcination of *Vitriol* made of

Copper. {We calcine our Copper to burn away its Salt tendencies. The rechanneled Sulphur, joined with its Mercury, purifies and perfects the Metal to surrender to the Gold in Tiphareth.}

6. Take therefore as much Copper as you please and dissolve it and calcinate it in *Aqua Fortis* to a fair green water; then set it 3 or 4 days to digest till the matter be clear, which pour out into a Limbeck, and in *Balneo* draw away the corrosive water so that the matter remain dry, for then it is calcined.

7. Then upon every two pounds of this calcined matter pour a gallon of distilled Vinegar and lute it up in a glass and set it in *Balneo* almost boiling the space of seven days, when it is cold put into a Limbeck to distill away all the Vinegar in *Balneo*, and in the bottom of the Alembick you will have your *Vitriol* very well congealed, for fairer than Roman Vitriol which is corporeal and metallic Vitriol.

8. Which *Vitriol* I do not dissolve in rain water like the Paracelsians, but rather with *Lac Virginis* as before is taught, or in Raymond's Calcination Water. And after its dissolution and perfect digestion, that is to say 15 days, I put it into a Limbeck and in *Balneo* draw off the *Lac Virginis*, which being done you will find an oily water, green and clear, upon which pour the Spirit of Wine; and after it has been digested seven days, and the Spirit of Wine distilled away in *Balneo*, you will find your green water perfectly rectified, made pure, subtle and spiritual and apt for putrefaction, for if it be not well dissolved and rarified it will not putrefy. {Die to the One-Ego in Tiphareth.}

9. But now that I may join with Paracelsus in the manner of putrefaction, I return to him and say with him, commanding to digest in a warm heat in a glass well closed the space of some months, and so long till diverse colors appear and be at length red, which shows the termination of its putrefaction.

But yet in this process this redness is not sufficiently fixed, but is to be more fully purged from its feces in this manner.

Resolve it or rectify it in distilled Vinegar till the Vinegar be colored, then filter it from its feces. This is its true Tincture and best resolution and rectification, out of which a blessed oil is to be drawn.

10. Then in sand or ashes lift up the Spirit gently and temperately, and when you see a fume ascend into the glass and red drops begin to fall out of the nose of the Limbeck into the Receiver, then the Red Oil begins to distill. Continue your distillation till all be come over. When it is done you will have the oil in the Receiver lifted up and separated from its Earth, more delightful and sweet than any balsam, or aromatic without any sharpness at all, which Oil is called the Blood of the Lamb. {In Hebrew, Blood of the Lamb is DMKR (Damcar), the metaphorical city in the Brother C.R.C. allegory. For a complete elucidation on Brother Christian Rosenkreutz and the Manifestoes, see *The True and Invisible Rosicrucian Order* by Dr. Paul Foster Case. For the Manifestoes and new translation of the *Hermetic Marriage*, see *A Rosicrucian Primer* (Holmes Publishing Group,

1994.)} In the bottom of the body you will find a white, shining Earth, like snow, which keep well from dust, and so you have the clear Earth separated from its oil.

Take this White Earth and put it in a glass vial and put thereto equal weight of the Oil or Soul and Body, which will receive it and embrace it in a moment. {To imply Virgin's Milk is Soul would be quite accurate in a great sense. It is responsible for our *Animation*. Without it we die. Also, see "The Tree of Venus" on page 97.}

But that it may be turned into a Medicine when you have joined these two together, set it into our furnace the space of forty days and you will have an absolute oil of wonderful perfection, wherewith Mercury and other imperfect metals are turned into Gold, as Paracelsus was pleased to say.

11. The Medicine being thus made, I now come to Fermentation, without which it is not possible to give form to it; neither will I adhere to the opinion of one man alone contrary to all the philosophers, that is to say Paracelsus, repugnant to the rest of the philosophers, because they all of them of necessity have decreed to give form to the Medicine by ferment and union, that is to say of an imperfect body, and by how much the ferment is more spiritual the Medicine will be of so much more penetration and transmutation. {The author called this item 11, Solution. Yet above he calls it Fermentation. They are the same, that is Meditation. Spiritual Ferment gives form to the Mind-Matter. The more exact the imagery (spiritual) the more transmutation.}

12. These things being promised, I do not think it fit that you should proceed to Projection upon Mercury instead of Fermentation as Paracelsus teaches, or that the *Pantarva* should be fermented his way with Gold, either corporeal or spiritual.

Which Gold will be the foundation of the first Projection. But what do the Philosophers command us to do? That Projection, that is to say, Fermentation, be made of a perfect foundation, and that upon imperfect bodies that Medicines may be made with foundation of the *Pantarva* or Elixir is not, except it be only the White or Red Ferment, in respect of which both Gold and Silver are said to be imperfect bodies. Therefore this *Pantarva* is to be fermented before it be projected upon the corporeal foundation or imperfect, that is to say, corporeal Gold.

13. Therefore join this Oil to the fourth part of the Oil of the Sulphur of Gold, and this is the true fermentation or conversion unto the Elixir.

14. Then augment it in virtue by solution and coagulation, and in quantity by projection, first upon the corporeal foundation, that is to say Gold, then upon purified Mercury, and that Medicine upon other bodies which are most fit for projection, that is to say most fusible, as Lead or Tin, which after they are purified, are most apt by reason of their easy melting.

And thus the inward parts of the Earth are visited and by reflection the hidden Medicine is found, the true Medicine out of the Green Lion of the Philosophers, and not of fools, and out of corporeal and metallic Vitriol, not terrestrial, and made of mineral Copperas. {This is typical of all True Alchemists. They caution us repeatedly that Alchemy is an inner process, and that they are not to be taken literally. Yet, so many believe this to be a blind.}

The Augmentation and Projection of the
Medicines of Metals Rosicrucian

First I will treat of the Augmentation of the virtue or quality, of which Raymond says: "The Augmentation in quality and goodness is by Solution and Coagulation of the Tincture, that is to say, by imbibing it with our Mercury and drying it." But let us hear Arnoldus more attentively: "Take one part of your prepared Tincture and dissolve it in three parts of our Mercury; then put it in a glass and seal it up and set it in ashes till it be dry and come to a powder; then open the glass and imbibe it again and dry it again. And the more often you do thus so much will you gain more tincture."

And also as it is found in *Clangor Buccinae*. "Dissolve it in the water of Mercury of which the Medicine was made till it be clear; then congeal it by light decoction and imbibe it with its oil upon the fire till it flow, by virtue whereof it will be doubled in tincture with all its perfections as you will see in projection because the weight that was before projected upon a thousand is now to be projected upon ten thousand, and there is no great labor in this Multiplication." {There is no labor at all since the process is done subconsciously.} Again the Medicine is multiplied two manner of ways: by solution of calidity, and solution of rarity.

By solution of calidity is that you take the Medicine, put in a glass vessel, and bury it in our moist fire seven days or more till the Medicine be dissolved into water without any turbulency.

By solution of rarity, is that you take your glass vessel with your Medicine and hang it in a new brass pot full of water that boils, and close up the mouth of the pot that the Medicine may dissolve in the vapor of this boiling water. But note that the boiling water must not touch the glass wherein the Medicine is to hang above it three fingers, and this solution will be above it in 2 or 3 days; after your Medicine is dissolved, take it from the fire to cool, fix and congeal and be hard and dry. This do often, and how much the more the Medicine will be dissolved it will be so much more perfect, and such a solution is the Sublimation of the Medicine and its virtual sublimation, which the oftener it is reiterated, so much more abundantly and more parts it tinges. {Meditations and visualizations must be repeated for subconsciousness to deduce suggestions from the conscious level.}

Whence Rhasis says the goodness of the Multiplication consists in the reiteration and fixation of the Medicine, and by how much more this order is repeated, it works so much more and is augmented; for so often as you sublime your Medicine and dissolve it, you will gain so much every time in projection, one upon a thousand, and if the first fall upon a thousand, the third upon a hundred thousand, the fourth upon a million and so infinitely. {There must be over forty trillion, ever-changing cells in the human body; no one knows how many for certain.} For Morienus the Philosopher says: "Know for certain that the oftener our *Pantarva* is dissolved and congealed, the Spirit and Soul is joined more to the body and is retained by it, and in every time the Tincture is multiplied." Whence we thus read in *Scala Philosophorum*, which also the philosophers say: "Dissolve and congeal." So without doubt it is understood of the Solution of the Body and Soul with the Spirit into water, and congelation makes the Soul and Spirit mix with the Body, and if with one solution and simple congelation, the Soul and Spirit would be perfectly joined to the Body, the philosophers would not say dissolve again and congeal, and again dissolve and congeal, that the Tincture of the *Pantarva* may grow if it could be done with one congelation only.

The Medicine is another way multiplied by Fermentation and the Ferment to the White is pure Silver, and the Ferment to the Red is pure Gold. Therefore project one part of the Medicine upon two of the Ferment (but I say 3 parts of the Medicine upon one of the ferment) and all will be Medicine, which put in a glass upon the fire and so close it that no air go in nor out, and keep it there till it be subtiliated {sic} as you did with the first Medicine and one part of the second Medicine will have as much virtue as one part of the first Medicine had. (But here again *Clangor Buccinae* has erred, for it should be written thus: One part of the second Medicine will have as much virtue as ten parts of the first Medicine had.) And thus by Solution and Fermentation the Medicine may be multiplied infinitely.

We have spoken enough of this Multiplication; we now come to the other way of Augmentation, which is called corporeal Multiplication, and according to Raymond is thus defined: "Augmentation is the Addition of quantity." Whence Avicenna writes: "It is hard to project upon a million and to predicate it incontinently." Wherefore I will reveal one great secret unto you; one part is to be mixed with a thousand parts of its nearest in kind (I call that nearest that is the body of the same metal whereof the Medicine was made or perfected). But to return again to Avicenna: "Close all this firmly in a fit vessel and set it in a furnace of fusion three days till it be wholly joined together, and the manner of the work is thus projected, one part of the aforesaid Medicine upon a 100 parts of melted Gold and it makes it brittle and will all be Medicine whereof one part projected on a 100 of any melted metal converts it into pure Gold, and if you project it upon Silver, in like manner it converts all bodies into Silver."

In *Scala Philosophorum* all sorts of projections are thus set down in few words.

You must know that first it is said project, that is to say, one upon 100, etc. Yet it is better to project *nunc dimittis upon fundamenta*, and *fundamenta* upon *verba mea* and *verba mea* upon *diligan te domine*, and *diligan te* upon *attendite*. This Enigma is thus expounded, it is nothing else but the words and opinion of the former author concealed under the *Aenigura* {enigma}. Therefore let us repeat the words of this *Aenigura* or Oracle.

> *Nunc dimittis super fundamenta*
> *Fundamenta super verba mea*
> *Verba mea super diligam te*
> *Diligam te super attendite.*

These are trifles for the hiding and concealing perfection of the art, if the expert Artist could be diverted with such simple words, which, though they are at first to young artists, yet they are thus explained. We therefore begin with the first sentence.

Nunc dimittis super fundamenta. {First project upon the fundaments.}

This is here allegorically taken for the almost last action of the work, which is called the Medicine *Pantarva*, which Medicine is to be projected upon the ferment, that is to say, upon the Oil of Sol or Luna, which are the ferments or foundations of the Art in spiritual augmentation (as before was said) upon molten Gold and Silver. And that spiritual ferment converted into Medicine is to be projected upon molten Gold or Silver which are corporeal ferments in corporeal augmentation and the corporeal fundaments of the Art upon Quicksilver. {There is profound gematria in these verses. *Fundamenta* = 89, that of GUPh (body), *Argentum* (Silver), and *nummus* (coin). Coins are the same ideas expressed in the *Turba* (Dicta 9 & 10), that of Corporeal Consciousness or the body cell structure. *Pantarva* is projected upon body cells, subconsciously (*argentum*). The *Turba* tells us: "Know that the key of this work is the Art of Coins." *Ars Nummae* = 93, that of *Regulus* (the King in Tiphareth and Gold). All this is done by the One Ego. We are also reminded by Paracelsus and others that Alchemy is a work of Fire. This whole first verse sums to 301, that of ASh, Fire.}

Fundamenta super verba mea {The fundaments upon my words}

This is also spoken allegorically because in the adage it is said words are wind, as if a word were nothing else but motion of the lips and exaltation of the lungs, which no sooner arise from motion but fly away and are turned to air, so likewise Quicksilver or Mercury goes out of the bodies of other Metals, and is so volatile in the fire or heat as words in the air. And therefore Mercury is likened

64

to words upon which the fundaments are to be projected. {*Verba mea* sums to 60, that of *Balneum* (bath). Healthy body cells are then set in *Balneo*.}

> *Verba mea* (viz. Mercury) *super diligam te.*
> {My words upon self-love}

That is to say, upon other metals which have most affinity with Quicksilver and easy of fusion, as Saturn and Jupiter, that is to say, Lead and Tin, which by this concord and love are easily by the penetration and aimiableness of the Medicine converted into Medicine. And no part of this Medicine converts other parts of metals into Gold or Silver according to the force and power of the Elixir, which other metals, because they are the substances of the other former bodies whereof the Medicines were made. They are the attendants of these medicines whereof the philosophers command that—

> *Diligam te* {self-love}

—be projected upon *attendite* {attention or attendants} that the second Medicine, or this last, projected upon metals, especially that whereof the Medicine (that is to say the *Pantarva*) was made, should turn that metal into Gold or Silver according to the property and quality of the Medicine. {*Diligam te* = 74, that of *Agnus Dei* and *aqua regis* (royal water). This is the self-love of Our Lord (*Domine*), within Tiphareth, who changes our physical blood into the royal water, healing every cell in our body. The whole hinted phrase "*Diligam te domine*" sums to 128. This is equal to *Microcosmus* (man, the miniature world), *menstruum* (solution of blood) and *vinum uter* (wine skin, in Mark 2:22). It must be kept in mind that the object of Alchemy is health, not wealth. Perfect health is seed to initiation and fourth dimensional awareness.}

But to put an end to this projection, take it according to the opinion of Arnoldus, gathered out of his 31st chapter: "Who wills to project one part of the Elixir upon 100 of Mercury purged, and all will be Medicine, afterward project one part of this Medicine last congealed upon 100 parts of Mercury washed, and all will be Gold or Silver in all trials according as the Elixir is white or red." Lastly that I may briefly rehearse the absolute manner of projection. First the Medicine is to be projected upon Gold or Silver molten, then upon Quicksilver purged, so long till it turn it into Medicine, and lastly upon metals most near, that they may be converted into pure Gold or Silver according to the properties and qualities of the Medicine.

Because we have said something of the propinquity of Metals, that is to say that the Elixir is to be projected upon that imperfect body out of which its Mercury and Sulphur was first extracted, therefore it will not be unnecessary to set down one example, that is to say, if the Medicine was made of Mercury, then it is to be projected upon Quicksilver for making Gold or Silver, because Quicksilver is a near body to Mercury, and so of the rest. Yet it is to be noted that all Elixirs may and ought to be projected upon Quicksilver, because Quicksilver is the Mother and Sperm of all Metals; therefore Quicksilver made and turned into medicine, is to be projected upon a body most near to it, which is Lead or Tin, upon which the Medicine is always to be projected, whether white or red, for the making and transmuting of metals; but both the Quicksilver and Lead are first to be purged that they may be purified and deprived of their filth. Enough has been said before of the purgation or putrefaction of Mercury. {This whole section on Augmentation may be put as: The cleansed Mercury (*Pantarva*) upon the Metals (Chakras); Perfected Metals upon the organs and blood; *Aurum Potabile* upon the cell structure.}

Of the Putrefaction of Lead

Melt your Lead in a Crucible and when it is melted let it stand in the fire a quarter of an hour, and put therein a little Salt Armoniack {*Sal Armoniac* or Vitriol}, and let it stand a while in the fire, and stir it with an iron spatula {*spatha*, in Latin =59. This is equal to Orsan in the 7th Treatise of *Splendor Solis*, where Hermes is quoted: "I have been observing a bird called the Philosophers' Orsan, which flies when in the Signs of Aries, Cancer, Libra or Capricorn." These are the Rule, Fall, Detriment and Exaltation of Mars. "Iron spatula" is "observed" continence of the Mars force, which energy is rechanneled to "stir" Lead, the Saturn (Muladhara) Chakra. Columba, also equal to 59, is Dove. The redeployed Mars energy is the Dove of Venus, Love.} till all the Salt Armoniack be gone away in fume, then scrape the skim away out of the Crucible that is upon the Lead, then let it stand to cool, and it will be much whiter and fairer. And thus you must purify your Lead or Tin before projection, because no other bodies are so fusible, and apt to melt. Wherefore every Elixir ought to be projected upon Quicksilver and upon Lead or Tin for making or transmuting metals. But to the end {that} the manner of projection may be yet more plain, I will set down two rules which must be carefully observed.

The first whereof is that the first Medicine, that is to say the *Pantarva*, be projected upon the ferment always three parts of the Medicine upon one of the ferment, and one part of this upon 10 or 100 of pure molten gold, and one part of this medicine thus made upon 100 parts of an imperfect body, that is to say, of Mercury for medicine.

The latter is that you must always consider the fortitude and debility of your Medicine for it is to be projected so often upon quicksilver as it brings it into a brittle medicine, and when it falls then project one part thereof upon Lead or Tin for making transmutation according to the order and form of the Elixir.

These being remembered you may easily conceive the order of augmentation in virtue and quantity.

These things being ended, the other three which follow are set down in order because we have spoken before of *Aurum Potabile, Argentum Potabile*, or Potable Gold or Silver. It is therefore necessary after we have made an end of projection to set down another method of the Elixir of Life in the next place, and after speak of its virtue and power as we find among all the ancient and modern philosophers.

But that we may come at last to the thing intended, observe this Manuduction.

You know that no Artificer can build, but the Earth must be the foundation to his building, for without this ground work his brick and mortar cannot stand. In the Creation, when God did build, there was no such place to build upon. I ask then where did He rest His matter, and upon what? Certainly He built and founded Nature upon His own Supernatural Center. He is in her and through her, and with His eternal Spirit does He support Heaven and Earth, as our bodies are supported with our Spirits. This is confirmed by that oracle of the Apostle: "*Omnia portat verbo virtutis sua.*—He bears up all things with the Word of His Power." From this power is He justly styled: "The infinitely powerful, and the All powerful power making power." I say then that Fire and Spirit are the pillars of Nature, the props on which her whole fabric rests, and without which it could not stand one minute. {AIN SUPh AUR is also the Alchemical Earth. Then Binah, the third sphere called Understanding, which is also Akasha, is that Substance which stands under, a substrata, or foundation of creation.} This Fire is the throne of the Quintessential Light, from whence He dilates Himself to generation as we see in the effusion of the Sun beams in the great world. In this dilatation of the Light consist the joy or pleasure of the passive spirit, and in its contraction, His melancholy or sorrow. We see in the great body of nature that in turbulent weather when the Sun is shut up and clouded, the air is thick and dull and our own spirits by secret compassion with the Spirit of the Air, are dull too. On the contrary, in clear, strong sunshine, the air is quick and thin and the spirits of all *Animals* are of the same rarified active temper.

It is plain then that our joys and sorrows proceed from the dilatation and contraction of our inward Quintessential Light. This is apparent in despairing lovers, who are subject to certain violent, extraordinary pantings of the heart, a timorous, trembling pulse, which proceeds from the apprehension and fear of the Spirit in relation to his miscarriage: Notwithstanding, he desires to be dilated, as it appears by his pulse or sally wherein he does discharge himself, but his despair checks him again and brings him to a sudden retreat or contraction. Hence it comes to pass that we are subject to sighs, which are occasioned by the sudden pause of the Spirit. For when he stops, the breath stops, but when he loses himself to an outward motion, we deliver two or three breaths, that have been formerly omitted, in one long expiration, and this we call a sigh.

This passion has carried many brave men to very sad extremities. It is originally occasioned by the Spirit of the Mistress or affected party, for her Spirit ferments or leavens the Spirit of the lover, so that it desires a union as far as nature will permit. This makes us resent even smiles and frowns like fortunes and misfortunes. Our thoughts are never at home according to that well grounded observation: "*Animus est ubi amat, non ubi animat*—The Soul dwells not where she lives, but where she loves." We are employed in a perpetual contemplation of the absent Beauty; our very joys and woes are in her power; she can set us to what humor she will. This and many more miraculous sympathies proceed from the attractive nature of the Fire; it is a Spirit that can do wonders. And now let us see if there be any possibility to come at him. Suppose then we should dilapidate or decompose some Artificial Building stone by stone. There is no question but we should come at last to the Earth whereupon it is founded. It is just so in Magic; If we open any Natural Body, and separate all the parts thereof one from another, we shall come at last to the Fire, which is the Candle and Secret Light of God. We shall know the Hidden Intelligence, and see that Inexpressible Face, which gives the outward figure to the Body. This is the Syllogism we should look after, for he that has once past the Aquaster enters the fire world, and sees what is both invisible and incredible to the common man. {This is AIN SUPh AUR, revealed to a seeker after persistent, prolonged meditations.} He will discover to the eye the miraculous conspiracy that is between the Fire and the Sun. He shall know the secret love of Heaven and Earth, and the sense of that deep Cabalism: "There is not an herb here below, but he has a star in Heaven above, and the star strikes him with her beam, and says to him: Grow." He shall know how the Fire-Spirit has his root in the Spiritual Fire-Earth, and receives from it a Secret Influx upon which he feeds, as herbs feed on that Juice and Liquor, which they receive at their roots from this Common Earth. This is it which Our Savior tells us: "Man lives not by bread alone, but by every Word that comes out of the Mouth of God." He meant not by ink and paper or the dead letter. It is a Mystery, and St. Paul has partly expounded it. He tells the Athenians that God made man, to the end that he should seek the Lord if haply he might feel after Him and find Him. Here is a strange expression, you will say, that a man should feel after God, or seek Him with his hands. But he goes on and tells you where you shall find Him. He is not far (says he) from every one of us; for in Him we live, move and have our being. {AIN SUPh AUR, the Black-Light Ocean of Awareness, is a solution throughout The Boundless. We and Universes are immersed in this *Aqua Vitae* as fish swim in an aquarium.} For the better understanding of this place I wish you to read Paracelsus, his *Philosophia ad Athenienses*. Again; he that enters the Center shall know why all Influx of Fire descends against the Nature of Fire, and comes from Heaven downwards. He shall know also why the same Fire, having found a body, ascends again towards Heaven and goes upwards.

To conclude: I say the Grand, Supreme Mystery of Magic, is to multiply the Fire, and place him in the most serene Aether, which God has purposely created to qualify the fire. For I would have you know, that this Spirit may be so chafed, and that in the most temperate Bodies, as to undo you upon a sudden, This you may guess yourself by the Thundering Gold, as the chemist calls it. Place him then as God has placed the Stars, in the condensed Aether of His Chaos, for there He will shine, not burn; he will be vital and calm, not furious and choleric. This secret I confess transcends the Common Process.

Now I will teach the blessed *PANTARVA ROSICRUCIAN*, their *Aurum Potabile* or the Elixir of Life, and also the way of making Malleable Glass.

1. Elixir of Life.
2. Gold Dissolved.
3. Silver Dissolved.
4. Gold Molten.
5. Melted Silver.
6. Projection of the Red Medicine.
7. Projection of the White Medicine.

I have now fully discovered the Principles of our Chaos. In the next place I will show you how you are to use them. You must unite them to a New Life, and they will be generated by Water and the Spirit. These two are in all things, they are placed by God Himself, according to that speech of Trismegistus: "*Unumquodque habet in se semen sui regenerationis.*" {"Each thing whatsoever bears within it the seed of its own generation."—*Lumen de Lumine*.} Proceed then patiently but not manually. The work is performed by an invisible Artist, for there is a secret Incubation of the Spirit of God upon Nature; you must only see that the outward heat fails not, but with the subject itself you have no more to do than the Mother has with the Child that is in her womb. {The outward heat is our desire for reunion, Our Sulphur.} The two former principles perform all, the Spirit makes use of the Water to purge and wash his body; and he will bring it at last to a Celestial, Immortal Constitution. Do not think this impossible. Remember that in the Incarnation of Christ Jesus, a *Quaternarius* or four Elements as men call them, were united to their Eternal Unity and Ternarius. Three and Four make Seven; the Septenary is the true Sabbaoth, the Rest into which the Creature shall enter. This is the best and greatest Manuduction that I can give you. In a word, Salvation itself is nothing else but Transmutation. "Behold," says the Apostle, "I show you a Mystery: We shall not all die, but we shall be changed in a moment, in the twinkling of an eye, at the sound of the last trumpet." God, of His great Mercy, prepares us for it. That from hard, stubborn flints of this world, we may prove Crysolites and Jaspers in the new, Eternal

Foundation. That we may ascend from this present, distressed Church, which is in captivity with her children, to the free Jerusalem from above, which is the Mother of us all.

Hermes, speaking of Fermentation, bids us to take the Sun and his Shadow. By the Shadow he means the Moon because in respect of dignity, luster and power she is much more weak and inferior than the Sun. And the Moon follows the Sun as a shadow does the body and is not illuminated except by the light of the Sun. We will first speak of the body, that is to say of Gold, and after come to the shadow, of which Gold it is written in a book of Chemical Art in this manner. The Rosicrucian *Pantarva* is made of Gold alone and only by Nature, and is more sublime than them which the philosophers affirm cures all infirmities. According to the opinion of this Philosopher, I propose to begin with Gold alone and the Medicine, which is a new and sole nature and ancient and sound Quintessence.

2. {The numeration of these paragraphs is not consistent in the MS. in any of the sections.} But to the end this Gold may be better and more pure, it may be purged two manner of ways, that is to say by Antimony and by dissolution in corrosive waters with which Copper plates are mixed as goldsmiths use to do, which is called Water Gold.

When you have thus prepared your Gold, project one part of your Red Medicine (or Red Elixir) upon a 100 parts thereof, when your Medicine is augmented in virtue and all that weight of molten Gold will be converted into a red, brittle mass, which grind upon a marble to an impalpable powder.

Then dissolve these hundred parts, or so much thereof as you please, in distilled Vinegar or in Spirit of Wine, and set it to digest in *Balneo* the space of a day or two, then distill the Spirit of Wine in *Balneo*, and in the bottom will remain the fixed and pure oil of the Gold, which is then the true *Aurum Potabile*, and Spiritual Elixir of Life. If you will give to anyone of this powder presently, before it be converted to oil, warm a little white or Renish wine and dissolve in either of them so much of the red powder as will tincture the same into a red color, and the wine so tinctured will be *Aurum Potabile*, but it would be better and more penetrating if it were tinctured with the aforesaid Oil.

In like manner is the White Medicine to be projected after the purification of the Silver in a corrosive water as is before declared.

And so the melted Silver will be converted into a brittle powder and white mass, which likewise is to be dissolved and turned into oil, and thus the White Elixir of Life is made and Potable Silver, curing and healing so far as it is able in human diseases, for it cannot be supposed that the Elixir of Luna has so great virtue as the Elixir of Sol, or *Aurum Potabile*.

Now whereas among the vulgar, and philosophers, Gold has this report, that being in his first disposition that it cures the Leprosy; and many other virtues. This is not, except by its complete digestion, because the excellency of the fire acting in it consumes all evil humors that are in sick bodies as well in hot as cold causes. But Silver cannot do this because it has not so much superfluity of fire, and is not so much digested and decocted with natural maturity; yet notwithstanding this, it has a fieriness occultly and virtually in it, but not so fully, because the fire causes not such elemental qualities, as in Gold. And therefore Silver, being in his first disposition, does not cure the Leprosy so potently unless it be first digested by Art, until it have the chief degrees of Gold in all maturity. Wherefore other sick metallic bodies more weakly cure infirmities according as they differ more from them in perfection and maturity. Some differ more, some less, which is by reason of the Sulphur, infected and burning, of which they were made at the beginning in their generation and coagulation, and therefore they cure not, whereas the fire in them is burning, and so infected with the elemental feces, with the mixture of other elemental qualities. {*Chylus*, the Virgin's Milk, is the crux of our immune system. We heal ourselves, despite ourselves, by small amounts released into the blood stream subconsciously. Alchemists, however, release extra amounts by Art. This, plus the Mature Metals influencing glands and organs to secrete additional essences into the blood stream, creates *Aurum Potabile*.}

4. Seeing, therefore, that Gold is of such vigor among the vulgar, and that being in his first disposition, what wonder is it, if it, being brought into Medicine (as is experienced) by Art, and his virtue be subtilated by digestion of decoction and purgation of the qualities, but it may then cure more, nay infinite, of all diseases.

It makes an old man young, as our Rosicrucian *Aurum Potabile* will do, it preserves health, strengthens nature, and expels all sicknesses of the body. It drives poison away from the heart, it moistens the arteries and, briefly, preserves the whole body sound. The manner of using this Medicine according to all philosophers is thus: If you will use to eat of the Medicine, then take the weight of two Florence Ducats of our *Aurum Potabile* and one pound of any confection, and eat of that confection the quantity of one dram in the winter. And if you do thus, it drives away all bodily infirmities from what cause soever they proceed, whether hot or cold, and conserves health and youth in a man, and makes an old man young, and makes gray hairs to fall; it also presently cures the Leprosy, and dissolves phlegm, mundifies the blood; it sharpens the sight and all the senses after a most wonderful manner, above all the medicines of the philosophers.

5. To which purpose we thus find in *The Rosary of the Philosophers*. In this (that is to say in the *Aurum Potabile*) is completed the precious gift of God, which is the Arcanum of all the Sciences in the world, and the incomparable treasure of treasures (for as Plato says): "He that has this gift of God has the dominion of the world (that is to say of the Microcosm) because he attains to the end of riches, and has broken the bonds of Nature, not only for that he has

power to convert all imperfect metals into pure medicines, but preserves both man and every *Animal* in perfect health.

To this purpose speaks Geber, Hermes, Arnoldus, Raymond Lully, Ripley, Aegidius, Roger Bacon, Scotus, Laurentius, Ventura and diverse, uncertain authors.

Lastly. I now come to the general consent of all philosophers and repeat what is found in their writings in the book *De Aurora Consurgeat* and in *Clangor Buccinae*. It is to be noted that the ancient philosophers have found 4 principal effects or virtues in the glorious repository of this treasure: First, it is said to cure man's body of all infirmities; Second, o cure imperfect Metals; Third, to transmute base stones into precious gems; and fourth, to make Glass malleable.

6. Of the first. All philosophers have consented that when the Elixir is perfectly rubified, it does not only work miracles in solid bodies, but also man's body, of which there is no doubt; for being taken inwardly it cures all infirmities. It cures outwardly by unction. The philosophers also say, if it be given to any in water or wine, first warmed, it cures them of the Frenzy, Dropsy and Leprosy, and all kinds of Fevers are cured by this Tincture, and takes away whatsoever is in a weak stomach; it binds and consumes the flux of peccant humors being taken, fasting; it drives away melancholy and sadness of the mind, it cures the infirmities of the eyes and dries up their moistness and bleariness, it helps the purblind, red or bloodshot eyes, it mollifies the web, the inflammation of the eyes and all other incident diseases are easily cured by this Philosophical Medicine of the Rosicrucians.

It comforts the heart and spiritual parts by taking inwardly, it mitigates the pain of the head by anointing the temples therewith; it makes the deaf to hear, and succors all pains of the ears; it rectifies the contracted nerves by unction; it restores rotten teeth by washing; also all kinds of imposthumes are cured by it, by ointments or emplasters or injecting the dry powder therein.

It cures ulcers, wounds, cancers, fistulas, noli me tangere and such like diseases, and generates new flesh. If it be mixed with corrupt and sour wine it restores it; it expels poison being taken inwardly; it also kills worms if it be given in powder; it takes away wrinkles and spots in the face by anointing therewith and makes the face seem young; it helps women in travail being taken inwardly, and brings out the dead child by emplaster, it provokes urine and helps generation; it prevents drunkenness, helps the memory, and augments the radical moisture; it strengthens nature, and also administers many other good things to the body.

2. Of the second it is written that it transmutes all imperfect metals, in colors, substance, lasting, weight, ductibility, melting, hardness and softness.

3. Of the third, that is to say of transmuting base and ignoble stones into precious gems.

4. Of the fourth it is written that it makes glass malleable by mixture (that

is to say of the powder of the white corporeal Elixir) when the Glass is melted. Thus far *Aurora Consurgens* and *Clangor Buccinea*.

Now if you desire to make pure and clear Malleable Glass, beware of what glass you make your metal, for you must not take glass of flints, wherewith glass of windows are made, but such as your Venice Glass is made of, and that is to be chosen out of the first metal of the glass which has stood molten in the fire, in the Glassmakers' furnace the space of a night, and then it will be without spots and pure. Therefore take as much of the said glass out of the furnace with your iron rod as you have a desire to convert, {The Glass Vessel is made clean and resilient from rechanneled reproductive energy. Two Latin words serve for rod, *virga* = 52 and *ferula* = 57. The symbolic images gathered from the gematria of these two numbers are far too numerous to exploit here. However, *ferula ferrea* (iron rod) sums to 106, that of TzChCh (tzachach), to be bright, pure; to flow. This hints the malleableness of the scintillating light in the aura. 106 is also the reputed age of Brother C.R.C., equal to NUN.} and when it is cold weigh it and melt it by itself in a pot; and when it is molten project your white corporeal Elixir upon it, and it will be converted into malleable metal, and fit and apt glass for all Goldsmiths' operations. And thus is Glass made malleable and prepared for any use; but if this were done with the Red Elixir it would be much more enduring, for there is nothing more precious.

To perfect this Great Work which all philosophers have concealed, observe my direction which by experience I found true: To Calcine, Dissolve and Separate the Elements; after, join them together, putrefy them or reduce them into Sulphur; Ferment, project, augment in virtue and quantity. This is the work of the philosophers. This Subject I call *Limus Coelestis*, and the Middle Nature. {Celestial Slime equals 163. As another term for the First Matter it is equivalent to OVLM HZH (olam ha-zeh), This World. The First Matter comprises this world and is the homogeneous, holy substance which reconciles all polar opposites.} The Philosophers call it the Venerable Nature, but among all pretenders I have not yet found one that could tell me why. This Chaos has in it the four Elements, which of themselves are contrary natures, but the Wisdom of God has so placed them that their very order reconciles them.

For example, Air and Earth are adversaries, for one is Hot and Moist, the other Cold and Dry. Now to reconcile these two God placed the Water between them, which is a Middle Nature, or of a mean complexion between both extremes. For she is Cold and Moist, and as she is Cold she partakes of the nature of the Earth, which is Cold and Dry; but as she is Moist, she partakes of the nature of the Air, which is Hot and Moist. Hence it is that the Air and Earth, which are contrary in themselves, agree and embrace one another in the Water, in a Middle Nature, which is proportionate to them both and tempers their extremities.

But verily this Salvo {living, alive; without breaking; this also suggests homogeneity. Its gematria, 60, equals *Balneum* (bath). A portion of the total salvo, which contains Mercury, Sulphur and Salt, is encircled within the aura and cleansed.} does not make up the breach, for though the Water reconciles two Elements like a friendly third, yet she herself fights with a fourth, namely, with the Fire. For the Fire is Hot and Dry, but the Water is Cold and Moist, which are clear contraries.

To prevent the distempers of these two, God placed the Air between them, which is a substance Hot and Moist; and as it is Hot it agrees with the Fire, which is Hot and Dry; but as it is Moist it agrees with the Water, which is Cold and Moist, so that by mediation of the Air the other two extremes, namely Fire and Water are made friends, and reconciled. Thus you see, as I told you at first, that contrary Elements are united by that order and texture wherein the Wise God has placed them. Now I tell you that this Agreement or Fellowship is but partial, a very weak love, cold and skittish; for whereas these principles agree in one quality, they differ in two, as you may easily compute. Much need, therefore, have they of a more strong and able Mediator to confirm and preserve their weak unity; for upon it depends the very eternity and incorruption of the Creature. This Blessed Cement and Balsam {Balsam is very appropriate. With gematria of 41 it equals ELI (my God). Amor (love) and fides (faith), both of which are embellished upon those who experience the Matter, each sum to 41.} is the Spirit of the Living God, which some ignorant scribblers have called a Quintessence {Quintessence has always been considered a misnomer by many writers.}; for this very Spirit is in the Chaos, and to speak plainly, the Fire is in His Throne, for in the Fire He is seated. This was the reason why the Magi called the First Matter their Venerable Nature, and their Blessed Stone. This Blessed Spirit fortifies and perfects that weak disposition which the Elements already have to Union and Peace (for God works with Nature not against her) and brings them at last to a beauteous, special fabric. Now if you will ask me where is the Soul, or as the Schoolmen abuse her, the form, all this while? What does she do? To this I answer, that she is as all Instrumentals ought to be, subject and obedient to the Will of God, expecting the perfection of her body; for it is God that unites her to the body, and the body to her. Soul and Body are the work of God, the one as well as the other. The Soul is not the Artificer of the House, for that which can make a body can also repair it and hinder death; but the Soul cannot do this, it is the Power and Wisdom of God. In a word, to say that the Soul formed the Body, because she is in the Body, is to say that the Jewel made the Cabinet, or that the Sun made the world since the Sun is in the world, and cherishes every part thereof. Learn, therefore, to distinguish between Agents and their Instruments, for if you attribute that to the Creature which belongs to the Creator, you bring yourselves in danger of Hell Fire, for God is a jealous God and will not give His Glory to another.

If you do know the First Matter, know also for certain you have discovered the Sanctuary of Nature. There is nothing between you and her treasures, but the door that indeed must be opened. If your desire leads you on to the practice, consider well with yourself what manner of man you are, and what it is that you would do, for it is no small matter. You have resolved with yourself to be a Co-operator with the Spirit of the Living God, and to minister to Him in His work of Generation. Have a care therefore, that you do not hinder His work; for if your heat exceeds the natural Proportion, you have stirred the wrath of the Moist Natures and they will stand up against the Central Fire against them, and there will be a terrible Division in the Chaos. But the sweet Spirit of Peace, the true eternal Quintessence, will depart from the Elements leaving both them and you to confusion; neither will He apply Himself to that Matter as long as it is in your violent, destroying hands.

I will now lay down plain instructions concerning:

1. The Elixir of Saturn.
2. Putrefaction into Sulphur.
3. The Oil of Sulphur.
4. Of the Conjunction.
5. Of the Salt.
6. Of the Oil of the Spirit.
7. Of Salt of Saturn, which contains the oil or Soul of the *Menstruum*.
8. Of White Mercury.
9. Of Red Water of Paradise.
10. Resolution.
11. Solution.
12. Distillation.
13. Hyle.
14. Purgation.
15. Resolution.
16. Of *Sericon*.
17. Of the Gum.
18. Of *Sericon* {Repeat of 16}
19. Of the Solution {Repeat of 11}
20. Of the Minium Ore
21. *Adrop*.
22. Of Calcination.
23. Of Minium {Repeat of 20}
24. *Adrop* {Repeat of 21}
25. Of Red Lead {Repeat of 20 & 23}
26. Of Calcination of Lead {Repeat of 22}.
27. Of *Aqua Fortis*. {These repeats are curious; maybe due to fatigue, maybe deliberate, to confuse. But if we keep the advice of Roger Bacon in

mind from an earlier section, we may understand all these to be but one operation, Meditation.}

Now see which way the Philosophers move. They commend their Secret Water, and I admire the Tears of *Beata Pulchra*. {Happy Beauty. The two adjectives sum to 98. TzCh (Tzach) in Hebrew means "pure, clear, bright," and equals 98. "Tears of *Beata Pulchra*," the bright light of the First Matter, is the Dew of Heaven. It appears like droplets or tears of light coming from inner realms toward physical manifestation.} I will tell you truly what she is; she is not any known water whatsoever, but a secret, Spermatic Moisture, or rather the Venus that yields that moisture. Therefore do not you imagine that she is any crude, phlegmatic, thin water, for she is a fat, thick, heavy, slimy humidity. But lest you should think I am grown jealous, and would not trust you with my mistress, Arnoldus de Villa Nova shall speak for me. Hear him: "I tell thee further," says he, "that we could not possibly find, neither could the philosophers find before us any thing that would persist in the fire, but only the Unctuous Humidity. A watery Humidity we see, will easily vapor away, and the Earth remain behind, and the parts are therefore separated, because their composition is not natural. But if we consider those Humidities, which are hardly separated from those parts which are natural to them, we find not any such but the unctuous, viscous humidities."

This Viscous Humidity is Water of Silver, which some have called Water of the Moon; but it is Mercury of the Sun and partly of Saturn, for it is extracted from these three metals, and without them it can never be made. {Both the Moon and Saturn are contractive powers within consciousness. They work to manifest Solar Light-Energy into tangible forms.}

Very many have written of Saturn or Lead, but none that I know of have written fully thereof in any particular treatise. Therefore I do not only here set down what I have gathered from them most briefly and truly, but also those things which I have found and proved by my own experience, which I have annexed to them that the work may be absolute and complete.

Of which, as they say, Mary the Prophetess, the sister of Moses, in her *Books of the Work of Saturn* is thus said to write: "Make your water running like the water of the two Zaibeth, and fix it upon the heart of Saturn." And in another place: "Marry the Gum with the true Matrimonial Gum and you will make it like running water," of which process, Mary, George Ripley, have these verses:

> *Maria mira sonat* {Admirably speaks Mary}
> *Quae nobis talia donat* {who gives us a sort}
> *Gummis cum binis* {of two-fold Gum when}
> *Fugitivum fugit in imis* {the fugitive flees to the bottom}
> *Horis in trinis* {in three hours}

Tria vinclat {?} fortia finis {a limit is bound by a three-fold strong}
Filia plutonis {daughter of the underworld}
Confortia jungit Amoris. {a shape forms of Love.}

{The translation may be rough. I could find no Latin form of *vinclat*, though the script was clear in the MS. The implication of the verses is clear. Deep within our consciousness lies the formative power of Binah which manifests with Love.}

The Heart of Saturn, you will find why in his body white and clear; the work is briefly thus described. That a Water be made out of the body of Saturn, like the water Ziabeth, {This term is spelled variously in the MS. I could not find an original Hebrew word to get its gematria.} and that water fixed upon the heart of Saturn. The direction for drawing out this water of Ziabeth and the way of making the heart of Saturn is hereafter at large declared, with reduction of the body of Saturn into his heart or Salt.

Note the power of Saturn and his Angel upon Earth, Cambriel, Hanael, Carcer, Tristitia and Lead thus prepared for Medicines and Telesmae. You see here the wonderful power of God, how He rules Heaven and Earth by ten names, ten Sephiroth, ten orders of the blessed Souls, ten Angels in their ten Spheres, seven Angels that carry their power to the seven Planets and the Earth; and here we teach you knowledge of their Seven Metals, and the miraculous Medicines of the Rosicrucians. {See "The Tree of Saturn" with commentary on page 99.}

6. {Here the author begins numbers, the five previous numbers are omitted in the manuscript.} Take 8 or 10 ounces of Lead in filing, and dissolve it in *Aqua Fortis* in double proportion and fortified with Salt Armoniack in an earthen vessel with a narrow neck and set in ashes till it be totally dissolved; and there will remain a white matter in the bottom like grains of white salt, which is a figure of perfect solution; then pour your matter that is dissolved in the water into a body, and set thereon a Limbeck, and in *Balneo* draw away the corrosive water till there remain a dry substance in the bottom, and so you have the body converted white by Calcination with corrosive water, out of which the heart of Saturn is to be drawn.

7. The way to wash away and purge the corrosive water from the body, pour warm water upon the substance in a Limbeck, and pour it off often till it has no sharpness at all upon the tongue, and then the body is prepared for drawing out the Salt. {One of the first operations in our meditations is to turn Sulphur in each of the Metals away from the Salt tendencies toward its own Mercury. Alchemists allude to this by "washing Metals of Salt" or by "turning Salt white".}

8. When your matter is well dried, dissolve it again in distilled Vinegar, and distill the Vinegar twice or thrice from it, and in the bottom you will have a lucid, clear and white, shining Salt, which is then called the Heart of Saturn.

9. Now I come to the practice of the other, greater work, that the verity of

the Medicine may be found, of which many have made mention in their books, as Raymond, who called it the Vegetable, Mineral, and *Animal* Medicine. Geber says there grows a Saturnian herb on the top of a hill or mountain, whose blood, if extracted, cures all infirmities. {The mount is found in meditation, which, if persistent, changes blood chemistry.}

10. Ripley wrote a whole book called his *Practical Compendium*, of the practice of the Vegetable Medicine, teaching the manner and form of operation; but because he neither set down the solution plainly nor perfectly, he has been the cause of much error and has not only deceived me but all those that followed him, until after a long time I found a way to dissolve Saturn, so that it could never, after by distillation, be turned into Lead again, which is the chief and greatest secret of the Vegetable Medicine.

11. But let us hear the words of Mary, the Prophetess, and Ripley, taken from her: "The Radix of our Matter is a clear and white body which putrefies not, but congeals Mercury or Quicksilver, with its odor makes its water like the running water of the Zaibeth and fix it upon the fixed heart of Saturn." Which words do most aptly agree with the properties of Lead; for if anyone be shot or wounded with a bullet, and the bullet remain in the body, it will never putrefy. {There is a Hebrew verb, ZUB (to flow, to drip). ZUBCh (zubech) sums to 23 by gematria, which equals ChIH (chiah), Life-Force; and the Latin *Aes*, Ore. ZUB may be the root-form of these variations of Zaibeth.}

12. And also if Quicksilver be hanged in a pot over the fume of molten Lead so as the fume of the Lead touch the Quicksilver it will congeal it. {Physical laboratory alchemists die from the fumes of mercury, lead or arsenic by following instruction like this literally.}

13. Thus far of the preparation of Lead. We now come to its denomination. They bid us fix the water Zaibeth upon the fixed body of the Heart of Saturn; now for the exposition of the body for the name of Saturn. Ripley called it *Adrop*, of which that is made which the Masters call *Sericon*; the water of *Sericon* they call their *Menstruum*, the two Zabieths {sic} joined together in one water are the two Mercuries, that is to say white and red, contained in one Menstruum, that is to say of the water and oil of the fixed body or Heart of Saturn. {Ida and Pingala of Kundalini sit coiled in the Sacral plexus, the Saturn Chakra.}

14. Isaacus also wrote a Treatise of Lead. He worked chiefly according to the doctrine of Mary, the prophetess, and labors much to fix the Earth of Saturn; and after to dissolve the body in distilled Vinegar; that by the addition of corroding the sharp things, his red Oil may be distilled, which he called the Water of Paradise, that he may imbibe his fixed Earth therewith: which way is much shorter than Ripley's, but the rubification and fixation of the Earth is long and uncertain; wherefore I have both forsaken Isaacus and Ripley in making the Earth, instead of which I have given the fixed Heart of Saturn.

15. But that the body may be prepared according to this Table and after my

intention and the desire of Ripley, we both will that the Oil of Water of Paradise be drawn out of the Gum of *Sericon* (whose Father is *Adrop*). *Sericon* is made of red Lead; therefore it is first necessary to show the way of making *Minium* of Lead. Take the description as follows and therewith the Composition of the Gum of *Sericon*.

16. Take ten or twelve pounds of Lead and melt it in a great Iron Vessel as plumbers use to do; and when it is molten, stir it still with an Iron Spatula {*Spatha* has been investigated earlier. *Spatha ferrea* (iron spatula) sums to 108, that of MNHIG (manehig), Leader, Driver. With regard the reproductive energy that force is the leader or driver in turning Lead and all the Metals.} till the Lead be turned to powder, which powder will be of a green color. When you see it thus, take it from the fire and let it cool, and grind that powder upon a marble till it be impalpable, moistening the powder with a little common Vinegar, till it be like thick honey; which put into a broad Earthen Vessel, and set it on a Trevet over a lent fire, to vapor away the Vinegar and dry the powder and it will be of a yellow color. Grind it again and do as before, till the powder be so red as red Lead, which is called *Adrop*. And thus is Saturn calcined into Red Lead or *Minium*. {*Minium*, Red Lead, equals 71 in Latin gematria. The Hebrew IVNH (yonah), means Dove, hinting again that Love is the key to turn Metals and is the resulting force when they are transmuted.}

17. Take a pound of Red Lead and dissolve it in a gallon of Vinegar, and stir it with a stick three or four times in a day, and so let it stand in a cold place the space of three days, then take your Earthen Vessel and set it in *Balneo* twenty-four hours, then let it cool and filter the liquor three times; and when it is clear put it in a bottom, the Gum of *Sericon* will remain like thick honey, which set apart and dissolve more new Lead as before for more Gum till you have ten or twelve pounds thereof.

18. Now give careful attention for we now come to the point and period of Ripley's error. For if you put four pounds of this *Sericon* to distill in a Limbeck, and from thence would draw a *Menstruum*, as Ripley teaches, perhaps you would have scarce one ounce of this Oil, and some part of a black earth will remain in the bottom, and most part of the Gum melted again into Lead, by which you may know that the *Sericon* is not well dissolved, nor as yet sufficiently prepared, that a Chaos may be made thereof fit for distillation, because it is not yet well dissolved. Therefore in Isaacus there is found a way resolving this Gum with distilled Vinegar, acuated with calcined Tartar and *Sal Armoniac*; wherefore says he, if you be wise, resolve the Gum; but I like not this acuation of the Vinegar, as I may call it, I rather choose to resolve the *Sericon* in Raymond's Calcination Water, which is a compounded water of the Vegetable Mercury, or fire natural, with the fire against nature, as Ripley testifies; and it is more verified by Raymond in his books of Mercury, where he teaches how to dissolve bodies with his Calcinative Water.

19. I will reveal unto you this water which is almost unknown. Note, therefore, that the Vegetable Mercury is the Spirit of Wine (instead of which we may sometimes use distilled Vinegar) and that the fire against Nature is a corrosive water made of Vitriol and Saltpeter.

20. Therefore take which you will, either Spirit of Wine rectified (or *Aqua Vitae*) or distilled Vinegar four pounds, and two pounds of corrosive water and mix them together. In this water thus compounded, resolve half a pound of Gum of *Sericon* in a circulatory and set it in *Balneo* four or five days, and the Gum will be totally dissolved into the form of water or Oil of a dusky red color.

21. Then distill away the water in *Balneo* and there will remain an Oil in the bottom which is then the Chaos out of which you may draw a *Menstruum* containing two Elements, and this is the true resolution of the Gum of *Sericon*. In this water you may resolve so much Gum as you please by reiteration.

22. Take two pounds of this Chathodical substance and prepare it for distillation in naked fire or sand, and lift up the clear red Oil, wherein both the Spirit and Soul do secretly lie hid, which Isaacus calls the Water of Paradise, which, when you have, you may rejoice, for you have gone through all the gross work and come to the Philosophical work.

Therefore proceed to conjunction and join the white Heart of Saturn with the red oil as it is found in the *Rosary, candida succincto jacet uxor nupta marito* {A wife lies back to put on white, a bride to marry.}, that is to say the red Mercury to the Salt if you proceed to the red work.

23. Therefore take four ounces of the Salt or Heart of Saturn, and as much of the red Oil or Water of Paradise, and seal them up in a Philosopher's Egg, and so soon as they shall feel the heat of the Balneum, the Salt will dissolve and be made all one with the Oil so as you will not know which was the Salt, nor which was the Oil.

Set your Glass in *Balneo* and there let it stand in an equal degree of fire till all your matter be turned white and stick to the sides of the Glass and shine like fishes eyes and then it is White Sulphur of Nature; but if you proceed to the red work then divide your White Sulphur into equal parts, reserving one part for the White Work, and go on with the other part, and in a new glass, well sealed up, set it in Ashes till it be turned into a red color.

24. When your Sulphur is thus converted, imbibe it again with equal weight of its Soul, dissolving and congealing till it remain in an oil and it will congeal no more, but remain fixed and flowing.

This then is to be fermented with the fourth part of the Oil of Gold.

We have set down already before of the augmentation in quantity and quality, therefore it is not necessary to repeat it here.

We will now return to the White Sulphur before reserved, that we may set down the manner of the White Work.

When you have your Red Oil, or Soul, if you desire to make the White

Elixir, set part of the said Oil in a Glass in *Balneo* to digest. Then take it out and put it into a body, and in a lent fire distill away the Spirit or White Mercury, which you must try and know whether it arises pure without water or not, as you do when you try the Spirit of Wine; for if it burns all up it is well; if it does not, rectify it so often, till it be without any wateriness at all; then have you rectified your Spirit, wherewith dissolve your White Sulphur till it remain fixed and flowing as you did before in the Red Work. Then ferment it and augment it with the fourth part of the Oil of the White Luminary, or Luna, as you did the Red, and it will be the White Elixir, converting imperfect bodies into perfect Silver.

25. Ripley divided the scope of this work into 4 operations, whereof the first is the dissolution of the body, the second the extraction of the *Menstruum* and the separation of the Elements; the third is not necessary in our work, because we cast away the Earth after every distillation instead of which we use our Salt or Heart of Saturn; the fourth is that there be a conjunction of our Salt as is before described.

Here Follows the Accurtation of the Work of Saturn

The way of extracting Quicksilver out of Saturn, found in Isaacus, of which I know how to make a special accurtation with his Water of Paradise, which I gathered partly from the aforesaid author and others. Ripley made his accurtation with Quicksilver precipitated with Gold, and imbibition with corrosive water, which I like not, because the Elixir so made will be the greatest poison, as himself confesses that it were better for a man to eat the eyes of a Basilisk than taste that Elixir.

26. But because I desire to set down this accurtation of Lead alone with his Elements, that no strange body may be added to our Elixir, and also that it may be made a Medicine for all uses, I have found out the way of making alone with the Mercury of Saturn and his own proper Tincture; for I make a body of one thing, which is a Spirit, and make that Medicine with its own proper Spirit. Read all the philosophers and you will never find a word of the process, nor none of the Ancients will teach you how to make the Mercury of Saturn.

Of the Medicine, Elixir Fermentation, Imbibition, Precipitation, Quicksilver, Saturn, Lead, and the Toad.

St. Christopher Heydon says in a manuscript of his: "The Alchemists know how by an easy Art to make current Mercury out of Lead." But what Art that was no other author of the ancients has showed us. "Keep seeking, keep seeking," says the first alchemist (so Paracelsus was pleased to say in imitation of him) "and you will find, knock and it will be opened to you." I tried many experiments, although they were repugnant to doctrine and philosophy; I almost despaired of that Art; yet because nothing is difficult to the industrious, by often knocking at last I found it apart, by which means I attained to the Art of such a felicity, that is to say, of making Quicksilver of Lead. This Art revealed is a great secret. The instruments necessary in this work are a Furnace, a Crucible and a pair of Tongs. Let the Furnace be filled with coals, whereunto put fire, and when the coals are well burnt, so that they give a clear flame and fire, take your Crucible, well annealed that it breaks not with the sudden heat, and put therein three ounces of filed Lead, having twelve ounces of Mercury sublimate, well ground, and Salt Armoniack six ounces mixed together, which put upon the filings of Lead into the Crucible, and when the fire is strong and glowing hot, take your Tongs and presently take up your Crucible, and put it into the hole in the top of the furnace till you hear a great noise and buzzing; then so soon as you can (lest the Quicksilver fly away with the Spirits) take away the Crucible with the matter therein and set it in an earthen dish filled with ashes to cool; and when it is cold, strike the lower part of the Crucible, so that the matter of the Lead may fall into an earthen dish, and you will find your Lead converted into Quicksilver.

This work is to be reiterated with new Spirits till you have a sufficient quantity of Quicksilver, with which proceed as follows. To precipitate this Quicksilver, that from a Spirit it may be converted into a fixed body by fixation.

Take of this Quicksilver so much as you please and put it to precipitate in a round glass, well luted, and set it in ashes to the top of the glass; yet let us stay here a while, that the understanding may be more enlightened.

Therefore understand that the intention of this work is to fire the Spirit, which may sooner be done with the Spirit of a fixed body, which before was homogeneal with the body, and which of its own nature desires to join again with its body.

Therefore Nature requires that she may be helped by Art in this work, to which the Artist consenting he administers thereto the pure and desired Metal, which it delights to adhere unto; which Metal is Gold, which is thus prepared that it be sooner parted by the Quicksilver, and stick thereunto.

Take as much pure Gold as you please, and dissolve it in *Aqua Regis* {Water of the King, gematria 90, that of MIM, Water, and MN, Manna. All refer to the First Matter, but cleansed.} mixed with equal part of *Acetum Acerrimum* {Sharp Vinegar, 148. This is equal to *Astrum Solis*, Star of the Sun. It implies that prolonged meditation is concentrated AIN SUPh AUR, as is our Sun. *Acetum* alone holds the value 57. The associations with words and phrases of equal value are lengthy, however, one important word glares. *Gummi*, Gum, is that substance within the pineal gland just prior to its final maturation.}, or *Lac Virginis*. Then set it to digest the space of a day, then put your dissolution into an Alembic, and set it in *Balneo*; so distill away the water as dry as you can, and do thus three times, and the third time distill it in ashes that the Salt Armoniac may sublime. Then put distilled Vinegar upon the matter remaining, and after it has stood three days in *Balneo*, distill the Vinegar away in ashes that all the substance of the Salt Armoniack may sublime, and do thus three times, always putting in new Vinegar, until the Oil of the dissolved Gold remain in the bottom; then take of your Quicksilver three times so much as your Gold and pour it upon the solution of the Gold that they may mix together and be united. Then put your Quicksilver with the solution in a round glass, stopped only with a piece of cotton, and with a stick put it down every day as it does ascend; and keep your glass in ashes the space of a month, till your quicksilver be turned into a red precipitate. Then again dissolve it in new, distilled Vinegar, till the whole substance of the Quicksilver be dissolved, and the Vinegar be colored into a golden color, then distill away the Vinegar in ashes and again precipitate the Quicksilver, which is in the bottom of a gold color, into a red and fixed body; and so have you the Mercury precipitate of Saturn.

It remains now that the Body be imbibed with its Soul, that this being from a Spirit reduced into a body, may again imbibe its Soul that it may be dissolved therewith. Therefore put it into a Glass, and add thereto equal proportion of its Soul or Water of Paradise, and shut your Glass well, the space of five days till the body be dissolved with the Soul. Then dry it in ashes till it penetrate and flow; and when it is dried, try it upon a hot iron plate if it be fixed and melt, if not, imbibe it again with half the weight of its water; and do so till you make it fusible and piercing by imbibing and drying. And when it will melt in the fire and penetrate, it is then the Medicine, and fit for Fermentation. And after Fermentation it will be the Elixir. Then it is to be augmented and projected as is before declared, and thus the work of Saturn is accurtated, of which George Ripley says: "*Adrop* is the Father of the Medicine, *Sericon* his brother, *Lympha* his sister, the Earth its Mother."

But if you desire to know all the secret of Saturn and Lead, I will set you down one process out of Paracelsus: "When you have well prepared the Heart of Saturn," says he, "take two or three ounces of that Heart and grind it small with double weight of Saltpeter and put it in a subliming Glass, with a head well luted to sublime, increasing the fire by little and little as long as anything will ascend or sublime." Thus far Paracelsus. Now if you find this true, Ripley will tell you what you will do in these words: "When by the violence of the fire in the distillation of the Gum of the *Sericon*, a certain white matter will ascend sticking to the head of the Limbeck, like ice, keep this matter, which has the property of Sulphur, not burning, and is a fit matter for receiving form. You will give it form after this manner by rubifying it in ashes; and when it is Red Sulphur give it of its Soul, until it pierce and flow, then ferment it."

Here I have delivered unto you all the ways and manners of Saturn which are found in any of the philosophers' books. To the end, therefore, that the work may be completed with a demonstration of this word *Plumbum*

Philosophorum as appears in the *Practical Compendium* of Ripley, I say that the Philosophers' Lead is not taken for Antimony, but for *Adrop*, being converted into the Gum of *Sericon*.

{The Elixir of Jupiter}

The Influence of Jupiter and his Angel upon Hismael, Advachiel, Amnitzel, Acquisitio, Laetitia and Tin, by Art and Nature fitted for man's use. Jupiter follows Saturn's steps for he is the offspring of Saturn and naturally born from him.

{This paragraph starts with the glyph of Jupiter's symbol} ♃ *representat STANNUM, sub quo aliquando Mercurius Sublimatus, et Sal Ammoniacum intelligitur.*

Cineritius ille probus justus Jupiter influentiam suam habet in terrestrem Jovem, qui post preparationem suam, se claro aerio suavi cum Sale Sulphureque lunari ostentat, et mortalibus virtutes suas prasentat. Habet quoque specialem suam influentiam bonus ille Jupiter in Jecur, sanat propterea illud, omnesque affectus, qui inde oriuntur. {— represents Tin from which Mercury Sublimate and *Sal Armoniack* is finally understood.}

Turned to ashes, that proper, just Jupiter holds influence on terrestrial Jove, who, after his preparation, shows itself clear, airy, agreeable with Salt and Sulphur of Luna, and presents his virtues by putrefaction. That good Jupiter also has his special influence on the Liver, for that reason he heals that and all effects which originate therefrom. {See "The Tree of Jupiter" with commentary on page 101.}

To Make the Elixir of Iron

Observe in this work:
1. Calcination.
2. Solution.
3. Separation.
4. Conjunction.
5. Putrefaction.
6. Sulphur.
7. Fermentation.
8. Elixir

Mars, being most earthly of all the planets or bodies, it is not to be doubted, but that it may easily be reduced into a body with little labor and therefore most easily converted into Salt, which is done by Calcination, I will therefore first show his Conversion into Salt. Understand therefore that hence arises a two-fold consideration, that is to say that it be calcined one way into its Body or Salt, the other way that the Body be prepared for Solution by Calcination.

The practice differs but a little, for whether you calcine Iron for its Salt or *Menstruum*, one only manner of preparation suffices. That is to say, that you take filings of Iron or Steel, as much as you please, and mix therewith equal weight of Sulphur in an earthen body with a Limbeck well luted thereto; then set it in ashes to sublime till all the Sulphur be sublimed from it; then dissolve the filings which remain in the bottom in *Aqua Regia* {Royal Water, gematria = 74}, and it will be converted into Salt, which will be cleansed from the said water, if you put thereon distilled Vinegar and distill it away. Do thus three times with new Vinegar, and you will have a yellowish, red Salt in the bottom, which then is a Body to be joined to the Soul, which keep in warm ashes till you use it.

Now for the practice of Iron for Dissolution; take filings of Iron or Steel, so much as you please, and put it in an Iron dish filled with Vinegar and set it in the flaming fire the space of three hours, then take it out and let it cool; reiterate this work four or five times, then calcine it with Sulphur as you did before.

When it is thus calcined, set it to dissolve in a corrosive water by adding equal weight of our *Acetum Acerrimum*, and let it stand till it has dissolved so much as it can in the cold; then set it in hot ashes, and let it stand there the space of four or five days. Pour off the water and dry which is not dissolved, and again calcine it and dissolve it; and when it is dissolved, so as the water be colored red, pour it out into a body and keep it till you have dissolved as much calcined Iron as you please.

Then take all your dissolutions, and with an Alembic distill away the water in *Balneo*, and put distilled Vinegar upon the matter remaining in the bottom and let it stand upon it in *Balneo* the space of seven days; then take out your Glass and filter the dissolution, and then again in *Balneo* distill off the Vinegar, and in the bottom will remain a thick oil of the Iron or Steel; but if it be not dissolved to your mind, reiterate your solution in Raymond's Calcinative Waters, but it would be better if it were edulcorated with *Aqua Vitae* {Water of Life = 88} drawing it away again in *Balneo*, and so you have your Iron dissolved into a Liquor.

Therefore proceed to distillation, that there may be a separation, and distill it in an earthen vessel in a strong fire, increasing the fire as much as you can, and receive the Oil or Soul or Red Tincture of Mars, separated from the remaining feces by the nose of the Limbeck, which oil is the most permanent tincture for coloring Sulphur for the Red Work or for exaltation of all Elixirs in color, for it makes it tinge and color higher.

When you have thus prepared the tincture then proceed to Conjunction and work with the Salt before reserved, taking three or four ounces of the Salt and equal weight of the Soul. Then seal it up and set it to putrefy in *Balneo* and keep it there till it passes through all colors and be white, and then it is Sulphur of Nature.

The Nature of Mars and his Angel upon Bartzabel, Malchidael, Barchiel, Puer, Rubeus and Iron, with the mixing of the Elements, the Medicine must be made when Mars ascends in Aries or Scorpio, in the hour of Mars, Puer projected in the Ascendant. {See "The Tree of Mars" with commentary on page 103.}

Then take out your Glass and set it in ashes in a greater degree of heat till it be red; then distill the Red Sulphur with its own Soul {Sulphur of Sulphur}, and again dissolve and fix it; dissolving it in *Balneo*, fixing it under the fire, and so it is prepared for Fermentation.

The Fermentation is, as has often been spoken of before, with the resolved oil of the Sulphur of Gold in a four-fold proportion to the Medicine, that by the addition of the ferment it may be made Elixir, transmuting all bodies. {Mars, transmuted, aids with turning all the other Metals.}

And note that the Elixir of Iron excels all other Elixirs, for it rubifies more and tinges higher and is better for man's body, for it prevails against the spleen, constringes the belly and cures wounds, it knits broken bones together, and stops the superfluous flux of the Courses, etc. {Crude Iron burns-up and destroys tissue cells. Mature Iron reproduces a healthier, more durable cell structure.}

I will now show the Operation of the Physical and Alchemical Tincture of the Red Lion and Glue of the Eagle.

It is chiefly to be remembered how I taught you to dissolve Antimony with our *Acetum Acerrimum*, which may be also well done if you dissolve it in our Calcinative Water, and after that Antimony is calcined, which hereafter shall be at large treated of, also of the Glue of the Eagle. You must understand that we attribute no other beginning to the accurtation, except that where before we took the Blood of the Red Lion and the Glue of the Eagle when they were both destroyed; we now join them sound and not hurt, together, that they, living, may mortify and dissolve themselves, which I have fitly called Corporeal Matrimony or the Union, for in this wedlock they die together, that they may be vivified in the Celestial Matrimony. It is not to be wondered if this differ from the other, for this pertains to the handling of Spirits, the other way teaches the manner of making the Elixir of bodies.

That I may plainly reveal all things unto you, take Antimony well ground, half a pound, and as much Mercury Sublimate likewise ground, and grind them both together upon a Marble till you cannot know them one from another; then set them in a cold place that the matter dissolving may drop into a Glass set underneath, for when the matters are well mixed together then, say, that they will both shortly be dissolved; when the water is perfectly dissolved it will be of a greenish color and a loathsome smell. Put this water with the thick part within into a Glass, and let it stand the space of three days in a fixatory under the fire, and in a short time you will have your dissolvedness of a brownish

THE SYMBOLIC TREES
OF THE PLANETS

TREE OF "UNIVERSAL" MERCURY

Jean d'Espagnet advises: "Our Stone is made from seven stones." The following seven symbolic Trees make Mercury of all those metals (stones). In turn, the sublimated virtues of all seven stones work together as processes toward union through the steps at the base of this Tree of Universal Mercury. At step 9 our consciousness dies to the pure desire (Sulphur) for total union. The Sulphur within our Glass burns to be joined with its Mercury mode, permeating our body (10) and Subconsciousness (11), where it multiplies in Quantity and Virtue (12 & 13). Eventually our fomenting, fermenting consciousness is rewarded with the inner vision, discovery and union with the Holy Mineral-Stone, the First Matter Elixir, AIN SUPh AUR.

The Tree of Mercury.

THE TREE OF THE MOON

This Tree illustrates the method of cleansing the Moon Center or *Ajna* Chakra, called the Metal Silver by alchemists. Within the overall meditation are exercises and visualizations that help purify subconsciousness, which are too involved to address in mere commentary.

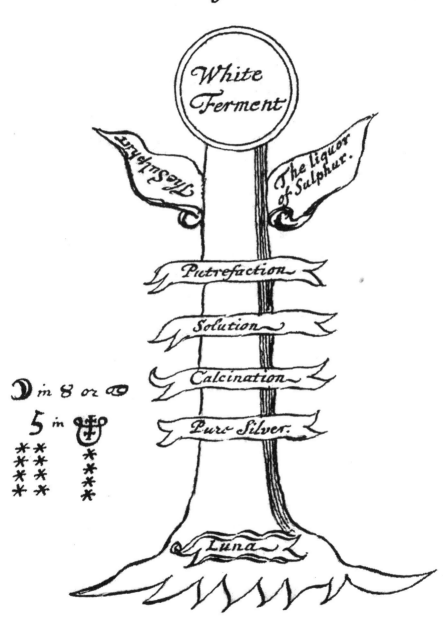

The Tree of the Moon

THE TREE OF "OUR MERCURY"

Sublimating "Our Mercury," the *Sahasrara* Chakra, is the theme of this illustration. Inceration is the process of impressing our creative imagery matrices upon the Universal First Matter, called "Wax" by many alchemists. By Dissiccation (exissiccation or desiccation) our author hints for us to temper the Water-Salt tendencies from our conscious intellects. Genuine repentance (Contrition) humble us before Our Lord while all Ferments deep within subconsciousness. Through steady desire and patience the Sulphur and Mercury modes within "Our Mercury" eventually conjoin as the Red Elixir. "Our Stone is made out of its own proper essence." Hence both Trees of Mercury have *Argentum Vive* at their roots.

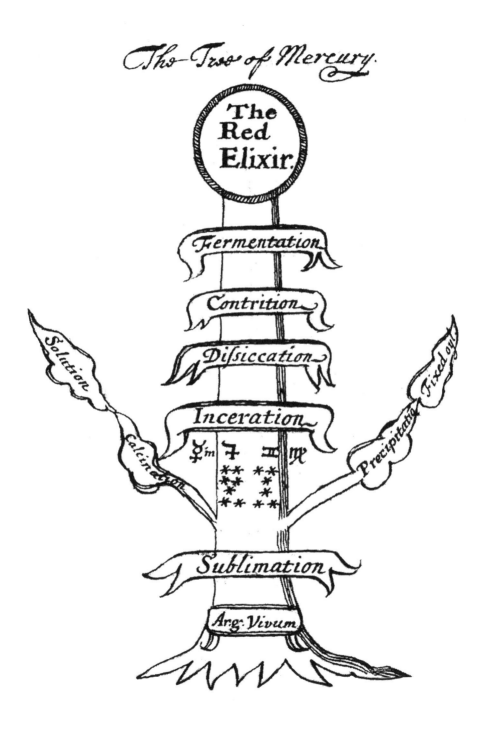

THE TREE OF THE SUN

Gold Salt is *Tamasguna* within the Heart or *Anahata* Chakra. This separative mode within our Metal must be Purged, Calcined and Dissolved by the Pure One-Gold. After the Putrefaction of all selfish elements we become a true Sun and Daughter of the One-Ego, which resides at the true center of all mankind. There is nothing in the top sphere as that is Kether, reflected in Tiphareth.

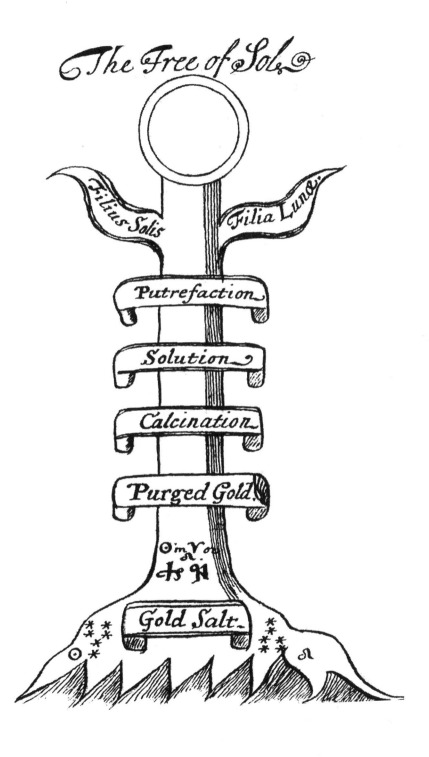

THE TREE OF VENUS

This is the manner of purification and perfection of the Metal Copper or the *Vishudda* (Venus) Chakra by meditation and redeployment of our Desire Nature. After Calcining Copper the Red Vitriol is slowly made White. Fermented by *Aqua Fortis*, Copper becomes Gold.

THE TREE OF SATURN

The Toad of Saturn hints of our earthy-water evolution. Our lower consciousness, condensed so tightly, alchemists metaphorically compare to Lead. Quicksilver (our crude conscious mind) begins to loosen or turn to Lead (and the *Muladhara* Chakra). This is accomplished through reading, studying, mindfulness, meditation and other uses of our intellect at the beginning of the Road of Return. We Imbibe (in a moral sense) the Precipitate influences of Jupiter's emanations. The Sulphur of Our Lead turns from its Salt, ferments to a Medicine confecting a tincture of Sulphur-Mercury Elixir. The very last section of this book, "Of the Spirit of Saturn or Tincture of Lead," might be read keeping this symbolic Tree in the mind's eye.

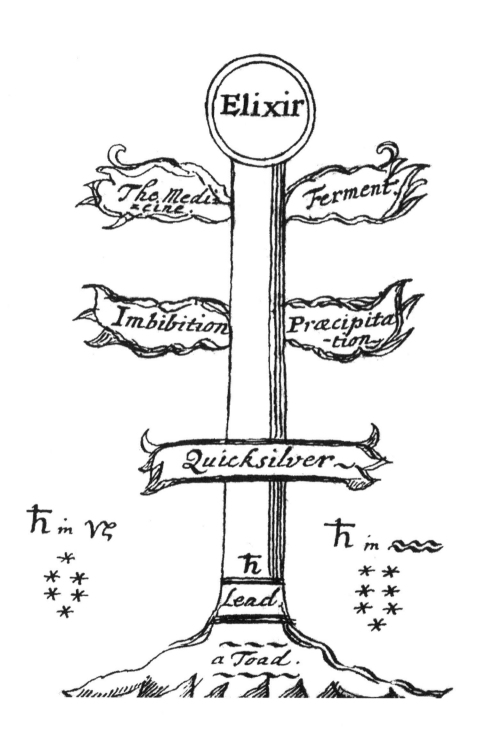

THE TREE OF JUPITER

The Tree of Jupiter illustrates the method of cleansing, sublimating and perfecting the Jupiter (Manipura) Chakra, or the Metal Tin. The Latin for Tin is *Stannum*. It sums to 90, to MIM, Waters, and the Hebrew letter Tzaddi, which is assigned to meditation by Qabalists. Tin in Hebrew is BDIL (bedil) and sums to 46.

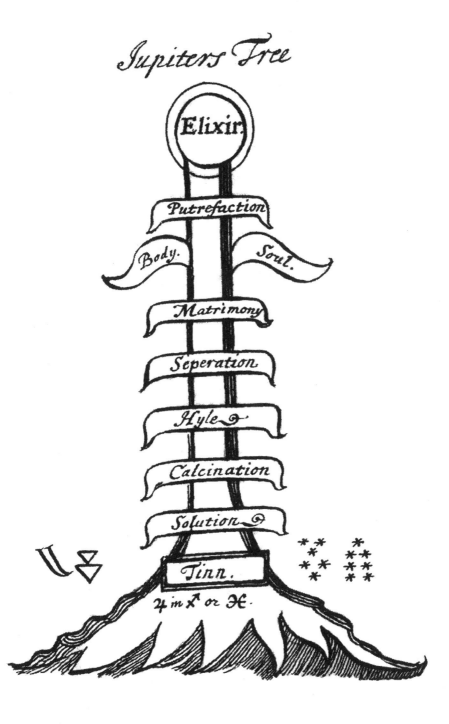

THE TREE OF MARS

The simplest of the Tree sketches outlines cleansing, sublimating and perfecting the Mars (*Svadishthana*) Chakra, or Iron. Iron is Key to the work as its nature is first involved with Dissolution of unwanted energies. It then applies its reproductive force toward rebuilding from the ashes. Iron steeped in Salt keeps us chained to the physical sphere of sensations. For this reason our author called Mars the "most earthly (intended) of all the planets or bodies" at the beginning of this section, even though Mars is a fiery planet. Notice he did not say "earthy."

The Tree of Mars.

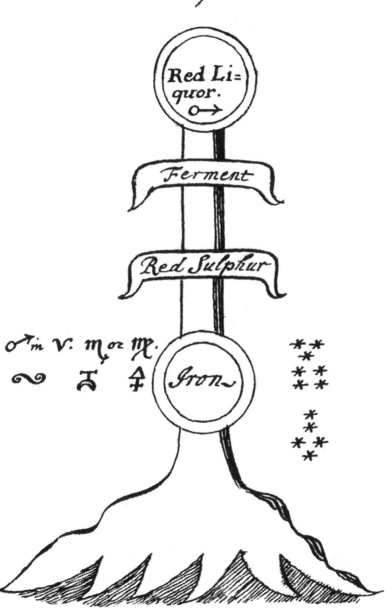

Geomancy—The Harmony in this Proportion

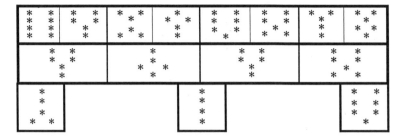

Commentary on the graph—This is a typical geomantic divination later outlined completely in the Golden Dawn papers. The top row from the left begins with the Four Mothers, the rest the Four Daughters. In the next row are the Four Resultants, derived from the eight above. The bottom center is the Judge derived from the flanking Left and Right Witnesses. The top twelve geomantic symbols were then placed within a Zodiacal House system and divined. It has value only to the one casting the divination.

Observe The Harmony of Geomancy in the Preparation

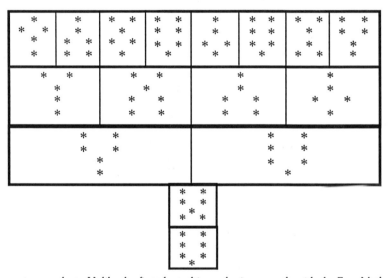

Commentary on chart—Unlike the first chart, this one begins correctly with the Four Mothers positioned at the upper right. In the same row, to the left, are the Four Daughters. The Four Resultants lay below the row of eight. The third row, below the Resultants, contains Left and Right Witnesses, the Judge below them. Under the Judge is a Reconciler, formed from the Judge and the Figure in the Particular House signifying the thing demanded. In this instance it could only be Fortuna Major, the first Mother, in the Tenth House.

104

black color, and after, that is to say, in the aforesaid time, it will be red, something higher than Red Lead.

Dissolve this calcined matter in Raymond's Calcinative Water, and when you have dissolved it all into a red liquor, or deep yellow, then is your matter brought well into its Chaos.

Put this Liquor into a fit body, with an Alembic and receiver, and by distillation separate the red oil or the red Mercury from the white body which remains in the earth, and if any matter ascend into the head of the Alembic, despise it not, but try if it is fixed; and if it be not fixed enough, sublime it till it be fixed.

Whereunto join equal weight of its Soul, for the Celestial Matrimony, and always leave out the Earth in the bottom, if you have any sublimate fixed; if not, take the white earth remaining in the bottom, with which proceed as before is said, and join the white body with the Soul. When they are thus joined, or married, set them to impregnate and revivify in *Balneo* till it pass through all colors, and at last be converted into red, which then is Medicine.

The manner of Fermentation, Augmentation, both in quantity, quality and projection, is spoken already.

And thus I have opened many choice secrets of the ancient philosophers, and also have amended many things in them. Their writings were rather published to conceal the Art, then to make it manifest or teach it; although it pleased Hermes Trismegistus, the first writer of this Art, both to say and protest that he had never revealed, taught nor prophesied anything of this Art to any, except fearing the Day of Judgement or the damnation of his Soul for shunning the danger thereof, even as he received the gift of faith from the Author of Faith, so he left it to the faithful. Yet when you read his writings either in his Smaragdine Table or in his *Apocaled* or his *Twelve Golden Gates*, and will find nothing plain or manifest, what will you think of such an author? Believe me, all the ancients have concealed the secret of their preparations in the Gross Work, although they wrote most famously of the Philosophical Operation; therefore I have used my endeavor to try, for out of their writings I found that the Elixir might be made of the Planets or Metals, and also of mean minerals, which came more near to a metallic nature. Then, reading more, I found a certain method amongst them all, as it were, with one consent or voice in this wise.

First and principally that bodies should be made incorporeal, that is to say discorporated or discompounded, which then is called the Hyle of Chaos. Secondly, that out of this Chaodical Substance, which is one thing, three elements {in this sense, Mercury, Sulphur and Salt comprising the One-Thing}, should be separated and purified. {Thirdly} that the separated and purified elements should be joined, the man and the woman, the Body and the Soul, Heaven and Earth, with infinite other names so called that the ignorant might think they were diverse, which only were nothing else but Water and Salt, or

105

the Body and Spirit or Soul, that is to say White Mercury and Red, which they joined together that a new and pure Body might be created in Putrefaction, and a Microcosmic infant might be created in imitation of the Creation, that is to say, Sulphur of Nature. Fourthly, that it should be fed with Milk, that is to say with its own proper Tincture, and after nourished by Fermentation, that it may grow to its perfect strength.

Having learned these I began to practice, and in the practice of every body and spirit, I found diverse errors; but reading more and trying more, at last I found the manner and true way of dissolving all bodies, separating and conjoining them; finding the composition of their secret of secrets, that is to say *Lac Virginis* or *Acetum Acerrimum*, and Raymond's Calcining Water, wherewith I dissolved all bodies at pleasure and perfected the Gross Work; wherefore I purposed to contrary the custom of the philosophers, reveal the whole work, lest I, being envious, should be the author of error like themselves. Therefore I have added their secrets to my own experiments and inventions, which are plainly and truly written. {The Gross Work is to become healthy as possible within and without.}

Alchemy Reveals & Opens Unto Us Four Other Secrets

The first is the Composition of Pearls far greater and fairer than natural ones, which cannot be perfectly done without the help of the Elixir.

The second is the manner of making precious stones of ignoble ones, by the same Art as we make Malleable Glass. {The precious stones are the force centers or chakras. "The Stone" is made from several stones as d'Espagnet advises, through meditation, as we do with the Glass Vessel.}

The third is the manner of making artificial Carbuncles in imitation of natural ones, which few or none have spoken of.

The fourth is the manner of making Mineral Amber, of which Paracelsus has only written in his *Book of Vexations of Philosophers* {This is a subtitle to *Coelum Philosophorum*}, and in the last edition of his work in the six {books} of his Archidoxes; but because they cannot be made without the help of the Elixirs, therefore they do serve a place among the Elixirs, where I shall discover the virtue or rather the vice of making Amber.

The Operation of the Making of Pearls

Consists of these parts, viz: *Lac Virginis*; Dissolved Pearls; Quicksilver; and The White Elixir.

{"Pearls" is a very clever metaphor. The Latin plural is *margaritae* = 86. There is numerous gematria with 86: *plumbum*, lead; *ruber Leo*, red Lion; *terra Adamica*, earthly Adam; *primus*, first; HTBO (hatayba) Nature; and NBDL (nibehal), to be divided, separated. The Hebrew plural is PhNINIM (pehninim) = 240, that of SPhQ (safek) Doubt; and OMLQ (amalek) the Amalekites (arch-enemy of the Jews). All these hints serve to describe something divided, crude, gross and fraught with negativity. This is our subconscious nature, which first must be purified and cleansed along with our self-conscious state. The "Composition of Pearls" makes the Pearl. The Latin singular is *margarita* = 81; that of ANKI (anokhi), I AM; *humidum*, humid; and KSA (kasa) Throne. The Hebrew singular is PhNINH (peninoh). At 195 it equals *vultus frigoris*; the appearance of Gold. Paracelsus writes of Pearl in *Coelum Philosophorum*: "Pearl is not a stone, because it is produced in sea shells. It is a white color. Seeing that it grows in *Animated* beings, in men or fishes, it is not properly a stony nature, but properly a depraved (otherwise transmuted) nature supervening upon a perfect work." The Pearl is the subconscious body cleared of dross, a "shell" of a watery nature previously "depraved." What follows is a method of cleansing.}

Take *Lac Virginis* or *Acetum Acerrimum*, so much as you think sufficient for dissolving the Pearls, as in double proportion to the Pearls; as if there be three ounces of the Pearls let there be six ounces of *Lac Virginis*, wherein dissolve the Pearls and set the Glass in *Balneo* {With respect to in *Balneo*, 86 equals *Balneo Mariae*, Mary's Bath, the *humidum* of subconsciousness.} to digest the space of a day. Then pour out the solution and distill it in *Balneo*, and in the bottom of the Glass you will find the thick Oil of the Pearls, whereunto add so much of your white, Corporeal Elixir {*chylus*} as suffice to make the matter like paste, and put thereto equal weight of the Pearls of Quicksilver. If the matter be too thin, put more powder of the Elixir; if it be too thick, add more *Lac Virginis* or Quicksilver, till it be like liver; grind this mass upon a stone till it be brought to a fit thickness.

Then make it up in what form you please. Therefore it is necessary that you have a pair of Brass or Iron molds in readiness (but it would be better if they were of silver) of what form you will, and fill them with this matter while it is soft; then pierce them through with a needle, or such like thing, and put as many of these in a Glass as you will (but first hang them upon a thread) and close well the Glass and bury it with the Pearls therein two feet under the earth and let it stand there the space of six months till they be congealed with the cold into a shining and clear substance like natural Margarites. These Pearls made and compounded in this manner are no less than natural ones, but much greater and more excellent by reason of the White Elixir.

The Operation of the Magistery of Carbuncles

Carbuncles have their birth or origin in the pits and golden mines of the earth, of the Spirit of Gold and Mineral Salt {This is very direct since *carbunculi* = 94, that of Sal Armoniac and Sol Pater, Sun Father.}, indurated and corporeal, being decocted and digested into the hardness of stone by the Archaeus of Nature, as well by the heat of the climate as by the great heat of the Sun; for they arise from the Spirit of the *minere* of Sol or Gold under the Earth, by whose influence they shine, as also from the hardened into the nature of the Stone; whence the philosopher intends and endeavors as he can to imitate nature by Art and to make and compound artificial Carbuncles above the earth with the same materials which nature forms them of under the earth; therefore he uses the same principles, operating with the Spirit and Soul of Sol undivided, and the most hard Salt of the Earth, whereof Venice Glass is made, which two are the Material Organs. For manual, three things are required, that is to say a Glass maker, Furnace of flaming fire, and a Crucible.

We now come to the materials, which are two and are to be joined together; the first gives the form, the other receives it. That which gives the form is the Spirit and Soul of Sol or Gold joined together in the Red Elixir, and is the Agent, and as it were, the Man; that which receives the form is the hardest Salt of the Earth contained in Glass, and is the power of Heaven impregnating the Earth; the Patient is the power of the Earth retaining the impression of the Heaven.

Having thus demonstrated the Theory, we now lay the foundation of the practice, which are two, whereof the first is as the preparation of the Elixir, the other of the Glass. Therefore your red corporeal Elixir is to be dissolved with the Oil or Tincture of Mars or Iron, because it has the greatest virtue above all other bodies, by whose Celestial Power the Earth, that is to say the Glass, is brought to the hardness of a stone, and converted into Stone. And so the Elixir is prepared for projection upon glass; but for the preparation of Glass there is no more required, but that it be made of the same matter that Venice Glass is made of; the Composition of which, if you know not, take as much Venice Glass as you please, and weigh it exactly, upon which project your Elixir. When you have so done, put your Glass in the Crucible to melt; and when it is well molten then take your Corporeal Red Elixir dissolved as before (or if you will, undissolved) as much as suffice to tinge the molten Glass, and put it tied up in a paper into the Crucible upon the molten Glass, stirring it a little with a rod, and there let it stand the space of an hour. Then take out the Crucible, and pour the matter into an ingot and it will be malleable, but as hard as Glass, and stone-like to the sight; and you may either cut it like a stone, or work it with a hammer. This Carbuncle Stone or Metal has the property of a Carbuncle in shining and glistening above all natural Carbuncles; and if you touch a Toad or Spider, they presently die, because it takes virtue from the Elixir against all poison. And if the sick carry this Carbuncle about him, so that it does touch the region of his heart, it takes away the cardiac passion and diminishes the strength of the disease.

Of the Composition of the Mineral Electrum of Amber as Natural as Artificial and the Bell Made of Amber used by Trithemius

Having finished these two secrets we now come to the Electrum. {*Electrum* is Amber in Latin and sums to 87 by Cabala Simplex.} But whether it is to be reckoned amongst Stones, or amongst bodies it may be doubted, because in the West Indies it is found written in the Spanish Decads of the virtue thereof; it is affirmed to be the greatest antidote against all poison, and far more noble than Gold. But if it be a Metal, it must necessarily be the chief and supreme of all Metals; for other Metals have the Origin from Sulphur and Mercury, but this Metal consists of Seven Metals, and is the best of all those which grow by the Ideas of the Earth. {Chakras cleansed of Salt become perfected force centers by the conjunction of their Sulphur and Mercury. Perfected Metals influence organs and glands to optimum health which then secrete subtle essences to the Amber Stone, perfecting it. PhZ (phez) is Fine Gold and sums to 87. This type of Gold is fashioned or beaten into crowns and fine jewelry. It hints a fabrication and composition of Amber from Seven Metals.} For where Gold is taken for the most noble of all metals by reason of its perfect color and digestion, this has a greater degree of digestion and color, having a higher color, that is to say, clear red, approaching nearer to the true color of the Sun. For as Gold is the Sun of other Metals, so this Electrum is to Gold as the Heaven to the Sun, wherein Nature, as it were, in Heaven has created certain Stars shining with clear beams of a silver color, showing plain to the eye that it consists of red and white metals mixed in the highest degree of digestion.

On the contrary it may be objected:

Objection 1. That there are only six metallic bodies, among which this is found to be none; therefore it is rather a Spirit than a Body.

Objection 2. The *Minere* of every Body or Metal is converted into Metal by fusion, but the *Minere* of Electrum, in melting, always remains, therefore it is no Metal.

Objection 3. There is nothing generated in the Earth but Stones, Spirits, Metals or mean Minerals; but Electrum is none of these; therefore it seems to be no Mineral.

1. To the first objection it is thus answered. We say that it is not apparent out of the books of any of the ancient philosophers, that they ever dreamed of this natural and mineral Electrum. But more to the purpose; those are called Spirits which fly from the fire; but the Electrum flies not from the fire; therefore it is no Spirit as Quicksilver and the rest, and also mean minerals.

2. We now come to the next. We grant that the *Minere* of every Metal is converted into Metal by the fire, which consists of Mercury and Sulphur. This Axiom is evident in those Metals which are imperfect and fly from the fire either in their Minere or in themselves after they be reduced into Metal; and also the Gold *Minere*, although before melting it flies from the fire, before the Gold be molten and converted into Metal; yet because Gold never flies after it is molten, but is found fixed in all probation, therefore it is accounted the worthiest of all Metals which consist of Sulphur and Mercury.

3. Now to the third. I say that I think it rather is of a stony and metallic nature joined together, by which mixture it differs from a stone and also from metal, but because it consists of Mercury, Earthly Salt and Sulphur mixed, therefore it gets unto it a mixed nature of them, so that it is half stone, half metal.

Wherefore it is to be judged that it consists of three natures mixed together; that is to say mineral, metallic and stony, and is the best of all those which grow in the Ideas of the Earth; for it exceeds mean minerals in fixation and constancy, because they pass away in fume by long melting and vanish to nothing, or else they melt easily in moisture as Salts, etc. But this Electrum or Amber remains fixed and constant, as well in the fire as water.

It exceeds metals in digestion, color and dignity. In digestion, because it is endowed with the sign of greater and more perfect digestion. For as Gold is more yellow, by reason of his greater heat and more perfect digestion, so the Electrum, because it has a higher color than Gold has, therefore it is more digested in color. For as Gold exceeds other metals in color, so Electrum exceeds Gold; for Gold is yellow, but Electrum is red, which is a higher color than yellow. And as Silver is the Luna of White Metals, so Gold is the Sol of Red Metals. So Electrum is to Gold as the Heaven is to Sol in dignity or value; for by how much Gold is more noble than Silver, so much this Electrum is more noble than Gold. {*Electrum* is the pineal body, pine-cone in shape. Within the gland is a yellowish, granulated substance called brain sand. The essences from perfected Metals mixed with the Virgin's Milk travel to the gland via the *Aurum Potabile*. Slowly, over years, the brain sand begins to gel. In later stages this is the Alchemist's Gum (*Gummi*). In a final stage Kundalini electrically charges this gland and the Gum is fused into a crystal, deep yellow-red, pyramidal in shape. It is the Stone of the Wise inside the Alchemist's body. For further reference see *Man, Grand Symbol of the Mysteries*, Chapter XVI, by Manly P. Hall.}

Lastly, it excels stones in shining and virtue; in shining because they shine by reason of their hardness; so this Electrum shows much sparkle, not by reason of its hardness but by reason of this completeness. {When completed, by the sole Grace of God, it "is visible to the clairvoyant as a vibrant spectromatic aura surrounding the outer body of the gland and pulsating with an electrical light."—Manly P. Hall} And as the Heaven is adorned with stars, so this Electrum with sparkling, because it has the clearness and brightness of all metals. And as the Heaven contains all the stars and planets, so this Electrum which is the Heaven of Metals, contains the Sun and Moon and the rest of the planets in itself; Gold and Silver as it were, the greater Luminaries, the other bodies or metals as the rest of the planets, mean minerals as stars in virtue. {The Amber Stone is the culmination of all previous stages in the Great Work and cannot be "composed" until the ingredients of all previous stages are, by Art, "confected" and perfected.}

For although many stones have singular properties and virtues, so that some help the sight, others the spleen, some the heart, some help blood, some hinder abortiveness, some hasten childbirth, some resist poison; yet there is no one found which takes away all infirmities, as Electrum does more than all mean minerals, metals or stones, according to his threefold conjunction, that is to say Mineral, Metallic and Lapidific. {What an understatement! Anyone possessing this Stone has instantaneous manifestation of any imagery. Such an one may disintegrate and reintegrate a physical body in this world plane or in any of the inner dimensions, at will. Does anyone believe such a person would stay in this world making Gold?}

Therefore, whatsoever others please to think of this natural Electrum, this seems most probable to me, that it is not simply a Metal, but of a nature exceeding Metal; for whereas stones, mean metals and minerals are generated of Salt, Sulphur and Mercury, this Electrum takes his origin from stones, minerals and metals.

From Stones it takes Salt, from minerals Mercury, from Metals Sulphur. These three being brought into one by the Ideas of Nature are its Elements, from a greater virtue and power of Nature; which Elements have formed a higher degree of perfection than in any other Stone, Mineral or Metal, as it were, by the Commandment of God, Nature should ascribe a Crown of Virtue, and dignity above all minerals.

But however it be, it is taken two manner of ways among the later Magicians and Rosicrucians, and that is to say, that which is made naturally, and {that} artificially. Naturally is that which grows in the natural Ideas of the Earth; the artificial is that which is made by Art above the Earth in imitation of nature. Whence Paracelsus, a worthy Master in Magic, seeing fully the nature of it, and the utility of Alchemy, commanding to make the Elixir thereof, when as its natural body cannot be had, in his *Book of the Vexations of Philosophers* and the sixth of his *Magical Archidoxes*, teaches to Compound an Artificial Electrum that the Elixir must be made thereof, as appears more at large in the said books, which I like not at all. He teaches how to make the Elixir out of Electrum; I contrarily, the Electrum out of the Elixir; he would make the Elixir out of the virtue of the Elixir. I leave his way to his own followers, but I desire mine not to weary and vex themselves in such a weak, but a more strong principle.

I make two kinds of Electrum one way, the first whereof is Spiritual, the other Corporeal. First of the former; after you have made your Red Corporeal Elixir by projection, in the same Crucible melt one ounce of Lead, and likewise another of Tin; and when they are hot, take the Crucible from the fire, and pour therein one ounce of Silver melted in another Crucible. And when these three white metals begin to be cold, take two ounces of Mercury, well purged, and put those two ounces of Quicksilver upon the molten metal by drops; then increase the fire gently, that too much of the Mercury do not fume away. {Beginning this paragraph we are advised that this is a spiritual method. Do not attempt to fume Mercury by taking all this literally.} Then in three other several Crucibles melt Iron, Copper and Gold, of each one ounce, which you must have in readiness molten. And first put your molten Gold into the Crucible, where your four white metals stand molten, and pour upon them the Copper and last of all your Iron, stirring the whole mass with a stick, that it may mix together; and let it stand in a melting heat the space of an hour; then take all out that it may mix together; and let it stand melting in the Crucible and consider well the weight of it; and according to the goodness of your Elixir, make projection for Medicine. And thus you have created and compounded Spiritual Electrum of the weight of Seven Ounces, consisting of Seven Metals, which Metals so converted into Medicine will be the Elixir of Electrum and an Universal Medicine, for you need not after regard upon what body (or metal) you project it. It is also the Chief Medicine for man's body; for although three or four of all the diseases of the Microcosm were united together, yet they may be cured with this one Medicine. If you dissolve part of this in Spirit of Wine, and distill away the same Spirit in *Balneo* and the Oil of the Medicine or Elixir remain in the bottom, you will have a most noble Rosicrucian Medicine of Life.

Note that if your Iron melt not well, then dissolve your Electrum in the Oil or Tincture of Mars, dissolving and congealing until it has imbibed a sufficient quantity.

·But if you desire to make Corporeal Electrum, when your Medicine begins to fail to convert Metals any more into Medicine, then in like manner project your Medicine upon your melted metals or bodies, and they will be converted into Corporeal Electrum, metallic and malleable. Of the abuse of this Electrum Paracelsus writes that Virgil Hispanus and Trithemius made a Diabolical Bell of this Artificial Electrum, upon which, when they would invoke spirits (which they called by a more decent name of Intelligences) they wrote the Character of what spirit they desired; and at the third ring of the Bell the spirits obeyed their desires so long as they desired to talk with them; and when they would talk no more, they hid the Character, and by the reverse ringing of the Bell the spirits departed; this Supernatural Magic is altogether infamous and unlawful. {Once again the Bell is the fully mature pineal gland. In the final Gum stages Kundalini power causes the tip of the gland to vibrate rapidly, which creates whirring and "ringing" sounds deep within the ears. After crystallization the ringing may continue and we not only "hear" discarnate life but see them as well. The fourth dimension and all therein is open to our new awareness.}

{*Particularia* or Preparation of the Seven Metals}

Before I come to the *Particularia* or the Preparations of the Seven Metals, I will discover some Arcanums belonging to Vitriol, Sulphur and Magnet.

There is a Subterranean Mineral Salt called *Vitriol*, which for dying of cloths and many other uses we cannot want. It is distinct from other Salts in its sharpness and quality in eating through. The Mineral of this Salt is strange, of a very hot and fiery quality, as apparent in its Spirit, the like not found in other Salts. It is white and red, and has an extraordinary medicinal quality. This Salt contains a combustible Sulphur, which is not in other salts. Therefore in metalline affairs, touching their transmutation, it performs more than others. It not only opens some but helps the generation of others by reason of its innate heat. When Vitriol is separated by fire, then its Spirit at first comes in a white form, after that there comes from its earth a spirit of a red condition. Staying in the Earth, the Salt, being united with its expelled Mercury and Sulphur can sharpen them. The remainder that stays behind is a dead Earth of no efficacy. Consider well this now kindled Ternary, for as you find in Vitriol's body three distinct things as Spirit, Oil and Salt, even so you may expect from its own Spirit again (which without the mingling of its Oil is driven from its matter) three distinct things as you did formerly from the body of Vitriol, which well deserves the name of *Speculum Sapientiae Physicae*. {Mirror of Common Sense Philosophy. Vitriol is another name for the First Matter, deep within the "subterranean" consciousness. It has the most profound dissolving quality with an intrinsic healing property.} Separate this Spirit of Vitriol as it ought, then that affords again unto you three principles, out of which only, without any other addition, since the beginning of the world the Philosophers' Stone has been made. From that you have to expect again a Spirit of a white form and an Oil of a red quality; after these two a Crystalline Salt. These three being duly joined in their perfection generate no less than the Philosophers' Great Stone; for that white spirit is merely the Philosophers' Mercury, the Red Oil is the Soul and the Salt is the Magnetic Body. As from the Spirit of Vitriol is brought to light the red and white Tincture, so from its oil there is made Venus, her Tincture, and in the Center they are much distinct asunder, though they dwell in one body. In this knowledge lay hid an irrecoverable error, worldly wits cannot conceive of it that the Spirit of Vitriol and the remaining Oil should be of so great distinction in their virtue. Touching their properties, the Spirit being well dissolved and brought into its three principles, Gold and Silver only can be made of it, and out of its oil only Copper, which will be apparent in a proof made. {Venus is fabled to have risen from the Foam of the Sea. That Sea is the unlimited ocean of awareness, and when cleansed Gold and Silver are conjoined. The King is returned to His Throne in Tiphareth and Venus is now the loving creativity of the Central Ego.} The condition of the Spirit of Vitriol, and its remaining Oil is this, that where there is Copper and Iron, the Solar Seed is not far from it commonly; and again where there is Seed of Gold at hand, Copper and Iron are not far from it, by reason of its attractive, magnetic quality and love, which they, as tingeing Spirits in a visible manner continually bear one to another. Therefore Venus and Mars are penetrated and tinged with the superabounding Tincture of Gold, and in them there is found much more the root of the Red Tincture than in Gold itself, unto which there belongs also the Minera of Vitriol, which goes beyond these in many degrees, because its Spirit is mere Gold, and *rubedo*, a crude, undigested tincture, and in very truth is not found out otherwise.

But this Spirit must be divided into certain distinct parts, as into a Spirit, Soul and Body. The Spirit is the Philosophic Water, which, though visibly parted asunder, yet can never be separated radically (because of their unavoidable affinity they bear and have one to another) as it appears plainly when afterward they are joined, the one in their mixture embraces the other, even as a Magnet draws the Iron, but in a meliorated essence better than they had before their dissolution. This Spirit (I can prove) is the essence of Vitriol, because this Spirit and Oil do differ much and were never united radically, because the Oil come after the Spirit, each can be received apart. This fiery Spirit may rather and more fitly be called an essence, Sulphur, and substance of Gold, and it is so, though it lies lurking in Vitriol as a Spirit.

This Golden Water, or Spirit drawn from Vitriol, contains again a Sulphur and a Magnet, its Sulphur is the *Anima*, an incombustible fire; the Magnet is its own Salt, which in the Conjunction attracts its Sulphur and Mercury, unites with the same and are inseparable companions. First in a gentle heat is dissolved the undigested Mercurial Spirit. By this is further extracted, after a Magnetic way by the Mercurial Spirit (so still the one is a Magnet unto the other) bearing Magnetic love one to another, as such things where the last together with the Medium is drawn forth by the first, and are thereby generated, and thus take there beginning. In this Separation and Dissolution the Spirit or Mercury is the first Magnet, showing its magnetic virtue towards the Sulphur and Soul, which it quasi magnes attracts. This Spirit, *per modem distillationis*, being absolved and freed, shows again its magnetic power towards the Salt, which it attracts from the dead earth; after the Spirit is separated from it, then the Salt appears in its purity. If that process be further followed, and after a true order and measure the Conjunction be undertaken and the Spirit and Salt be set together into the philosophic furnace, then it appears again how the heavenly Spirit strives in a magnetic way to attract its own Salt, it dissolves the same within 40 days, brings it to an uniform water with itself even as the Salt has been before its coagulation. In that destruction and dissolution appears the deepest blackness and eclipse and darkness of the Earth that ever was seen. But in the exchange thereof a bright, glittering whiteness appearing, then the case is altered, and the dissolved, fluid, watery Salt turns into a Magnet; for in that dissolution it lays hold on its own Spirit, which is the spirit of Mercury, attracts the same powerfully like a Magnet, hiding it under a form of a dry, clear body, bringing the same by way of uniting into a deep coagulation and firm fixedness by means of a continued fire, and the certain degrees thereof.

Note that from all Metals, especially from Mars and Venus, which are very hard and almost fixed Metals, of each a part can be made a Vitriol. This is the Reduction of a Metal into a Mineral; for Minerals grow to Metals, and Metals were at first Minerals, and so Minerals are *proxima materia* of Metals, but not *prima*. From these Vitriols may be made other reductions, namely a Spirit is drawn from them by the virtue of the fire.

This Spirit being driven over, then there is again a reduction of a Mineral into its spiritual essence, and each Spirit in its reduction keeps a Metalline property; but the Spirit is not the *prima materia*.

Of the Sulphur and Ferment of the Philosophers

I have formerly told you plainly how the Philosophers' Sulphur is made; *loco masculi* {in a masculine place} pour this Spirit upon purged and fined Gold. Let it dissolve and putrefy 14 days in *Balneo Mariae*, distill it and pour the water again on the Gold Calx, and cohobate this until the Gold pass over with the water; set this again to distill, abstract the water gently, leave a third part of it in the bottom then set it into a Cellar; let it Coagulate and Crystallize, wash these Crystals with distilled water, amalgamate them with Mercury Vive, evaporate the Mercury gently, then you have a subtle powder; put it in a glass, lute it, reverberate it for three days and nights, do it gently; thus is the Philosophers' Sulphur well prepared for your work, and this is Purple Mantle or Philosophic Gold. Keep it safe in a Glass for your Conjunction.

Of the Philosophers' Vitriol

After the Philosophers' Sulphur is made, which loco masculi is to make the King or man, {The gematria of *loco masculi* sums to 109. While it may hint something or somewhere else it equals *vas naturae*, the Vase of Nature as used by Artephias for womb or belly, and that of AM KL ChI (am kol hay) Mother of all Living Things. The masculine and feminine, King and Queen, reside deep within the Womb of the Subconscious.} now you must have the female or wife, which is the Mercury of the Philosophers, or the *Materia Prima Lapidis* {This equals 176, that of *fons miraculorum*, the Fountain of Miracles. The First Matter of the Stone is the source of everything.}, which must be made artificially; for our AZOTH {AZUTh = 414, that of AIN SUPh AUR} is not common Vinegar, but is extracted with the common AZOTH and there is a Salt made of *materia prima* or Mercury of the Philosophers, which is coagulated in the belly of the Earth. When this matter is brought to light it is not clear and it is found everywhere; {AZOTH is revealed as greenish or aqua-marine. The *Turba* also mentions a spissitude, from the Latin, *spissus*, dense.} it is ponderous and has a scent of a dead body. Take this matter, distill, calcine, sublime and reduce it to ashes; for if an artist want ashes, how can he make a Salt, and he that has not a Metalline Salt {When we discover the First Matter we experience a salty-metallic taste.} how can he make the Philosophers' Mercury?

Therefore if you have calcined the matter, then extract its Salt, rectify it well, let it shoot into the Vitriol, which must be sweet without any corrosiveness or sharpness of Salt. Thus you get the Philosophers' Vitriol, or Philosophic Oil; make further of it a Mercurial Water. Thus you have performed an artificial work. This is called the Philosophers' Azoth, which purges Laton, but is not yet washed. For Azoth washes Laton, as the ancient philosophers have told two or three thousand years ago. For the Philosophic Salt or Laton must, with its own humidity or its own Mercurial Water be purged, dissolved, distilled, attract its Magnet and stay with it. And this is the Philosophers' Mercury, or *Mercurius duplicatus*, {Clever, *mercurius* and *duplicatus* each add to 115, totalling 230.} and is two Spirits, or a Spirit and a Water of the Salt of Metals. Then this water bears the name of *Succus Lunariae* {162}, *Aqua Celestis* {133}, *Acetum Philosophorum* {222}, *Aqua Sulphuris* {169}, *Aqua Permanens* {129}, *Aqua Benedicta* {95}. {The foregoing gematria leads us to further imagery in all directions. For example, 95 is also the number for *vera medicina* and *tinctur*, as the Blessed Water tincts our cells and imbues us with true medicine.} Take 8 or 10 parts of this water, and one part of the Ferment or Sulphur of Sol; set it into the Philosopher's Egg, lute it well, put it in the Athanor, into that vaporous, and yet dry fire; govern it to the appearance of a black, white and red color, then you get the Philosophers' Stone.

Of the Philosophers' Magnet

Hermes, the Father of Philosophers, had this Art and was the first that wrote of it and prepared the Stone out of Mercury, Sol and Luna of the Philosophers, whom some hundred laborators have imitated. I do assure you for a truth that the Philosophers' Stone is composed of two bodies, the beginning and ending of it must be with Philosophic Mercury.

And this is now *Prima Materia* and is coagulated in the Entrails of the Earth, first into Mercury, then into Lead, then into Tin and Copper, then into Iron, etc. Thus the Coagulated Mercury must by Art be turned into its *Prima Materia* of water, that is Mercurial Water. {Cleansed *Prima Materia* perfects Metals, which perfect organs and glands in the entrails of the Earth, our body.}

This is a stone and no stone, of which is made a volatile fire, in form of a water, which drowns and dissolves its fixed father and its volatile mother.

Metalline Salt is an imperfect body which turns to Philosophic Mercury, that is into a Permanent or Blessed Water, and is the Philosophers' Magnet, which loves its Philosophic Mars, sucks unto him and abides with him. Thus our Sol has a Magnet also, which Magnet is the first root and matter of our Stone. {*Magnes* = 53, that of ABN (ahben) Stone, and ChMH (khammaw) Sun, which attracts Iron. The rechanneled reproductive force becomes the Desire of Aspiration, drawing *Magnesia*. Aspire long and ardently and revelation of the First

Matter is our reward. Sendivogius wrote: "The Air generates the Magnet, and the Magnet generates or makes out Air to appear and come forth. I have here entirely showed thee the truth." In this respect *aether*, Latin for Air, is 53. Deep breathing during meditation generates *Magnesia*. Khunrath suggests we perceive *Magnesia* as "magnes-IAH," the Magnet of Jah.} If you conceive of and understand my saying and what Hermes says, three things are required for the work; first a volatile or Mercurial Water, *Aqua Coelestis*; then *Leo viridis* {The Green Lion is the raw will-sex urge before transmutation and redeployment. Its gematria is 111.}, which is the Philosophic Luna; thirdly *aes Hermetis*, Sol or Ferment. {*Aes*, at 23 is the Latin for Ore and is used profusely in the *Turba*. This number equals ChIH (chiah), Life-Force, and the astrological symbol for the Sun, which is a circle (22) around a point (1). *Aes Hermetis* = 112, that of *Lac Virginis*, *semen solare*, *Prima Materia* and *gemma pellucida*, the Transparent Jewel (referring to the mature pineal gland).}

Lastly note, Philosophers had two ways, a wet one, which I made use of, and a dry one. Herein you must proceed philosophically; you must purge well the Philosophers' Mercury and make Mercury with Mercury, adding the Philosophic Salt, Ferment or Sulphur of the Philosophers, and then you have the Philosophers' Magnet, that is the Philosophers' Mercury; secondly, the Metalline Salt, or Philosophic Salt; thirdly, *aes Hermetis* or Philosophic Sulphur.

A Process upon the Philosophic Work of Vitriol

{There is a marginal note in the MS. which states: "This process Dr. Dee had from Dr. R. set down in a letter October 19th 1605."}

Take 10 pounds of Vitriol dissolved in distilled rain water, being warmed, let it stand for a day and a night. At that time many feces were settled. I filtrated the matter, evaporated it gently, *ad cuticulam usque* {all the way to the skin}. I set it on a cool place to crystallize. This unshot Vitriol I exiccated, dissolved it again in distilled rain water, let it shoot again, which work I reiterated so, till the Vitriol got a celestial green color, having no more any feces about it, and lost all his corrosiveness and was of a very pleasant taste.

This highly putrefied Vitriol, thus crude and not calcined I put into a coated Retort, distilled it in open fire, drove it over in 12 hours space by an exact government of fire in a white fume. When no more of these fumes came, and the red corrosive Oil began to come, then I let the fire go out. The next morning, all being cold, I took off the receiver, poured the gift in the receiver into a body, and some of the lute being fallen into, I filtered it, and had a fair Menstrual water, which had some phlegm because I took that Vitriol uncalcined, which I abstracted in *Balneo*, not leaving one drop. I found my Chaos in the bottom of a dark redness, very ponderous, which I poured into a Vial, sealed it Hermetically, set it on a three-foot ///into a wooden globe into a vaporous Bath made of water, where I left it so long till all was dissolved. After some weeks it separated into two parts, into a bright, transparent water and into an Earth, which settled to the bottom of the glass in form of a thick black corrosive-like pitch.

I separated the white spirit from it and the fluid black matter I set in again to be dissolved. The white spirit which was dissolved of it, I separated again. This work I reiterated leaving nothing in the bottom, save a dry red earth. After that I purged my white Spirit *per distillationem* very exactly; it was as pure as the tear that falls from the eye. The remaining earth I exiccated under a muffle; it was as porous and as dry as dust. On this I poured again my white Spirit, set it in a digestion. This Spirit extracted the Sulphur or Philosophic Gold and was tinged of a red-yellow. I canted it off from the matter and in a body I abstracted the Spirit from the Sulphur; that Sulphur stayed behind in form of an Oil, very fiery, nothing like unto its heat, as red as Ruby. This abstracted white Spirit I poured on the earth again, extracted further in Sulphur and put it to the former. After this that *Corpus Terrae* looked of a paler color, which I calcined for some hours under a muffle {*Surdus* = 92. The value is shared with *vitrum*, Glass; *Mercurio*, in Mercury; and *assa foetida*, Stinking Bath. To put something "under a muffle" is the same as placing it in *Balneo*.}, put it into a body; on it I poured my white Spirit, extracted its pure, white, fixed Salt. The remaining earth was very porous, good for nothing which I flung away; thus these three principles were fully and perfectly separated.

After all this I took my Astral, Clarified Salt which, weighed half an ounce after the weight at Strasbourg in Germany, {Our original author was not void of humor.} and of the white Spirit, which weighed four ounces, of Mercury one ounce and a quarter of an ounce. These I divided into two parts, whose quantity was half an ounce and one dram. I put this Salt to one part of the water in a Vial and nipped it, set it in digestion; there I saw perfectly how the Salt dissolved itself again in this Spirit, therefore I poured to it the other part, which was half an ounce and one dram. No sooner this was put to it then presently the body, together with the Spirit, turned as black as a coal, ascended to the end of the glass; and having no room to go any further, it moved to and fro. Sometimes it settled to the bottom; by and by it rose to the middle, then it rose higher. Thus it moved from the fourth of July to the seventh of August, namely thirty-four days, which wonderful work I beheld with admiration. At last, these being united and turned to a black powder, staying on the bottom, and was dry. Seeing that it was so I increased my fire in one degree, took it out of the wet and set it in ashes; after ten days the matter on the bottom began to look somewhat white, at which I rejoiced heartily. This degree of fire I continued till the matter above and below became as white as the glittering snow. But it was not yet fixed, making trial of it; I set it in again, increased my fire one degree higher; then the matter began to ascend and descend, moved on high, stayed in the middle of the glass, not touching the bottom of it. This lasted 38 days and nights. I beheld them as well as formerly, at the 30 days a variety of colors which I am not able to express.

At last this powder {which} fell to the bottom became fixed, made projection with it, putting one grain of it to one, and a quarter of an ounce of Mercury, transmuting the same into very good Lune. Now it was time to restore unto this white tincture her true *Anima*, and imbibe it, to bring it from its whiteness unto redness and to its perfect virtue.

Thereupon I took the third principle, namely the *anima*, which hitherto I had reserved; in quantity it was one ounce and one dram; poured to it my reserved Spirit of Mercury, whose quantity was one ounce and a quarter of an ounce, drew it over several times *per alembicum* so that they in the end united together. Those I divided into 7 equal parts; one part I poured on my clarified earth or tincture, which greedily embraced its *anima*, together with its Spirit, and turned to a ruddiness in 12 days and nights, but had no tinging quality as yet, saving Mercury Vive and Saturn, it transmuted into Lune, which Lune at the separating yielded 3 grams of Gold. I proceeded further with my imbibition and carried all the seven parts of *anima* into; at the fourth imbibition one part of my work tinged ten parts of Copper into Gold; at the fifth imbibition one part tinged an hundred parts; at the sixth it tinged a thousand parts; at the seventh it tinged ten thousand parts. At this time I got of the true Medicine four ounces, half an ounce and one dram.

Of the Preparation of the Seven Metals and First of the Sulphur of *Sol*, whereby Luna is tinged into good Gold

Take of pure Gold, which is three times cast through Antimony, and of well purged Mercury Vive, being pressed through Leather, six parts; make of it an *Amalgama*; to the quantity of this *Amalagama* grind twice as much of common Sulphur, let it evaporate on a broad pan in a gentle heat under a muffle, stirring it still well with an Iron hook {Hook, spatula or rod…Iron is the key}; let the fire be moderate that the matter do not melt together. This Gold Calx must be brought to the color of a Marigold flower, then is it right. Then take one part of Saltpeter, one part of *Sal Armoniack*, half a part of ground pebbles; draw a water from it. Note, this water must be drawn warily and exactly. To draw it after the common way will not do it; he that is used to Chemic preparations knows what he has to do. And note you must have a strong stone Retort, which must be coated to hold the Spirits closely; its upper part must have a pipe upward of half a span's length, its wideness must bear two fingers breadth, it must be set first in a distilling furnace, which must be open above that the upper pipe may stand out directly. Apply a large receiver, lute it well. Let your first fire be gentle, then increase it that the Retort look glowing hot. Put a spoonful of this ground matter in at the pipe, close the pipe suddenly with a wet clout; the Spirits come rushing into the receiver. These Spirits being settled, then carry in another spoonful. In this manner you proceed till you have distilled all. At last give time to the Spirits to be settled, to turn into water. This water is a hellish, dissolving, strong one, which dissolves instantly prepared Gold Calx and laminated Gold into a thick solution. This is that water which dissolves not only Gold but brings it to a volatility, carrying it over the helmet, whose *Anima* may afterwards be drawn from its torn body.

Note, the Spirit of Common Salt effects the same if drawn in that manner, which I shall mention afterward. If three parts of this Salt Spirit be taken, and one part of *Spiritus Nitri*, it is stronger than *Sal Armoniack* water, and is better because it is not so corrosive, dissolves Gold the sooner, carries it over the helmet, makes it volatile and fit to part with its Soul. You have your choice to use which you think best and may easier be prepared thus: Take one part of the prepared Gold Calx and three parts of the water which you make choice of. Put it into a body, lute a helmet to it, set it in warm ashes, let it dissolve; that which is not dissolved, pour three times as much water upon, that all dissolve. Let it cool, separate the feces, put the solution into a body, lute a helmet to it; let it stand in a gentle heat day and night in *Balneo Mariae*. If more feces be settled, separate them, digest them again in *Balneo* nine days and nights, then abstract the water gently to a spissitude like unto an Oil in the bottom. This abstracted water must be poured on that spissitude; this must be iterated again and often that it grow weary and weak. Remember to lute well at all times. To the oiliness on the bottom pour fresh water which was not yet used; digest day and night, firmly closed, then set it in a sand Capel, distill the water from it to a thickness; make the abstracted water warm, put it into a body, lute it, abstract it, iterate this work and make all the Gold come over the helmet.

Note, at the next drawing always the fire must have one degree more. The Gold being come over into the water, abstract the water gently from it in *Balneo* to the Oiliness; set the glass into a cold place; there will shoot transparent Crystals. These are the Vitriol of Gold. Pour the water from it, distill it again unto an oiliness, set it by for shooting; more Crystals will shoot; iterate it as long as any do shoot. Dissolve these Crystals in distilled water, put to it of purged Mercury three times as much, shake it about, many colors will appear, an *Amalagama* falls to the ground; the water clears up. Evaporate the *Amalgama* gently under a muffle, stirring it still with a wire. At last you get a purple colored powder, scarlet like. It dissolves in Vinegar into a blood redness. Extract its *Anima* with prepared Spirit of Wine mixed with the Spirit of common Salt, entered together into a sweetness, this Tincture of Sol is like a transparent Ruby, leaving a white body behind. {It could be noted here that as the cellular life within the body becomes more imbued with cleansed Limitless Light, a sweet odor may be detected. The Spirit of Wine (*Spiritus Vini* = 168), that is our Tinctured

Blood, prepares the body and Metals. Father of Metals, *Pater Metallorum*, equals 168.}

Note, that without information you cannot attain unto the Spirit of Salt. If it be not sweet it has no attractive power; to the attaining hereof observe these following manuals. Take good Spirit of Salt, dephlegmed exactly, driven forth in that manner as you shall hear anon.

Take one part of it, add half a part to it of the best Spirit of Wine, which must not have any phlegm, but must be a mere Sulphur of Wine and must be prepared in that manner as I shall tell you anon. Lute a helmet to it, draw it over strongly, leave nothing behind; to the abstracted, put more Spirit of Wine, draw it over somewhat stronger than you did the first time, weigh it, put a third time more to it, draw it over again well luted. Putrefy this for half a month or so, long as it be sweet, and it is done in *Balneo* very gently. Thus the Spirit of Wine and Salt are prepared, lost its corrosity, and is fit for extracting.

Take the Ruby-red prepared Gold powder, put of this prepared Spirit of Salt and Wine so much that it stand two fingers breadth over it; set it in a gentle heat. The Spirit will be red tinged; this red Spirit must be canted off. Pour a new spirit on that which remains on the bottom, set it luted into a gentle heat, let it be tinged deeply, then cant it off. This work must be iterated, that the body of Sol remain on the bottom like *Calx Vive*, which keep, for therein sticks yet more of the Salt of Gold, which is effectual in ways of Medicine as will be shown anon.

Those tinged spirits put together, abstract them gently in *Balneo*; there will be left a red subtle powder in the bottom, which is the true tincture *Animated*, or Sulphur of Gold. Dulcify it with distilled rain water. It will be very subtle, tender and fair. Take this extracted Sulphur of Sol as you were taught, and as much of Sulphur of Mars, as you will hear anon when I treat of Mars. Grind them together, put it in a pure glass, pour on it so much of Spirit of Mercury, let it stand over it two fingers breadth that the matter in it may be dissolved. See to it that all dissolve into a Ruby-like Gold water, jointly drive it over, then is it one, and were at first of one stem. Keep it well that nothing of it evaporate. Put it to separated Silver Calx, being precipitated with pure Salt and afterwards well edulcorated and dried; fix it together in a fiery fixation that it sublime no more; then take it forth and melt it in a wind-oven; let it stream well; then you have united Bride and Bridegroom and brought them unto Gold of a high degree. Be thankful to God for it as long as you live.

I shall hereafter at large set forth, how this extracted Soul of Sol may be made potable. I will now set forth how the white solar body will further be anatomized, and that by Art its Mercury Vive and its Salt may be obtained. The process of it is thus.

Take the white body of Sol, from which you have drawn its *anima*, reverberate it gently for half an hour, let it become corporeal, then pour on it well rectified honey water which is corrosive. Extract its Salt in a gentle heat. It is done in ten days' space. The Salt being all extracted, abstract the water from it in *Balneo*, edulcorate the Salt with iterated distillings with common distilled water, clarify it with Spirit of Wine, then you have *Sol Auri*, of which you will hear more in its due place {and} of the good qualities it has by way of medicine upon man. On the remaining matter pour Spirit of Tartar, of which elsewhere because it belongs unto Medicinals. Digest these for a month's time, drive it through a glass Retort into cold water, then you have quick Mercury of Sol; many strive to get it but in vain.

There is one Mystery more in Nature, that the white Solar body, having once lost its *Anima*, may be tinged again, and brought to be pure Gold, which Mystery is revealed to very few. I shall briefly declare it; as also about the Universal Stone of the Philosophers, how it rests merely upon the White Spirit of Vitriol, and how that all three principles are found only in this Spirit, and how you are to proceed in and to bring each into its certain state and order.

Take the Philosophic Sulphur, which in order is the second principle and is extracted with the Spirit of Mercury; pour it on the white body of the King, digest it for a month in a gentle Balny, then fix it in ashes and at last in sand, that the brown powder may appear; then melt it with a fluxing powder made of Saturn, then will it be malleable and fair Gold as it was formerly, in color and virtue nothing defective.

But note the Salt must not be taken from the Solar Body. There may be prepared yet another transparent Vitriol of Gold in the following manner.

Take good *Aqua Regis* made with *Sal Armoniack* one pound, *id est*, dissolve four ounces of *Sal Armoniack* in Aqua Fortis, then you have a strong *Aqua Regis*. Distill and rectify it often over the helmet, let no feces stay behind. Let all that ascends be transparent. Then take thinly beaten Gold rolls, cast formerly through Antimony, put them into a body, pour on it *Aqua Regis*, let it dissolve as much as it will, or as you can dissolve in it.

Having dissolved all the Gold, pour into it some Oil of Tartar or Salt of Tartar dissolved in fountain water till it begins to hiss. Having done hissing, then pour in again of the Oil. Do it so long till all the dissolved Gold be fallen to the bottom and nothing more of it precipitate, and the *Aqua Regis* clear up. This being done, then cant off the *Aqua Regis* from the Gold Calx, edulcorate it with common water eight, ten or twelve times; the Gold Calx being well settled, cant off that water, and dry the Gold Calx in the air where the Sun does not shine. Do it not over a fire, for as soon as it feels the least heat it kindles, and great damage is done, for it would fly away forcibly that no man could stay it. This powder being ready also, then take strong Vinegar, pour it on, boil it continually over in a good quantity of Vinegar, still stirring it that it may not stick unto the bottom, for 24 hours together, then the fulminating quality is taken from it; be careful you do not endanger yourself; cant off the

Vinegar, dulcify the powder, and dry it. This powder may be driven *per Alembicum* without any corrosive, blood-red, transparent and fair, which is strange, and unites willingly with the Spirit of Wine, and by means of coagulate may be brought to a Solar Body.

Do not speak much of it to the vulgar. If you receive any benefit by my plain and open information, keep these Mysteries secret to your dying day. I shall impart unto you this Arcanum also, and entrust you upon your conscience with it.

Take good Spirit of Wine, being brought to the highest degree, let fall into it some drops of Spirit of Tartar, then take your Gold powder, put to it three times as much of the best and most subtle common Flowers of Sulphur, grind these together, set it on a flat pan under a muffle, give to it a gentle fire. Let the Gold powder be in a glowing heat, put it thus glowing into the Spirit of Wine, cant off the Spirit of Wine, dry the powder against a heat, it will be porous. Being dried, then add to it again three parts of *Flores Sulphuris*. Let them evaporate under a muffle, neal the remaining powder in a strong heat and put it in Spirit of Wine; iterate this work six times. At last this Gold powder will be so soft and porous as firm butter; dry it gently because it melts easily. Then take a coated body, which in its hinder part has a pipe; lute a helmet to it, apply a receiver, set it freely in a strong Capel; let your first fire be gentle, then increase it; let the body be almost in a glowing heat, then put in the softened, well dried Gold powder, being made warm, behind at the hollow pipe. Shoot it in nimbly; there come instantly red drops into the helmet. Keep the fire in this degree so long till nothing more ascends and no more drops fall into the Receiver. Note, in the Receiver there must be of the best Spirit of Wine into which the Drops of Gold are to fall.

Then take this Spirit of Wine into which the Gold Drops did fall, put it in a pelican, seal it Hermetically, circulate it for a month. It turns then to a blood-red Stone, which melts in the fire like wax. Beat it small, grind among it Lunar Calx, melt it, then you find much good Gold, as the Gold powder and the Spirit of Wine together with the Moiety and the added Lunar Calx did weigh, but one moiety of the Lunar Calx is not tinged, the other is as good as it was to be used. If you hit this rightly, then be thankful to God. If not, do not blame me, I could not make it plainer.

Now if you will make this Vitriol, then take the powder formerly made, boiled in Vinegar, pour on it good Spirit of common Salt, mingled with Saltpeter Water, and the Spirit of Salt of Nitre. This Saltpeter Water is made as *Aqua Tartari* is made, with Saltpeter. Gold is dissolved in the water, which being done then abstract the water to a thickness; set it in a cellar; then there shoots a pure Vitriol of Sol. The water which stays with the Vitriol must be canted off. Distill it again to a spissitude, set it in the cellar; more of the Vitriol will shoot. Iterate this work as long as any Vitriol shoots. If you are minded to make the that way, then be first acquainted and ask counsel of your purse and prepare ten or twelve pounds of this Vitriol, then you may perform the work very well, and the Hungarian Vitriol, and others dug out of mines will permit you to do it. You may extract from this Vitriol also its Sulphur and Salt with Spirit of Wine, which is all easy work.

The Particular of Lune, and of the Extraction of its Sulphur and Salt

Take of *Calx Vive* and common Salt and neal them together in a wind oven; then extract the Salt purely from the Calx with warm water; coagulate it again, put to it an equal quantity of new Calx, neal it, extract the Salt from it, iterate it three times, then is the Salt prepared.

Then take the prepared Lunar Calx, stratify the Calx with prepared Salt in a glass viol, pour strong water on it, made of equal quantities of Vitriol and Saltpeter, abstract the *aqua fort* from it (iterated a third time) at last drive it strongly; let the matter well melt in the Glass, then take it forth; your Lune is transparent and bluish, like an ultra-marine. Having brought Lune thus far then pour on it strong, distilled Vinegar; set it in a warm place, the Vinegar is tinged with a transparent blue, like a Sapphire, and attracts the tincture of Lune, being separated from the Salt; all which comes from Lune goes again into the Vinegar, which must be done by edulcoration; then you will find the Sulphur of Lune fair and clear. Take one part of this Sulphur of Lune, one half part of the extracted Sulphur of Sol {with} six parts of the Spirit of Mercury. Join all these in a body, lute it well, {then} set it in a gentle heat in digestion; that liquor will turn to a red-brown color, having all driven over the helmet, and nothing stand in the bottom; then pour it on the matter remaining of the Silver you drew the Sulphur from, lute it well, set it in ashes for to coagulate, and to fix it eleven days and nights, or when you see the Lunar body be quite dry, brown and nothing of it does any more rise, or fume; then melt it quickly with a sudden flux-fire before the blast; cast it forth, then you {have} transmuted the whole substance of Silver into the best, most malleable Gold.

I formerly told you that the Spirit of Salt can destroy Lune, so that a potable Lune can be made of it, of which potable Lune will hereafter be set forth as to the preparation and the use thereof in Medicine.

When you perceive that the Sulphur of Lune is wholly extracted and the Vinegar takes no more tincture from her, nor the Vinegar does taste any more of Salt, then dry the remaining calx of Silver, put it into a glass, pour on it corrosive honey water as you did to the Gold, yet it must be clear and without any feces; set it in warmth for four or five days, extract Lune's Salt, which you may perceive when the water grows white. The Salt being all out of it, then abstract the honey water, edulcorate the corrosiveness by distilling, and clarify

124

the Salt with Spirit of Wine; the remaining matter must be edulcorated and dried. Pour upon it the Spirit of Tartar, digest it for half a month, then proceed as you did with the Gold; then you have Mercury of Lune. The said Salt of Lune has excellent virtues upon man's body. The efficacy of its Salt and Sulphur may be learned by this following process.

Take of the sky-colored Sulphur, which you extracted from Lune and is rectified with Spirit of Wine, put it in a glass, pour on it twice as much of Spirit of Mercury, which is made of the White Spirit of Vitriol. In like manner take of the extracted and clarified Salt of Silver, put to it three times as much of Spirit of Mercury. Lute well both glasses; set them in a gentle Balney for eight days and nights; look to it that the Sulphur and Salt loose nothing, but keep their quantity as they were driven out of the Silver. Having stood these eight days and nights, then put them together into a glass, seal it Hermetically, set it in gentle ashes, let all be dissolved and let it be brought again into a clear and white coagulation. At last fix them by the degrees of fire, then the matter will be as white as snow. Thus you have the white tincture which with the volatile, dissolved *Anima* of Sol you may *Animate*, fix, bring to the deepest redness, and at last ferment and augment the same, *ad infinitum*, the Spirit of Mercury being added thereunto. And note, that upon Gold a process is to be ordered with its Sulphur and Salt.

If you understood how their *primum mobile* is to be known, then is it needless in this manner and to that purpose to destroy Metals; but you may prepare every thing from or of their first essence and bring them to their full perfection.

Of the Particular of Mars, together with the Extraction of its *Anima* and Salt

Take of the red Vitriol Oil, or Oil of Sulphur one part and two parts of ordinary well water. Put these together; dissolve therein filings of Steel. This dissolution must be filtered, and being warmed, let it gently evaporate a third part of it; then set the glass in a cool place. There will shoot Crystals as sweet as sugar, which is the true Vitriol of Mars. Cant off that water, let it evaporate more, set it again in a cold place; more Crystals will shoot. Neal them gently under a muffle, stirring it still with an Iron wire; then you get a fair purple-colored powder; on this powder cast distilled Vinegar, extract the *Anima* of Mars in a gentle Balney, abstract again the Vinegar, and dulcorate the *Anima*. This is the *Anima* of Mars, which, being added to the Spirit of Mercury and united with the *Anima* of Sol, tinges Line into Sol, as you heard about the Gold.

Of the Particular of Venus, what Mysteries there are hid therein, and of the Extraction of its Sulphur and Salt

Take as much of Venus as you will and make Vitriol of it, after the usual and common practice. Or take good Verdigris sold in shops, it effects the same. {Alchemists frequently called the First Matter their Venus. Vitriol is another name for that same Venus, cleansed. Verdigris is spelled verdigreece in the MS.; it is a Greek green. Venus (or Aphrodite) maintained her grove and alter on Cyprus in the eastern Mediterranean. Our image making faculty is situated at the back of the brain, at the East. This is more than enough alchemical hint toward "what mysteries are hid therein."} grind it small, pour on it good distilled Vinegar set in a warmth; the Vinegar will be transparent green, {Azoth has a spissitude, a density which blots out the Light. Meditation cleanses the green to a transparency.} cant it off, pour on the remaining matter on the bottom new Vinegar; iterate this work as long the Vinegar takes out any tincture and the matter of the Verdigris on the bottom lies very black. Put the tinged Vinegar together, distill the Vinegar from it to a dryness, else a black Vitriol will shoot, thus you get a purified Verdigris. Grind it small, pour on it the juice of immature grapes, let it stand in a gentle heat; this juice makes a transparent tincture, as green as a Smaraged, and attracts the red tincture of Venus, which affords an excellent color for painters, Limners and others for their several uses. {See the Tree of Venus with commentary on page 97.}

When the juice extracts no more of the tincture, then put all the extraction together, abstract the moiety of this juice gently, set it into a cool place; there shoots a very fair Vitriol. If you have enough of that, then you have matter enough to reduce the same and to make of it the Philosophers' Stone, in case you should make a doubt to perform this great mystery by any other Vitriol. The common Azoth is not the matter of our Stone, but our Azoth or *Materia Prima* is extracted with the common Azoth, and with the wine, which is the outpressed juice of unripe Grapes, and with other waters also must be prepared. These are the waters wherewith the body of Venus must be broken and be made into Vitriol, which you must observe very well, then you may free yourselves from many troubles and perplexities. {Our images, formed of the cleansed Venus substance, comprise our world of objects by a cooling-down process. Our world is really "frozen" mind-matter of the Universal Subconscious Sea of Awareness, the dream-stuff substance.}

But especially note that it may be done with great profit if you drive forth the Red Oil of Vitriol, {These are separative, selfish and personal desires.} and dissolve Mars in it {The rechanneled reproductive force}; and Crystallize the Solution, as you were told when I treated of Mars. For in this dissolution and coagulation Venus and Mars are united. This Vitriol must be nealed under a muffle unto a pure red powder, and must be extracted further with distilled Vinegar as long as there is any redness in it. Then you get the *Anima* of Mars, and of Venus doubled; of this doubled virtue, after the addition of the *Anima* of Sol, which you made in the before quoted quantity, take twice as much of Silver Calx and fix it. But note that there must be twice as much of the Spirit

126

of Mercury than there was allowed in that place; but in the rest the process is alike. The Salt of Venus must be extracted when the Juice takes no more of the green tincture; then take the remaining matter, dry it, pour honey water upon it, then that Salt goes in that heat for five or six days, and clarify it with Spirit of Wine; then is the Salt ready for your Medicine.

Of the Particular of Saturn; Together with the Extraction of its Soul and Salt

Saturn, the highest of the Celestial Planets, has the meanest authority in our Magistery, yet is he the chiefest Key in the whole Art. Saturn is not to be slighted by reason of its external, despicable form. If he be wrought in due process after the philosophers' way he is also to requite all the Laborer's pains bestowed on him, for the great virtues of it in Medicine for man's health and for meliorating of metals the Preparation of it is thus. {The sphere of Saturn on the Tree and the Saturn Chakra (Lead) are the extremes of the Art. Binah is the Door of the Art, the Crow. Universal AIN SUPh AUR is limited down into form by its influence. Light is twisted into and through an unfathomable darkness, shaped into our physical reality. Compacted Light is Darkness. Kundalini, coiled at the Sacral Plexus (Saturn Chakra or Lead), reverses the process with expansion of consciousness. Saturn is key in both directions. It is of primary consideration when traversing the Road of Return via the Great Work.}

Take red *Minium*, or Ceruse, laminate it thinly, hang these Lamens in a large glass filled with strong Vinegar, in which is dissolved a like quantity of the best *Sal Armoniack*, sublimed thrice with common Salt. Stop the glass's mouth very closely that nothing evaporate, set the Glass in ashes of a gentle heat, otherwise the Spirits of Vinegar and *Sal Armoniack* ascend and touch the Saturnal Lamens. At the tenth or twelfth day you will spy a subtle Ceruse hanging on these Lamens; brush them off with a hare's foot; go on, get enough of this Ceruse. Take a quantity of it, put it in a body, pour strong Vinegar on it, which several times has been rectified, and was fortified at the last rectification with a sixteenth part of Spirit of vulgar Salt, dephlegmed and drawn over. Stop the body well or, which is better, lute a blind head to it, set the body in ashes to be digested, swing it often about. In few days the Vinegar begins to look yellow and sweet at first; iterate it a third time, it is sufficient.

The remnant of the Ceruse stays in the body's bottom, unshapely; filter the tinged Vinegar clearly, that is of a transparent yellowness; put all the tinged Vinegar together, abstract two parts of it in *Balneo Mariae*; let the third part stay behind. This third part is of a reasonable *Rubedo*; set the Glass in cold water, then the Crystals will shoot off the sooner; being shot, take them out with a wooden spoon, lay them on a paper for to dry; these are as sweet as Sugar and are of great energy against inflamed symptoms. Abstract the Vinegar further in *Balneo*, in which the Crystals did shoot, set that distillation aside for the shooting of more Crystals and proceed with these as you did formerly.

Now take all these Crystals together. They in their appearances are like unto clarified sugar or Saltpeter. Beat them in a mortar of glass or Iron, or grind them on a marble unto an unpalpableness, reverberate it in a gentle heat to a bloodlike redness. Provide {that} they do not turn to a blackness. Having them in a scarlet color, put them in a glass, pour on a good Spirit of Juniper abstracted from its oil and rectified several times into a fair, white, bright manner; lute the glass above, set it in a gentle heat; let the Spirit of Juniper be tinged with a transparent redness like blood, then cant it off neatly from the feces into a pure glass, with that proviso that no impure thing run therewith; on the feces pour other Spirit of Juniper, extract still, as long as any Spirit takes the tincture; keep these feces, they contain the Salt.

Take all these tinged Spirits together, filter them, abstract them gently in *Balneo*, there remains in the bottom a neat Carnation powder, which is the *Anima* of Saturn. Pour on it rain water, often distilled. Distill it strongly several times to get off that which stayed with the Spirit of Juniper, and so this subtle powder will be edulcorated delicately. Keep it in a strong boiling, cant it off, then let it go off neatly; let it dry gently. For safety's sake reverberate it again gently for its better exsiccation. Let all impurity evaporate, let it grow cold, put it in a Viol, put twice as much of Spirit of Mercury to it, seal it Hermetically. Set it in a vaporous Bath, called the Philosophers' *fimus equinus*, let it stand in the Mystical Furnace for a month, then the *Anima* of Saturn closes daily with the Spirit of Mercury and both become inseparable, making up a fair, transparent, deeply tinged Red Oil. Look to the government of the fire, be not too high with it else you put the Spirit of Mercury as a Volatile Spirit to betake himself to his wings, forcing him to the breaking of the Glass. But if these be well united, then no such fear look for, for one nature embraces and holds up the other.

Then take this oil or dissolved *Anima* of Saturn out of the Vial; it is of a gallant fragrance. Put it into a body, apply a helmet to it, lute it well, drive it over, then Soul and Spirit are united together and fit to transmute Mercury precipitated into Sol.

The Precipitation of Mercury is done thus: Take one part of the Spirit of *Sal Nitre* and three parts of Oil of Vitriol; put these together, cast into it half a part of quick Mercury, being very well purged, set it in sand, put a reasonable strong fire to it, so that the Spirits may not fly away; let it stand a whole day and night. Then abstract all the Spirits; then you find in the bottom a precipitated Mercury, somewhat red. Pour the Spirits on it again, let it stand day and night, abstract it again, then your precipitate is at the highest *rubedo*; dulcify it with distilled water; let it strongly be exsiccated, then take two parts of this precipitated Mercury one part of the dissolved Saturnal Oil, put these together, set it in ashes. Let all be fixed; not one drop must stick anywhere to the glass. Then it must be melted with due additionals of Lead; they close together, afford Gold, which afterward, at the casting through Antimony, may be exalted.

Note, that Mercury must not be precipitated unless with pure Oil of Vitriol or Oil of Venus, with the addition of the Spirit of *Sal Nitre*. Albeit such Mercury cannot be brought to its highest fixation, by way of precipitating, but its fixed coagulation is found in Saturn. Beat the above said Mercury small, grind it on a stone, put it in a Vial, pour on it the Saturnal dissolved oil.

It enters instantly, if so be, you proceeded right in the precipitation. Seal the Vial Hermetically, fire it in ashes, at last in sand, to its highest fixation. Then you have bound Mercury with a true knot and brought him into a fixed coagulation, which brought its form and substance into a melioration, with an abundance of riches. If you carry it on a white precipitate, then you get only Silver, which holds but little of Gold.

One thing more I must tell you about this process; that there is yet a better way to deal upon Saturn with more profit. Take two parts of the above said dissolved oil, or of the Saturnal Soul, one part of *Astrum Solis*, and of Antimonial Sulphur, whose preparation follows afterward, two parts, half as much of Salt of Mars as all they are, weigh them together, put all of them into a vial; let the third part of it be empty; set them together to be fixed, then the Salt of Mars opens in this compound, is fermented by it and the matter begins to incline to a blackness; for ten or twelve days it is eclipsed, then the Salt returns to its coagulation, laying hold in its operation on the whole compound. Coagulate it first into a deep brown mass, let it stand thus unstirred in a continual heat; it turns to a blood red body. Increase the fire that you may see the *Astrum Solis* to be predominant, which appears in a greenish color, like unto a Rainbow; keep this fire continually, let all these colors vanish; it turns to a transparent red stone, very ponderous, needless to be projected on Mercury but tinges after its perfection and fixation all white metals into the purest Gold. Then take of the prepared, fixed, red stone, or of the powder one part, and four parts of any of the white Metal. First let the Metal melt half an hour and let it be well clarified, then project the powder upon it; let it drive well, and so that it be entered into the metal and the metal begin to congeal; then is it transmuted into Gold. Beat the pot in pieces, take it out; if it has any Slacks drive them with Saturn, then is it pure and malleable. If you carry it on Lune, then put more of the powder to it than you do upon Jupiter and Saturn, as half an ounce of the powder tinges five ounces of Lune into Sol. Let this be a miracle; fool not your Soul with imparting this mystery unto others that are unworthy of it. Proceed with Salt of Saturn as you were informed about Mars and Venus. Only distilled Vinegar performs that which honey water did by the others, and clarify it with Spirit of Wine.

Of the Particular of Jupiter, with the
Extraction of its *Anima* and Salt

Take Pumice Stones sold in shops, neal them, quench them in old, good wine, neal them again, and quench them as you did formerly; let this nealing be iterated a third time, the stronger the wine is you quench with, all the better it is. After that dry them gently, thus are they prepared for that purpose. Pulverize these Pumice Stones subtly, then take good Tin, laminate it, stratify it in a cementing way in a reverberating Furnace, reverberate this matter for five days and nights in a flaming fire; it draws the tincture of the Metal. Then grind it small, first scraping the Tin lamens; put it in a glass body, pour on it good, distilled Vinegar, set it in digestion; the Vinegar draws the tincture which is red-yellow. Abstract this Vinegar in *Balneo*, edulcorate the *Anima* of Jupiter with distilled water, exiccate gently; proceed in the rest as you did with the *Anima* of Saturn, viz., dissolve radically in or with the Spirit of Mercury, drive them over, pour that upon two parts of red Mercury precipitated; being precipitated with this Venerean, sanguine quality, then coagulate and fix; if done successfully, you may acknowledge Jupiter's bounty that gave leave to transmute this precipitate into Gold, which will be apparent at their melting. It performs this also, it transmutes ten parts of Lune into Gold, if other Sulphurs be added thereunto; force no more upon Jupiter, its all he is able to do, being of a peaceable disposition, he told all what he could do. The Process about this Salt is to extract it with distilled Rain water, clarified with Spirit of Wine.

Of the Particular of Mercury *Vive* and of its Sulphur and Salt

Take of quick Mercury, sublined several times, *Lib. semis* {half a pound}, grind it very small, pour on it a good quantity of sharp Vinegar, boil it on the fire for an hour or upward, stirring the matter with a wooden spatula. Take it from the fire, let it be cold, the Mercury settles to the bottom and the Vinegar clears up. If it be slow in the clearing, let some drops of Spirit of Vitriol fall into the Vinegar. It does precipitate the other. For Vitriol precipitates Mercury Vive, Salt of Tartar precipitates Sol, Venus and common salt does precipitate Lune, and Mars does the like to Venus; a *lixivium* {Wood-ash lye, used as detergent.} of Beech ashes does it to Vitriol, and Vinegar is for common Sulphur, and Mars for Tartar, and Saltpeter for Antimony. Cant off the Vinegar from the precipitate; you will find the Mercury like a pure washed Sand. Pour on it Vinegar, iterate this work a third time, then edulcorate the matter; let it dry gently.

Take two ounces of *Anima* of Mars, one ounce of *Anima* of Saturn, one ounce of *Anima* of Jupiter, dissolve these in six ounces of Mercurial Spirit; let all be dissolved, then drive it over, leave nothing behind; it will be a golden water like a transparent dissolution of Sol. Your prepared and edulcorated

Mercury must be warmed in a strong viol, pour this warmed water gently on it, a hissing will be, stop the viol, then the hissing is gone; then seal it Hermetically, set it in a gentle Balney; in ten days the Mercury is dissolved into a grass-green Oil. Set the viol in ashes for a day and a night, rule the fire gently; this green color turns into a yellow Oil. In this color is hid the *Rubedo*; keep it in this fire and let the matter turn to a yellow powder like unto Orpiment; when no more comes over, then set the Glass in Sand for a day and a night, give a strong fire to it, let the fairest Ruby *rubedo* appear, melt it to a fixedness with a fluxing powder made of Saturn; it comes now to a malleableness. One pound of it contains two ounces of good Gold, as deep as ever Nature produced any.

An Oil Made of Mercury and its Salt

Take quick Mercury, being often sublimed and rectified with *Calx Vive*, put it in a body, dissolve it in a heat in strong nitrous water. Abstract the water from it; the corrosiveness which stays there must be extracted with good Vinegar well boiled in it. At last abstract the Vinegar. The remainder of it must be dulcified with distilled water and then exiccated. Afterward on each pound must be poured one pound of the best Spirit of Wine. Let it stand luted in putrefaction, then drive over what may be driven, first gently, then more strongly. From that which is come over abstract the Spirit of Wine per Balneum; there stays behind a fragrant Oil, which is Astrum Mercurii, an excellent remedy against venereal diseases.

Seeing the Salt and *Astrum* of Mercury is of the same Medicinal operation, I hold it needful to write of each in particular and will join their operation into one and declare of it in the last part about the Salt of Mercury, because they are of one effect in Medicinal operations. Take the made Oil or *Astrum Mercurii*, which by reason of its great heat keeps its own body in a perpetual running, casting it on the next standing earth, from which you formerly drew the Oil. Set it in a heat, the Oil draws its own Salt. That being done, put to it a reasonable quantity of Spirit of Wine; abstract it again, the Salt stays behind, dissolved in the fresh Spirit of Wine, being dulcified by cohobation. Then is the Mercurial Salt ready and prepared for the Medicine. Mercury is able to do no more, neither particularly nor universally, because he is far off from Philosophers' Mercury, although many are deceived in their fancies to the contrary.

Of the Particular of Antimony; Together with the Extraction of its Sulphur and Salt

Take good Hungarian Antimony, pulverize it subtly to a meal, calcine it over a gentle heat, stirring it still with an Iron wire, and let it be albified that at last it may be able to hold out in a strong fire. Then put it into a melting pot, melt it, cast it forth, turn it to a transparent glass, beat that glass, grind it subtly, put it in a glass body of a broad, flat bottom, pour on it distilled Vinegar; let it stand luted in a gentle heat for a good while. The Vinegar extracts the Antimonial Tincture, which is of a deep redness. Abstract the vinegar. There remains a sweet, yellow, subtle powder, which must be edulcorated with distilled water. All acidity must be taken off; exiccate it. Pour on it the best graduated Spirit of Wine; set it in a gentle heat. You have a new extraction, which is fair and yellow. Cant it off, pour on other Spirit, let it extract as long as it can, then abstract the Spirit of Wine. Exiccate. You find a tender, deep, yellow, subtle powder of an admirable, Medicinal operation {and} is nothing inferior unto potable Sol.

Take two parts of this powder, one part of Solar Sulphur. Grind these small, then take three parts of Sulphur of Mars, pour on it six parts of Spirit of Mercury, set it in digestion, well luted, let the Sulphur of Mars be dissolved totally, then carry in a fourth part of the ground matter of the Sulphur of Antimony and of Sol. Lute and digest; let all be dissolved, then carry in more of your ground Sulphurs. Proceed as formerly, iterating it so long till all be dissolved; then the matter becomes a thick, brown Oil. Drive all over jointly into one, leave nothing behind in the bottom, then pour it on a purely separated Lunary Calx. Fix it by degrees of fire, then melt it into a body, separate it with an *Aqua Fort*; six times as much of Sol is precipitated than above the ponderosity the compound did weigh. {This last is verbatim from the MS.} The remainder of Lune serves for such works as you please to put it unto.

The Antimonial tincture being extracted totally from its *vitrum*, and no Vinegar takes more hold of any tincture, then exiccate the remaining powder, which is of a black color; put it into a melting pot, lute it, let it stand a reasonable heat. Let all the sulphurous parts burn away, grind the remaining matter, pour on it new, distilled Vinegar, extract its Salt, abstract the Vinegar, edulcorate the acidity by cohobation. Clarify it so long, so that the water be white and clear. If you have proceeded well in your manuals, then the lesser time will be required to extract the Antimonial Salt as you will hear of it, whereby you may observe that the Antimonial Sulphur is extracted in the following manner, and is of the same Medicinal operation, but is of a quicker and speedier work, worthy to be observed.

A Short Way To Make Antimonial Sulphur And Salt

Take good Vitriol, common Salt, and unslacked Lime, of each one pound, {with} four ounces of Salt Armoniack. Beat them small, put them in a glass body, pour on it three pounds of common Vinegar. Let it stand in digestion, stopped for a day. Put it afterward into a Retort, apply a receiver to it; distill it as usually in an *Aqua Fort* is distilled. Take of the off-drawn liquor, and of common Salt one pound of each, rectify them once more; let no muddiness come over with it; all must remain clear. Then take one pound of pulverized, antimonial glass, pour this Spirit on it, lute it well, digest and let all be dissolved. Then abstract the water in *Balneo Mariae*; there remains in the bottom a black, thick, fluid matter, but somewhat dry. Lay it on a glass table {and} set it in a Cellar; a red oil flows from it, leaving some feces behind. Coagulate this red Oil gently upon ashes, let it be exiccated there. Then pour the best Spirit of Wine on it; it extracts a Tincture which is blood red. Cant off that which is tinged, pour other Spirit of Wine on the remainder, let all redness be extracted. Thus you have the tincture or Antimonial Sulphur, which is of a wonderful Medicinal efficacy and is equivalent unto potable Gold as you were told before. This black matter which stayed behind after the extraction of Sulphur must be well exiccated {To remove moisture from a substance. The modern spelling is exsiccate}. Extract its snow-white Salt with distilled Vinegar, edulcorate it, clarify it with Spirit of Wine, observe its virtues in Medicine.

I have mentioned and demonstrated that all things are made and compounded of three essences, viz., of Mercury, Sulphur and Salt. But know this, that the Stone is made of one, two, three, four and five: of five, that is the quintessence of its matter; of four are understood the four Elements; of three, they are the three principles of all things; of two, for that is the double Mercurial Substance; of one, that is the Ens {AIN} *Primum* of all things, which flowed from the fiat of the first creation.

Many well-minded Artists may be doubtful by these sayings, to attain the foundation and discovery hereof. Therefore I shall first very briefly speak of Mercury, secondly of Sulphur, thirdly of Salt; for these are essences of our matter of the Stone. {For cross reference, see the 14th chapter of the *Bhagavad-Gita*: The Three Modes of Material Nature.}

First know that no common *Argent Vive* is made of the best Metal by the Spagyric Art. {Our *Vivum* is} pure, subtle, clear, splendent as a fountain, transparent as Crystal, without any impurity. Of this make a water or incombustible Oil. For Mercury was at the first Water, as all philosophers agree.

In this Mercurial Oil dissolve its proper Mercury, out of which the water was made, and precipitate that Mercury with its proper Oil; then have you a double Mercurial Substance. And know that your Gold must be first dissolved in a certain water, after its purification, and must be reduced into a subtle Calx, as hereafter will be declared at large. And then the said Calx must be sublimed by Spirit of Salt and precipitated again, and by reverberation reduced into a subtle powder; then its own proper Sulphur will the more easily enter into its own substance and be in amity with it, for they wonderfully love each other. So have you two substances in one, and is called the Mercury of the Philosophers, and yet is but one Substance, that is, the First Ferment.

Your Sulphur you must seek in the like Metal, then you must know how to extract it out of the Body of the Metal by purification and destruction of its form and reverberation without any corrosive. Then dissolve this Sulphur in its own proper blood, whereof it was made before its fixation according to its due weight; then have you nourished and dissolved the True Lion with the Blood of the Green Lion; for the fixed blood of the Red Lion is made out of the volatile Blood of the Green Lion, therefore are they of one nature. {The Lion, representative of the raw, *Animal* will-sex urge within humanity, naturally tends toward sensation or Salt. At 28, Leo = Sal. In this stage it is commonly called *Crudus Leo* (106) or *Viridis Leo* (111), and rightly is the beginning of the Art. Through Art and meditation the crude urge is refined by essences that actually change the blood chemistry. Gradually our wine becomes the Blood of the Red Lion when Sulphur is firmly fixed with Mercury. Maturity makes the Old Lion (*senex Leo* = 87). Our purified blood, mixed with Water (Mercury), becomes the Force of the Eagle, soon to be united with the Eagle Stone.} And the volatile blood makes the fixed blood volatile, and the fixed likewise makes the volatile blood fixed, as it was before its solution. Then set them together in a gentle heat until the whole Sulphur be dissolved; then have you the Second Ferment, nourishing the fixed Sulphur with the volatile as all philosophers agree with me herein. This afterwards is driven over with Spirit of Wine, red as blood, and is called *Aurum Potabile*, whereof there is no reduction to a body.

Of the Salt of the Philosophers

Salt makes fixed and volatile, according as in its degree it is ordered and prepared. For the Spirit of Salt of Tartar, if it be drawn *per se* and without addition, makes all metals volatile by resolution and putrefaction and resolves them into a true Vive or current Mercury as my practice declares.

Salt of Tartar per se fixes most firmly, especially if the heat of *Calx Vive* be incorporated with it, for both these have a singular degree of fixing.

So also the vegetable Salt of Wine both fixes and makes volatile according to the diverse preparation thereof, as its use requires, which certainly is a great Mystery of Nature and a wonder of the Philosophical Art.

If a man drink wine and out of his urine a clear Salt be made that is volatile and makes other fixed things volatile, and carries it over the helmet with it, but it fixes it not, and although the man drink nothing but wine, out of whose urine the Salt was made, yet it has another property than the Salt of Tartar or of the feces of wine. For there is made a transmutation in the body of man, so that out of a vegetable, that is, out of a Spirit of Wine, an Animal Spirit of Salt is made. Horses, by the corroboration of their natural virtue do transmute oats, hay, and such like, and convert it into fat and flesh; so does the bee make honey out of the best of flowers and herbs. So understand of other things. This Key and cause consists only in putrefaction, from whence such a separation and transmutation takes its original. {This paragraph contains the bulk of the alchemical process. Commentary would call for a separate chapter. Perhaps gematria of a few terms may help the Miner's own explorations: urine (*urina* = 57); dung (*fimus* = 62); horse dung (*fimus equinus* = 158); feces (*faeces* = 37); Salt of Tartar (*Sal Tartari* = 107); Tartar = 70; wine (*vinum* = 70); Spirit of Wine (*spiritus vini* = 168)}

The Spirit of Common Salt, which is drawn after a peculiar manner, makes Gold and Silver volatile, if a small quantity of the Spirit of the Dragon {The Dragon is the most common symbol for the First Matter or the Universal Mercury in the Orient.} be added to it, it dissolves it and carries it over with it *per alembicum*, as also does the Eagle with the Dragon's Spirit, which dwells in stony places; but if anything be melted with Salt, before the Spirit be separated from its body, it fixes much more than it volatilizes.

If the Spirit of common Salt be united with Spirit of Wine, {*Spiritus Salis* = 173, plus 168 = 341. This equals the sum of the Three Mother letters: A, M and Sh (the First Matter), and MN-HMDBR (men-ha meedebar) Manna from the Wilderness (Cant.3:6)} and both be three times distilled over together, then it waxes sweet and looses its acrimony. This prepared Spirit does not corporeally dissolve Gold, but if it be poured on a prepared Calx of Gold, it extracts its highest tincture and redness, which if it be rightly done, it reduces pure and white Luna into the same color whereof its body was before it was extracted. Also, the old body will again attain its color by the love of enticing Venus, being descended from the same original, state and blood. Know also the Spirit of Salt destroys Luna, and reduces it into a Spiritual Essence, from whence afterwards *Luna Potabile* may be prepared, which Spirit of Luna is appropriated to the Spirit of Sol as man and wife by the copulation and conjunction of the Spirit of Mercury or its Oil.

The Spirit lives in Mercury; seek the tincture in Sulphur and the coagulation in Salt; then have you three matters, which may again produce some perfect thing, that is the Spirit in Gold fermented with its own proper Oil. Sulphur is plentifully found in the propriety of most precious Venus, which inflames the fixed blood of her. {Both Sulphur and Venus are Desire, albeit different expressions.} The Spirit of the Philosophic Salt gives victory to coagulation, although the Spirit of Tartar and Spirit of Urine, together with the true acetum may do much; {*Acetum* is Vinegar. It sums to 57, that of *urina*. The summation of *Acetum*, the Spirits of Tartar and Urine require too much space to develop. However, the gist is that meditation alters blood chemistry.} for the Spirit of Vinegar is cold, and the Spirit of *Calx Vive* is very hot, therefore are they esteemed and found to be of contrary natures. This I faithfully declare. Seek your matter in a Metalline Substance, make thereof Mercury, which ferment with Mercury; then a Sulphur, which ferment with its proper Sulphur, and with Salt reduce it into order; distill them together, conjoin them all according to their due proportion, then will it become that one thing, which before came from one; coagulate and fix it by a continual heat, then multiply and ferment it three times.

The Key of the Process, discovering the Tincture, is thus. When the

Medicine, and Stone of the Philosophers, is made and perfectly prepared out of the true *Lac Virginis*, take thereof one part of the best and purest Gold, melted and purged by Antimony, three parts, and reduce it into as thin plates as possible, you can put these together into a Crucible wherein you use to melt Metals. First give a gentle fire for twelve hours, then let it stand three days and nights continually in a melting fire; then are the pure Gold and the Stone made a mere Medicine of a subtle, spiritual and penetrating quality. For without the ferment of Gold the Stone cannot operate or exercise its tingeing quality, being too subtle and penetrative; but being fermented and united with its like ferment, the prepared tincture obtains an ingress in operating upon other bodies. Then take of the prepared ferment one part to a thousand parts of melted metal, if you will tinge it, then know for a very certain truth that it will be transmuted into good and fixed Gold. For the one body embraces the other, although they be not alike, yet by the force and power added to it, it is made like unto it, like having its original from its like.

Note well that out of black Saturn and friendly Jove a Spirit may be extracted, {This is an essence from organs and glands influenced by the perfected chakras, Saturn and Jupiter.} which is afterwards reduced into a Sweet Oil as its noblest part, which Medicine particularly, does most absolutely take away the nimble, running quality from common Mercury and brings him to an amelioration.

Having thus attained the matter, nothing remains but that you look well to the fire, that you observe its Regimen, for herein is the highest concern and the end of the work. For our fire is a common fire, and our furnace is a common furnace, although some philosophers, to conceal the Art, write contrary. The fire of the lamp with the Spirit of Wine is unprofitable; the expense thereof would be incredible. *Fimus Equinus* spoils it, for it cannot perfect the work by the right degree of fire.

Many and various furnaces are not convenient, for in our threefold furnace only the degrees of fire are proportionally observed. And as our furnace is common so is our fire common, and as matter is common, so is our Glass likened, to the Globe of the Earth. {These things are common because everybody has them. The Glass (our aura) is the globe around our body, the Earth.}

Of Mercury

There are several sorts of Mercury. Mercury of Animals and Vegetables is merely a fume of an incomprehensible being, unless it be caught and reduced to an Oil, then is it for use. But Mercury of Metals is of another condition, as that also of Minerals; though the same also may be compared with a fume, yet is it comprehensible and running. One Mercury is better and nobler than the other, for the Solar Mercury is the best of them all. Next unto that is the Lunar Mercury, and so forth. There is a difference also among Salts and Sulphurs.

Among the Mineral Salts, that carries away the Bell which is made of Antimony; and that Sulphur which is drawn from Vitriol is preferred before all others. Mercury of Metals is hot and dry, cold and moist; it contains the four qualities.

There are Medicaments prepared of it of a wonderful efficacy, of several sorts and forms, which is the reason why there is such a variety of virtues therein. In Mercury lies hid the highest Arcanum for man's health, but is not to be used crude, but must first be prepared into its essence. It is sublimed with Copper Water and is further reduced into an Oil. There is an Oil made of it per se, without any corrosiveness, which is pleasant and fragrant. Several sorts of Oils, with additionals, can be made of it, good for many things. It is prepared also with Gold, being first made into an Amalgama; there is made a precipitate of it in water, wherein it dissolves Green, like unto a Smaragad or Chrysolite. The Volatile Mercury serves for outward use, if a Separation is made by some means, and is brought into a subtle, clear Liquor and then to a red-brown powder, and its received corrosiveness is separated, then it may do well for other uses.

The Mixed Mercury serves for inward use. Mercury, being purged, is precipitated with the Blood of Venus, is well digested with distilled Vinegar, and thus his corroding quality is taken off. Have a care what quantity you minister; if given in a true dose, then it does its part very well. But for its operation, it is not equally sublimed unto the fixed, its coagulation is found in Saturn, his malleableness is apparent, when he is robbed of his life; he contains his own Tincture upon white and red, being brought in his fixed coagulation unto a white body, is tinged again by Vitriol Water and being reduced unto Gold is graduated by Antimony. Though that blood thirsty Iron Captain, with his spear assaults Mercury very much, yet he alone cannot conquer him unless cold Saturn come in to hide him and Jupiter command the peace with his Scepter. Such Process being finished, then the Angel Gabriel, the Strength of the Lord, and Uriel, the Light of God, has shown Mercy unto humble Michael, then Raphael can make right use of the highest Medicine.

Of Antimony

It is very difficult to find out all the mysteries that are hid therein. Its virtue is miraculous; its power is great; its color, hidden therein, is various; its crude body is poisonous; yet its essence is an antidote against poison, is like unto Quicksilver, which ignorant physicians can neither comprehend nor find, but the knowing physician believes it to be true, as having made many experiments with it.

This Mineral contains much of Mercury, much of Sulphur and little of Salt, which is the cause why it is so brittle and applicable; for there is no malleableness in it by reason of the small quantity of Salt. The most amity it bears unto Saturn is by reason of Mercury, for Philosophers' Lead is made out of it and is

137

affected unto Gold by reason of its Sulphur; for it purges Gold, leaving no impurity in it. There is an equal operation in it with Gold if well prepared and ministered to man medicinally. It flies out of the fire and keeps firmly in the fire, if it be prepared accordingly. Its volatile Spirit is poisonous, purges grievously not without damage unto the body; its remaining fixedness purges also, but not in that manner as the former did, provokes not to stool but seeks merely the disease wherever it is, penetrates all the body and the members thereof, suffers no evil to abide there, expels it and brings the body to a better condition. In brief, Antimony is the Lord in Medicinals. There is made out of it a *Regulus* out of Tartar and Salt; if at the melting of Antimony some Iron filings be added, by a Manual used there comes forth a wonderful Star, which philosophers before me called the Signet Star. This Star being several times melted with cold Earth Salt, it grows then yellowish, is of a fiery quality and of a wonderful efficacy. This Salt afterwards affords a liquor which further is brought to a fixed, incombustible Oil, which serves for several uses.

Besides there are made of common *Regulus* of Antimony curious Flowers, either red, yellow or white, {Pingala, Sushumna, Ida respectively; also called *Flores Sulphuris* (196)} according as the fire has been governed. These Flowers being extracted and the Extract, without any addition, per se being driven into an oil, have an admirable efficacy. This Extraction may be made also with Vinegar of crude Antimony, or of its *Regulus*, but it requires a longer time, neither is it so good as the former preparation.

And being reduced into a *Philistea* there is a glass made of it *per se*, which is extracted also; then abstracted, there remains a powder of incredible operation, which may safely be used after it has been edulcorated. This Powder, being dissolved, heals wounds, sores, etc., causing no pains. This Powder being extracted once more with Spirit of Wine or driven through the Helmet with some other matter, affords a sweet oil.

Antimony is melted also with cold Earth Salt, dissolved, and digested for a time in Spirit of Wine. It affords a white, fixed powder, is effectual against *Morbus Gallicus* and breaks inward Imposthumus. It has several virtues besides.

There is made an Oil also of Antimony, the Flying Dragon being added thereunto, which, being rectified thrice, then it is prepared. Though a Cancer were never so bad and the wolf never so biting, yet they, with all their fellows, be they fistulas or old ulcers, must fly and be gone. The little powder of the Flying Dragon prepared with the Lion's Blood, must be ministered also, three or four grains for a dose according to the party's age and complexion.

A further Process {Many "processes" are hinted in this work. We are not to understand that they are ongoing operations or a series of functions or system of actions that bring about an end result. It is a subconscious awakening. Something dormant within us is suddenly made functional due to our evolution. We could not chew until we grew teeth; we could not walk until we had bones strong enough to

138

support us. So is it in alchemical processes. We cannot infuse extra amounts of *Lac Virginis*, for example, until our organism is sufficiently evolved with the Light Substance.} may be made with this Oil with the addition of a Water made of Stone Serpents, and other necessary spices; not those that are transported from the Indies. This powder is of that efficacy that it radically cures many chronic diseases. There is made a red Oil of Antimony, *Calx Vive*, Sal Armoniac, and common Sulphur, which has done great cures in old ulcers; with Stone Salt or with common Salt, there is forced from Antimony a red Oil which is admirably good for outward symptoms.

There is made a Sublimate of Antimony with Spirit of Tartar and Salmiac, being digested for a time, which by means of Mars, is turned into quick Mercury. This Antimonial Mercury has been sought of many but few have gotten it, which is the reason why his praise is not divulged, much less is his operative quantity known. If you know how to precipitate it well, then your arrow will hit the mark to perform great matters; its quality ought not to be made common. It is needless to describe its combustible Sulphur, how that is made of Antimony. It is easy and known; but that which is fixed is a secret and hidden from many. If an Oil be made of it in which its own Sulphur is dissolved, and these be fixed together, then you have a Medicine of rare qualities, in virtue, operation and ability far beyond vegetables.

Quicksilver being imbibed with Quicksilver melted with Antimony for some hours in a Wind Oven, the Salt of the remainder being extracted with distilled Vinegar, then you have the Philosophers' Salt, which cures all manner of Agues.

There is an *acetum* made of Antimony, of an acidity as other *acetums* are; if its own Salt be dissolved in this acetum, and distilled over, then this *acetum* is sharpened, which is an excellent cooler in hot swellings and other inflamed symptoms about wounds, especially if there be made an unguent of it together with *Anima* of Saturn.

There is a quintessence of Antimony which is the highest Medicine, the noblest and most subtle found in it, and is the fourth part of an Universal Medicine. Let the preparation of it be still a mystery; its quantity or dose is three grains. There belong four Instruments to the making of it, the furnace is the fifth, in which Vulcan dwells; the Manuals and the government of fire afford the ordering of it.

Of Copper-Water

Copper is a Mineral whose Salt is set forth in the highest manner, whose great and good qualities are of that transcendency that reason is not able to comprehend or to conceive of them. It went generally by the name of Copper-Water to make the meaning and sense of it plain. {In the century this was written it was plain in alchemical terms. Copper, or the imagery of desire, working upon the fluid substance was rightly termed Copper-Water. Images are the matrix to which the *Magnesia* (fluid First Matter) adhered.} And be thus informed that Vitriol contains two Spirits, a white and a red one; the White Spirit is the White Sulphur upon white, the Red Spirit is the Red Sulphur upon red.

Observe it diligently. The White Spirit is sour, causes an appetite and a good digestion in a man's stomach. The Red Spirit is yet more sour and is more ponderous than the white; in its distilling a longer fire must be continued because it is more fixed in its degree. Of the white, by distilling of Sulphur of Lune is made *Argentum Potabile*. In the like manner the Gold, being destroyed in the Spirit of common Salt and made spiritual by distilling and its Sulphur taken from it and joined with a Red Spirit in a due dose, that it may be dissolved, and then for a time putrefied in Spirit of Wine to be further digested, and often abstracted that nothing remain in the bottom, then you have made an *Aurum Potabile* of which great volumes have been written, but very few of their processes were right.

Note that the Red Spirit must be rectified from its acidity and be brought into a sweetness subtly penetrating, of a pleasant taste and sweet fragrancy.

The sweet Spirit is made of Sulphur of Vitriol, which is combustible like other Sulphur before it is destroyed. For the Sulphur of the Philosophers is not combustible. Note this well. The preparation is easy, requires no great pains nor great expenses to get a combustible Sulphur out of Vitriol. This sweet Oil is the essence of Vitriol and is such a Medicine which is worthy the name of the Third Pillar of the Universal Medicine. The Salt is drawn from Colchotar and is dissolved in the red or white oil or in both and is distilled again; if it be fermented with Venus it performs its office very well for it affords such a Medicine which at the melting tinges pure Iron into pure Copper.

Colchotar of Sulphur affords true fundamentals unto healing of perished wounds, which otherwise are hardly brought to any healing, and such sores, which by reason of a long continued white redness, will admit of no healing. Colchotar affords an ingress thereunto, setting a new foundation that quality and virtue is not in the Colchotar, but the Spirit, together with the Salt, are the Masters which dwell therein.

There is made of Copper and Verdigris a Vitriol of a high degree, and is far spread in its tincture. There is a Vitriol made of Iron also which is of a strange quality; for Iron and Copper are very nigh kind one to another; belong together as man and wife. This mystery I would have concealed.

If Vitriol be corroded with Salt Armoniac in its Sublimation, there arises a combustible Sulphur together with its Mercury, of which there is but little because it has most of Sulphur. If the same Sulphur be set at liberty again by the Eagle, with Spirit of Wine, there can be made a Medicine of it, as I told you before, though there be a nearer way to make a combustible Sulphur out of Vitriol, as of its precipitation upon a precedent dissolution by the Salt, or liquor of Tartar, as also by a common *lixivium* made of Beech ashes; yet this is the best reason, because the body of Vitriol is better and more opened with the Key of the Eagle. There is not found in its nature neither cold nor moist quality, but is of a hot and dry substantial quality, and is the reason why, by its super abounding calidity, it heats other things, digests them and at last it brings them to a full maturity, the fire being continued for a certain time.

Of Common Sulphur

The usual common Sulphur is not so perfectly exalted in its degree and brought unto maturity, as it is found in Antimony and Vitriol. There is made of it *per se* an Oil against putrid, stinking wounds, destroying such worms which grow in them, especially if the little Salt in it be dissolved from its Sulphur.

There is made of it a Balsam with Salad Oil or Oil of Juniper, in like manner with the white Spirit of Turpentine, and is of a red color, made thus: Take Flowers of Sulphur made with Colchotar of Vitriol, digest them for a time in Horse Dung. This Balsam may safely be used for such that are in a consumption of the lungs, especially if rectified several times with Spirit of Wine, drawn over and separated, that it be blood red. This Balsam is a preservative against corruption and rot.

The Quintessence of Sulphur is in a Mineral, where sulphurous flint is generated. Thus, beaten pebbles, put in a glass, and on it be poured a strong *Aqua Fort*, made of Vitriol and Saltpeter, and let dissolve what may be dissolved; abstract the water, the remainder must be well dulcified and reverberated to a redness; pour on that Spirit of Wine, extract its tincture, afterward circulate for a time in the Pelican. Let all the essence of Sulphur be separated. It stays below the Spirit of Wine like fat salad Oil, by reason of its ponderousness; its dose of six grains is found to work sufficiently. If you digest in this essence of Sulphur, Myrrh, Aloes and other Spirits, it extracts virtues and makes it into a Balsam, which suffers no flesh or other parts that are subject to putrefaction to fall into rot, for which cause the ancients have put this name to it: *Balsamus Mortuorum*. {gematria 214} There may be made an Oil of it which is found very useful. The Sulphur must be sublimed in a high Instrument with a good heat, which Sublimation in a long time changes into a liquor or oil, standing in a humid place.

There may be cocted a Liver out of common Sulphur, which is turned into milk; and it may also be changed into a red Oil. Many other Medicinals may be made out of Sulphur. Its Flowers, Essence and Oil are preferred before the rest, together with the white and red fixed Cinnabar which are made of it, because in them is found a mighty virtue.

Of *Calx Vive*

The secrets of Quicklime are known to few men and few there are who attained to a perfect knowledge of its qualities. {*Calx Vive* = 86 by Cabala Simplex.} But though Lime is contemptible yet there lies great matters therein, and requires an understanding Master to take out of it what lies buried in it. I mean to expel its pure Spirit, which collaterally stands in affinity with Minerals, is able to bind and help to fix the volatile Spirits of Minerals, for it is of a fiery essence, heats, concocts and brings unto maturity in short time, when in many years they could not be brought to it. The gross earthly body of it does not do the feat, but its Spirit does it, which is drawn out of it. This Spirit is of that ability that he binds and fixes other volatile Spirits. For note the Spirit dissolves *Oculi Cancerorum* {Crabs' Eyes, gematria = 148. This equals *Spiriti Damnati*, Reprobate or Condemned Spirits.}, dissolves Crystals into a liquor; these two being duly brought united *per modum distillationis* {Through a mode of distillation, gematria = 255.} (I will say nothing now of Diamonds and such-like stones) that water dissolves and breaks the stone or the bladder and the gouty Tartar settled into the joints of hands and feet; suffers not any gout to take root in those parts. This is a rare secret. Quicklime is strengthened and made more fiery and hot by a pure and unsophisticated Spirit of Wine, which is often poured on it and abstracted again; then the white Salt of Tartar must be grinded with it, together with its additionals which must be dead and contain nothing, then you will draw a very hellish Spirit, in which great Mysteries lie hid.

Of Arsenic

Arsenic is in the kindred of Mercury and Antimony as a Bastard in a family may be. Its whole substance is poisonous and volatile, even as the former two. In its external color to the eye, it is white, yellow and red, {Ida, Sushumna and Pingala again} but inwardly it is adorned with all manner of colors like to its metals, which it was fain to forsake, being forced thereunto by fire. It is sublimed *per se* without addition and also in its subliming there are added several other matters as occasion requires. If it be sublimed with Salt and Mars, then it looks like a transparent Crystal, but its poison stays still with it, unfit to be joined or added to Metals. It has very little efficacy to transmute any Metal.

The Subterranean Serpent {Kundalini} binds it in the union of fire, but cannot quite force it that it might serve for a Medicine for man and beast. If it be further mixed with the Salt of a Vegetable Stone, which is with Tartar, and is made like unto an oil, it is of great efficacy in wounds which are of an hard healing. It can make a Coat for deceitful Venus, to trim her handsomely, that the inconstancy of her false heart may be disclosed by her wavering servants, without gain, with her prejudice and damage. "When Antimony and Mars are as my companions, and I am exalted by them to the top of Olympus, then I afford a Ruby in transparence and color like that which comes from the Orient and I am not to be esteemed less than it. If I am proved by affliction, then I fall off like a flower which is cut off and withers; therefore nothing can be made of me to fix any metal or tinge it to any profit." {*Arsenicum*, the Latin, sums to 93 and equals *Ars Nummae*, the Art of Coins. This hints arsenic as the function of consciousness that coagulates the white First Matter (*Calx Vive*) into forms. Arsenic restricts or constricts, like a Saturnine function. *Calx Vive* disintegrates previous form while Arsenic reintegrates the fluid energy into new shapes. The Comte de St. Germain is reputed to have perfected flawed jewels by this very manner. The Hebrew for Arsenic (or Orpiment) is ZRNIK (zarenic) and sums to 286.}

Of Saltpeter

Two Elements are predominant in me, as fire and air; the lesser quantity is water and earth; I am fiery, burning and volatile. There is in me a subtle Spirit, I am altogether like unto Mercury, hot in the inside and cold on the outside; am slippery and very nimble at the expelling of my enemies. My greatest enemy is common Sulphur, and yet {he} is my best friend also, for being purged by him and clarified in the fire, then am I able to allay all heats of the body within and without and am one of the best Medicaments to expel and keep of the poisonous plague.

I am a greater cooler outwardly than Saturn, but my Spirit is more hot than any. I cool and burn according as men will make use of me and according as I am prepared. When Metals are to be broken I must be a help, else no victory can be obtained, be the understandings great or small. Before I am destroyed I am a mere Ice, but when I am anatomized, then I am as hellish fire. {This is *Sal-Nitre* of the alchemists, and Kama-rupa of the Yogis. It is the principle of Animal desire, burning fiercely during Life in Matter. It is considered inseparable from Animal existence. So Sulphur is its greatest enemy, and best friend, depending where we direct our Animal desire. Yet *Sal-Nitre* sums to 88 in Cabala Simplex. This value is shared with *Aqua Vitae* and *Filius Dei*. In downward expression Salt-Peter burns and acts upon the Water of Life. Turned, it burns toward evolution to become the Son of God in regeneration.}

Of Sal Armoniack

Sal Armoniack is none of the meanest Keys to open Metals thereby, {*Sal Armoniac* = 94, but *Armoniac* = 66, that of *granum* (seed) and IVN, Dove, in Cant.6:9.} therefore the ancients have compared it with a volatile Bird. It must be prepared, else you can do no feats with it, for if it be not prepared it does more hurt than good unto Metals; carries them away out of the Chimney hole. It can elevate and sublime with its swift wings the tincture of minerals and of some Metals to the very mountains, where store of snow is found usually, even at the greatest heat of the Summer. If it be sublimed with common Salt, then it purges and clears and may be used safely.

He that supposes to transmute Metals with this Salt, which is so volatile, surely he does not hit the nail on the head, for it has no such power; but to destroy Metals and make them fit for transmutation, in that respect it has sufficient power, for no Metal can be transmuted, unless it be first prepared thereunto.

Of Tartar

This Salt is not set down in the book of Minerals, but is generated of a vegetable seed, but its Creator has put such virtue into it, that it bears a wonderful love and friendship unto Metals, making them malleable. It purges Lune unto a whiteness and incorporates into her such additionals which are convenient for her; being digested for a time with Minerals or Metals and then sublimed and vilified, they all come unto a quick Mercury, which to do there is not any vegetable Salt besides it. Many mysteries lie hid in it. It is a good remedy either outwardly or inwardly in Medicine; its Salt being made spiritual and sweet it dissolves and breaks the stone in the bladder and dissolves the coagulated Tartar of the Gout settled into the joints or anywhere else. Its ordinary Spirit, which is used for opening of metals, being used and applied outwardly, lays a foundation for healing of such ulcers which admit hardly any healing, as Fistulas, Cancers, wolves and such-like. {The physical description of Tartar is a deposit from grapes inside wine casks. Its affiliation with wine is hint enough. Add the fact that Tartar carries a numeral value of 70 and we are drawn to a profound conclusion. For 70 is also the value of Wine both in Hebrew (IIN) and in Latin (*Vinum*). In Greek, *Hagnia* (purity or chastity), also sums to 70. Our author says Tartar is not "in the book of minerals" but "generated of vegetable seed". We must conclude that Tartar is coded as human blood, which is generated of vegetables and has such virtue as to aid Metals. Purified blood (through Art) carries such deposits throughout our body to and from various organs and glands that they may function optimally. Indeed "many mysteries lie hid within it...and is a good remedy" to every body.}

Of Vinegar

In Alchemy and Medicina nothing, almost, can be prepared but Vinegar must set a helping hand to it. In Alchemy it is used to set Metals and Minerals into putrefaction. It is used also for to extract the essences and tinctures, being first prepared thereunto even as the Spirit of Wine is usual to extract the tinctures from Vegetables. {Meditation does all this to alter a chemical balance of the blood. In Hebrew Vinegar is ChMO and shares numeral value 138 with *Aurum Potabile* Since Alchemy is entirely an internal process, it is true that nothing can be done in The Work without it.}

In Physics it deserves its praise also, for it takes the pure from impure and is a separator and takes from Mineral Medicaments their sharpness and corrosiveness, fixes that which is volatile and is a great defender against poison. Vinegar is used inwardly also and both men and beasts are benefited thereby.

Outwardly it is applied to hot inflammations and swellings for a cooler. Spirit of Wine and Vinegar are of great use both in Alchemy and physics; both have their descent from the Urine, are of one substance, but differ in the quality by reason of putrefaction, the Vinegar got there. {*Urina* and *Acetum* each sum to 57.} But this is not the Philosophers' Vinegar. Our Vinegar or *Acetum* is another Liquor, namely a matter itself for the Stone of the Philosophers, made out of AZOT of the Philosophers, which must be prepared with ordinary distilled AZOT, with Spirit of Wine and with other waters besides, and must be reduced unto a certain order. {57 is also the value of *lumen* (light), that is, Astral Light or AZOT. Vinegar, urine, *acetum* or ChMO is that Universal Liquor which is "personalized" as our conscious mode of mentation. It is "distilled" as conscious direction toward the Great Work.}

Note this for a Memorandum, if distilled, pure Vinegar be poured upon destroyed Saturn and is kept warm in Mary's Bath, it loosens its acidity altogether, is as sweet as any sugar; then abstract two or three parts of that Vinegar, set it in a Cellar, then you will find white transparent stones like unto Crystals. These are an excellent cooler and healer of all adust and inflamed symptoms.

If these Crystals are reduced into a red oil and poured upon Mercury, precipitated by Venus, and proceeded in further as it ought; if that be his rightly, then neither Sol nor Lune will hinder thee from getting riches.

Of Wine

The true Vegetable Stone is found in Wine which is the noblest of all Vegetables. It contains three sorts of Salt, three sorts of Mercury, and three sorts of Sulphur.

The first Salt sticks in the wood of the Wine, which if burnt to ashes, and a *lixivium* {Gematria = 106} made of it to have its Salt drawn forth, which must be coagulated. This is the first Salt.

The second Salt is found in Tartar, if that be incinerated, then draw its Salt forth, dissolve and coagulate it several times and let it be sufficiently clarified.

The third Salt is this. When the Wine is distilled it leaves feces behind, which are made to powder; its Salt can be drawn out with warm water.

Each of these Salts has a special property; in their Center they stand in a harmony, because they descend from one root.

It has three sorts of Mercury and three sorts of Sulphur. The first Oil is made of the Steam, the second Oil is made out of crude Tartar, the third is the Oil of Wine.

There is a strange property in the Spirit of Wine, for without it there cannot be extracted any true tincture of Sol, nor can there be made without it any true *Aurum Potabile*; but few men know how a true Spirit of Wine is made, much less can its property be found out wholly. Several ways have been tried to draw and to get the Spirit of Wine without sophistication, as by several instruments and distillings with metalline Serpents and other strange inventions, of Sponges, papers and the like. Some caused a rectified *Aqua Vitae* be frozen in the greatest frost, expecting the phlegm thereof should turn to Ice, the Spirit thereof to keep liquid, but nothing was done to any purpose.

To Make a True Spirit of Wine

Take *Vinum Adustum* {Burned Wine, gematria = 159. *Spiritus Vini*, Spirit of Wine = 168. Both reduce to 15} and put it into a strong Vessel, which will endure the fire; light it with a Match of Brimstone and put quickly a head of Iron or Copper upon it and the true, fiery Spirit will be resolved into a water in the Receiver {15 is also the number of ADI (aydee) Vapor or Steam} which must be large. This is the true aerial, fiery Spirit of Wine. It must be subtle, penetrating, without any phlegm, pure, airial and volatile, so that air in a magnetic quality may attract it; therefore it had need to be kept close in. It is of a penetrating and effectual operation.

There are three which are the noblest Creatures in the world; these three bear a wonderful affection one to another. Among *Animals* it is man, out of whose Mummy is made an *Animal* Stone, in which Microcosm is contained. Among Minerals Gold is the noblest, whose fixedness is a sufficient testimony of its noble offspring and kindred. Among Vegetables there lies hid a Vegetable Stone. Man loves Gold and Wine above all other creatures, which may be beheld with the eyes. Gold loves Man and Wine, because it lets go its noblest part if Spirit of Wine be put to it, being made potable, which gives strength to man and prolongs his life in health. Wine bears affection to man also and to Gold, because it easily unites with the tincture of Sol, expels melancholy and sadness, refreshes and rejoices man's heart. These stones renew men and beasts, cure Leprous Metals, cause barrenness to become fruitful with a new birth.

The True Preparation of *AURUM POTABILE*
without Sophistication

First; what is that true and highest *Aurum Potabile* and Universal Medicine. After this in order there follows another *Aurum Potabile* made of the fixed Red Sulphur or Soul of the corporeal Gold, most highly purged, and is prepared with the Conjunction of the Universal Spirit of Mercury. After this there follows another particular Medicine, which is half an *Aurum Potabile*, showing its efficacy and power in many trials. Then I will add thereunto a description of *Aurum Potabile*, because it traces the steps of Gold and it shows wonderfully its great energy and virtues.

The highest and chief *Aurum Potabile* which the Lord God has laid into nature is the excocted, prepared and fixed substance of our Stone before it is fermented.

A higher, greater and more excellent Universal Medicine and *Aurum Potabile* cannot be found nor had in the Circumference of the whole world; for it is a heavenly Balsam because its first principles and original comes from heaven, made formal in earth or underground, and is afterwards, being exactly prepared, brought into a *plusquam* {what is more than} perfection, of which first principle and Nativity of this heavenly substance I have already written sufficiently. {The above describes universally diffused AIN SUPh AUR incorporated into the blood stream "in Earth or underground."}

Now as this excocted and perfect substance is the highest, chief and greatest Universal Medicine unto man, even so, on the other side, the same matter, after its fermentation, is a Tincture also and the chief, greatest and most powerful Universal Medicine upon all Metals whatsoever, and thereby {the Metals} may be transmuted into their highest amelioration and health, namely into the purest Gold. This is the first, chief and greatest *Aurum Potabile* and Universal Medicine of the whole world, of which alone great volumes could be written, whose preparation is already written.

Now I will declare the true and full process how a true *Aurum Potabile* is to be made.

How true *Aurum Potabile* is to be had and prepared from Gold, which in the best manner is exactly putrefied. Take the extracted Soul of Gold, draw {it} forth with the sweet Spirit of common Salt, as I informed you about the Particular of Gold, where the body of Gold appeared very white; abstract the Spirit of Salt from it; edulcorate the *Anima* of Sol ten or twelve times; at last let it be purely exiccated; weigh it; pour on it four times as much of Spirit of Mercury; lute it well; set it in the vaporous Bath; putrefy it gently. Let the *Anima* of Sol be quite dissolved and be turned into water or its *Prima Materia*. Both will turn into a blood-red liquor, fair and transparent, no Ruby on the earth is comparable to it.

But note, when the *Anima* of Sol begins to be dissolved and brought into its *Prima Materia*, that at the first, on the side round the Glass where the matter lies, there be seen a green Circle, on it a blue, then a yellow. Afterwards all the colors of a Rainbow join and make appearances, which do last but a little while. The *Anima* of Sol, being wholly dissolved into the Mercurial Spirit, and nothing is seen in the bottom, then pour to it twice as much of the best rectified Spirit of Wine, brought to its highest degree. The glass must be luted exactly; digest and putrefy gently for twelve or fifteen days together, then abstract per alembicum; the matter comes over in a blood-red, transparent color. The abstracting must be iterated; nothing must be left in the bottom which is corporeal; then you have the true *Aurum Potabile*, which can never be reduce into a body.

But note, the Gold, before its destruction and extraction of its Soul, must be purged in the highest degree. There is made another *Aurum Potabile*, and artificially prepared, which, though it cannot be said or set down in writing to

147

be the full and true Potable Gold, yet is it more than half an *Aurum Potabile* counted, because it is transcending effectual in many diseases in which Nature might have stood in great doubts. This half *Aurum Potabile* is made in a twofold manner, where the latter is better and more effectual than the former and asks more pains and time than the former.

Take this extracted Soul of Gold, drawn forth with the sweet Spirit of common Salt, edulcorate it most purely and exactly; at last exiccate it; put it in a spacious vial or body of Glass; pour on it red Oil of Vitriol, which was dephlegmed and rectified *per retortam* that it be transparent, clear and white and you may see, that it seizes on the Gold and dissolves it and is tinged deeply red. Put so much of the Oil to it that in it may be dissolved Sulphur of the Soul of Gold. Let it putrefy in *Balneo Mariae*; {In Mary's Bath—some commentators have attributed this bath to something Mary the Prophetess had devised. Whether she was the first to call it such is not certain. The Bath, however, is the area enclosed by the Glass Vessel, the human aura. Within it plays Mercury, Sulphur and Salt (the cleansed *Azoth*), a Light of the Lord. *Lux Domini* sums to 107 as does In *Balneo Mariae* and *Sal Tartari. Balneum* = 60; in *Balneo* = 64. The various spellings are referenced to different ideas concerning the Glass Vessel by their gematria.} put a reasonable fire to it that you may see that the Soul of Gold is quite dissolved in the Oil of Vitriol. The feces which it has settled must be separated from it; then put twice as much of the best rectified Spirit of Wine to it, which rectification you will be further informed of. Seal the Glass; let no Spirits of the Wine evaporate, set it again in putrefaction in *Balneo*; let it be there for a month, then the sharpness of Vitriol is mitigated by the Spirit of Wine, and loses its acidity and sharpness; both together make an excellent Medicine. Drive both over; let nothing stay behind in the bottom, then you get more than half an *Aurum Potabile*, in form and color of a deep yellow liquor.

Note that some Metals in this manner may be proceeded withal. First a Vitriol may be gotten out of the Metal, then a Spirit is further driven from it and joined in this manner with the Soul, dissolved and further digested with Spirit of Wine. All must enter together into a Medicine as I formerly said, which have their special efficacy.

The second way to prepare this half *Aurum Potabile*, which though it but be half an *Aurum Potabile*, yet in virtue and efficacy, is far preferred before the other now spoken of and is done as follows.

Take the extracted Solar Soul spoken of above, put it into a viol, pour on it the extracted Philosophic Sulphur, which is the second Principle, which is drawn with Spirit of Mercury from the Philosophers' Earth and Mercury, or the Spirit of Mercury, unto an Oleity, which now is Sulphur again and must be abstracted gently *per modum distillationis*.

Of this Philosophical Sulphur pour on it as much that the Solar Soul may be dissolved. Let it stand in a gentle Bath, let the dissolution be made, then pour more of the best Spirit of Wine to it, digest gently, draw these over, let nothing stay behind in the bottom, then you have a Medicine which does not want above two grains of the right and true *Aurum Potabile*.

These are the chief ways to make the corporeal *Aurum Potabile*. This I close, and proceed further with a short but true process how the Silver, which is the next to Gold concerning perfection, is made potable also. This process must be done in the following manner.

Take the sky-colored Sulphur or Spirit of Lune, which was extracted with distilled Vinegar as I informed you in the particular of Lune. Edulcorate it, rectify it with Spirit of Wine, exiccate it, put it in a viol, pour to it three times as much of Spirit of Mercury, which is prepared from the white Spirit of Vitriol as I taught you before. Lute the glass firmly, set it in putrefaction in the vaporous Bath, let all be dissolved and nothing more seen in the bottom. Then put to it an equal quantity of the best Spirit of Wine, set it in digestion for half a month, drive all over, let nothing stay behind, then you have the true potable Luna, which in its efficacy is admirable and does wonders when it is used.

A Description of the Fiery Tartar

Distill of good wine a Spirit of Wine, {Spirit of Wine is not alcohol.} rectify it with white, calcined Tartar, let all come over; put that which is distilled over into a viol. Put four ounces of well sublimed *Sal Armoniack* to one quart of Spirit of Wine, set a Helmet upon it, set a great Receiver into cold water; drive the volatile spirits gently in *Balneo Mariae*. Leave but a little quantity of it behind. Note the Alembic must always be cooled with wet clothes, then the Spirits will be dissolved and turn into a liquor. Thus is prepared this hot Spirit of Wine.

Of the Salt of Tartar

First you must note that the Philosophers Tartar is not the Vulgar Tartar, {Our author could not be more clear on points as this.} wherewith the Lock is opened, but it is a Salt which comes from the Root {Ain SUPh AUR} and is the only Mystical Key for all Metals and is prepared thus:

Make a sharp *Lixivium* of the ashes of Sarments or Twigs of the Vine; boil away all its moisture. There stays behind a ruddy matter which must be reverberated for three hours in a flaming fire. Stirring it still, let it come to a whiteness, which white matter must be dissolved in distilled Rain water. Let the feces of it settle, filter and coagulate them in a Glass, that the matter in it be dry, which dry matter is the Salt of Tartar from which the true Spirit is driven.

Note, as precious stones have many rare virtues and qualities, so there are many despicable and ignoble stones, which have great virtues; for example, the

Limestone, *Calx Vive*, which in men's judgements is held of no great value and lies contemptibly in obscurity, however, there is a mighty virtue and efficacy in it which appears if application be made of it to the most heavy diseases, seeing its triumphant and transcendent efficacy is almost unknown for the generality; therefore for the good of such which are inquisitive into natural and supernatural Mysteries I will discover this Mystery concerning *Calx Vive* and show how its Spirit is driven from it, which work, indeed, requires an expert Artist who is well informed before hand of its preparation.

Take unslacked Lime as much as you will; beat and grind it on a well dried stone to an impalpable powder; put on it so much of Spirit of Wine as the pulverized Calx is able to drink. There must not stand any of that Spirit upon it. Apply a Helmet to it, lute it well and put a receiver before it, abstract the Spirit gently from it in *Balneo*; this abstracting must be iterated eight or ten times. This Spirit of Wine strengthens the Spirit of Calx mightily and is made more fiery hot. Take the remaining Calx out of the body, grind it very small, put to it a tenth part of Salt of Tartar, which is pure, not containing any feces.

As much as this matter weighs together, add as much of the additional of Salt of Tartar thereunto, namely the remaining matter from which was extracted the Salt of Tartar, and it must be well exiccated. All this must be mingled together, and put in a well coated Retort. Three parts of the Retort must be empty. Take a great Receiver or body to it very strongly. Note, the body into which the Retort's nose is put must have a pipe of a finger's breadth unto which may be applied another body and a quantity of Spirit of Wine in it. Then give a gentle fire to it. At first there comes some of the phlegm, which falls into the first applied body. The phlegm being all come over, then increase the fire; there comes a white spirit to the upper part of the body, like unto the white Spirit of Vitriol, which does not fall among the phlegm but slides through the pipe into the other body, draws itself into the Spirit of Wine, embracing the same as one fire does join with the other. Note, if the Spirit of Calx be not prepared first by the Spirit of Wine and drawn off and on as I told, then he does not so, but falls among the phlegm where he is quenched and loses also its efficacy. Thus difficult a matter is it to search Nature thoroughly, reserving many things unto herself. This Spirit being fully entered into the Spirit of Wine, then take off the body, put away the phlegm, but keep carefully the Spirit of Wine and Spirit of Calx.

Note, both these Spirits are hardly separated because they embrace closely one another and being distilled they come over jointly.

Therefore take these mixed and united Spirits, put them into a jar-glass, kindle it; the Spirit of Wine burns away, the Spirit of Calx stays in the glass. Keep it carefully. This is a great Arcanum; few of other Spirits go beyond its efficacy, if you know how to make good use of it. This Spirit dissolves *Oculi Cancrorum*, the hardest Crystals; these three being driven over together and often iterated in that distilling, three drops of that liquor being ministered in warm wine break and dissolve any gravel and stone in man's body, expelling their very roots, not putting the patients to any pain.

This Spirit of Calx at the beginning looks bluish, being gently rectified, looks white, transparent and clear, leaving few feces behind. This spirit dissolves the most fixed jewels and precious stones. On the other side he fixes all volatile Spirits with his transcendent heat.

This Spirit conquers all manner of podagrical symptoms, be they never so nodose and tartarous; dissolves them and expels them radically.

Of Vitriol and its Preparation; Also of its Power and Virtue

Take good Hungarian Vitriol, calcine it till it be of a yellowish color and no higher. Grind this calcined Vitriol small, put it into a distilling vessel of Glass, with a long neck, well luted, *luto sapientiae* {of impure knowledge}. Put thereto a large Receiver and begin to distill day and night with a very gentle fire that gives not a stronger heat than the Sun does in a hot day. Afterwards increase the fire by degrees, forcing at last the Spirits with the strongest fire, till red, visible drops do come over, which work has taken up three days and nights. This being done take that which is left in the distilling vessel, commonly called *Caput Mortuum* {162}, and grind it small. Pour on it clear rain water, first distilled, and boil therein the Cholcotar and the Salt of the Vitriol will go into the water. The water being settled and clear, filter it that the feces may be separated. Let the water vapor away in some Glass Vessel til the Salt be dry; dissolve the Salt again in rain water first distilled and let it vapor away again to dryness. Repeat this operation the third time and the Salt of Vitriol will be very fair, clean and clear. Put this dry Salt into a Cucurbit of Glass and pour on it the above made Spirit of Vitriol; lute the Glass {*luto sapientiae*} and set it in digestion for some days. This being done, open the Glass and put the materials together into a Retort of Glass and distill them first gently; and when it ceases to drop increase the fire, and force it over till nothing will come more. Let it become cold and then take the Spirit out of the Receiver, which must be somewhat large and strong. Put the Spirit into a Glass body and rectify it by distillation till it be freed from the phlegm and the matter in the Glass body appear to be of a red, deep-brown color.

Then take the Glass body and set it with the said matter in a Cellar, and there will shoot from it very fair, white, clear, transparent Crystals. Put these transparent Crystals into a large Phial with a very large and long neck and pour on them the first white Spirit of Turpentine and it will boil up and foam; therefore you must be careful and not over hasty in doing this. The Crystal will dissolve, and the Spirit of Turpentine will grow transparent, as red as blood. This being done, pour on it three times the weight of Common Spirit of Wine,

151

freed fully from its phlegm, so that it stand two fingers high above it. Then put a little head of glass upon the neck of the Phial, luting it well, join to it a Receiver and distill very gently the Spirit of Wine in *Balneo Mariae* and the tincture of Vitriol comes over very pleasant with the Spirit of Wine and that which is corrosive remains behind with the oily parts of the Spirit of Turpentine. The Spirit of Wine being come with the Tincture, put it together into another Phial and pour on it some fresh Spirit of Wine and distill it again gently in *Balneo Mariae* as you did before; if any corrosive become over with the fire it will now stay behind. Repeat this operation the third time and the work is done and perfect. Put this fair, red, transparent Spirit of Vitriol into a Pelican, add to it at once half an ounce of well pulverized Unicorn's Horn and let it stand in circulation in a gentle heat a whole month. Then pour it off very clear from the feces and the Tincture of Vitriol is prepared for the Medicine, of a very pleasant taste, and is to be used after this manner following, to wit: Let him that is troubled with the falling sickness take half a dram of it in a spoonful of *Lillium Convallium* water when the fit is coming upon him. Thus let him use it three times and the Medicine will cure him by the help of God. He that is mad and distracted should take it likewise in Wine for the space of eight days and he will have reason to give God thanks for it. Moreover if it be taken in Wine it does resolve any hardness settled in the nerves and if it be constantly used for some time, even the Gout itself is consumed and cured thereby.

Likewise it makes those who are melancholy and troubled with sadness, if it be used as before, very cheerful and light-hearted; dispels all sadness and breeds good and pure blood. It has been found very excellent in swimmings and giddiness in the head; it comforts the brain and preserves the memory. If it be administered in consumptions of the lungs and any other coughs in the manner aforesaid, it will cure those distempers and is very useful for many other things.

An Addition

Take Sal Armoniac, dissolve a considerable quantity of it in the strongest Vinegar and add to it filings of Copper. Let it putrefy in heat till the filings are all grown friable so that they may be ground into powder and you will have a yellow powder, which edulcorate well.

Having done so, dry the powder and pour on it the red *Aqua Vitae Vitrioli* {191}, which has been distilled over with its proper Salt, so that it covers it all over. Set it thus in heat and the powder of the Copper will be dissolved in the oil, but there must be some fair water mixed with it. Then draw it off in Sand to dryness and the phlegm comes over. The remainder force out of a retort in an open fire and you will find an *Oleum Veneris*, {oil of Venus or Love, 141} green, transparent, like an Emerald. Put again into this *Oleum* some of the powder of Copper and it will be perfectly dissolved in it. Then coagulate it to dryness and you have a powder, half an ounce whereof will transmute a whole pound of Iron, being in flux, into very good Copper.

Of the Sweet Essence of Vitriol

The sweet Essence of Vitriol, whereby many wonderful cures may be wrought, is only prepared out of its Sulphur, which burns like other Brimstone. To obtain this proceed after this manner. Take of the best Vitriol you can get, dissolve it in fair fountain water; after this take Pot-ashes, such as dryers use for their dyeing; these dissolve likewise in fair fountain water; let it settle well and then pour off the clear from the dregs and add it to the solution of Vitriol and one will inflame the other and cause a separation. Make a considerable quantity of it and edulcorate it from all impurity. Afterwards dry the same Sulphur, which will burn like other Sulphur, being cast upon glowing coals.

Take now this Sulphur and sublime it by itself without any addition and there will remain some feces, which separate and put away. Then take the Sulphur and grind together with it half its weight of common Salt of Tartar and distill them together through a retort and there will come over a reddish oil. Pour to this oil some distilled Vinegar and there will precipitate a brown powder and the Spirit of Tartar remains in the water. Edulcorate the same powder very well, for therein is the treasure to be looked after. This work being done, pour some Spirit of Wine on the said powder and let it circulate in heat for eight days. Thus the excellent, sweet Essence of the Sulphur of Vitriol goes into the Spirit of Wine and swims upon the top, in *forma olei*, like an oil of cinnamon. Then separate the essence from the Spirit of Wine by means of a separating glass and keep it very carefully for use, it being a great treasure.

The Use of this Medicine

This Essence of Sulphur, four grains of it being taken in Balm water, dries up the bad humors of the blood, strengthens and incites men and women to copulation, cleanses the womb, hinders the rising of the mother and breeds good seed for the procreation of children.

The same quantity being taken in parsley water and continued for a fortnight, does consume all phlegmatic humors of the whole body, cures the dropsy radically, drives out the putrefied blood, opens impostumes; yea, you will find it does wonderful cures if you will be industrious and careful in the preparation thereof; but you must never while you live forget God your Creator, to call upon Him for a blessing and to render to Him thanks for all His Fatherly benefits He has bestowed upon you.

The Preparation of the Stone *Ignis*

{*Lapis Ignis*, Stone of Fire, sums to 104. This is the number of *Lux Mundi* and *Mons Sion* (esoteric name for the fully mature pineal gland).} Now I will teach you the chief Preparation of Antimony and the use of it in Medicine. In this Antimony are hidden and found so many wonderful Mysteries that there is none too old to learn and to search to find them out. I will instruct you to make some Preparations which are also required to other things.

Take pure Mineral Antimony, which is brought from Hungary, grind it small and wash it very clean, that the Earth may be separated from it. Take then a pound of it, mix with it as much of fluxing powder and melt it once again and then the *Regulus* will be clear and pure.

Add to this *Regulus* its weight of Nitre and melt it down. Pour it out together, and beat off the *Scoriae* and put again to the *Regulus* its weight of Nitre and melt it. Repeat this till all the *Regulus* is gone into *Scoriae*, which you must carefully keep; they will burn upon the tongue like fire. This being done, take the matter so gathered, grind it small and edulcorate the Saltpeter from it and there remains a brown-yellow powder, which dry and keep; it looks like ground Glass. Take now a common *Regulus* of Antimony made with Saltpeter and Tartar, grind it small and put it into a round Glass, which must not be too high, and fasten a head to it. Sublime your *Regulus* in Sand by itself without any addition, sweep the Sublimate with a feather again into the Glass and Sublime it again. Repeat this so long till nothing do rise, but remain red and fixed in the bottom. Then take this fixed Antimony and put it upon a Stone in a Cellar and in time it will be dissolved into water, which distill in *Balneo Mariae* until the sixth part only of the water remains in the Glass. Set this in a cold place and there will shoot reddish Crystals, which dissolve in rain water. Filter it and draw off the phlegm to a thickness, set it by as before and the Crystals will shoot white and very pure, like unto Saltpeter. This is the Salt of Antimony.

Take these Crystals and pour upon them pure distilled Vinegar and they will dissolve in the Vinegar. Then distill the Vinegar, the Glass being very close luted, forcing at last the Spirits into the Vinegar and then the Vinegar is prepared. Take this Vinegar and pour it on the prepared brown-yellow powder and set it in some warm place and the Vinegar will draw out the Tincture of Antimony, altogether red, within half or quarter of an hour. Pour off this Extraction together and set it to digest for twenty days in *Balneo Mariae*.

Afterwards distill from it the Vinegar through an Alembic in Sand, forcing in the end the Oil into another Glass, which comes over with many strange and wonderful veins. Rectify this Oil in ashes and the rest of the Vinegar, if any be left, will come off and the Oil remains very sweet and of a pleasant red color like a Ruby. Thus have you joined the Sulphur with the Salt of Antimony and brought it over like an *Aqua Vitae*, which keep very carefully. Furthermore take again a common *Regulus* of Antimony made with Saltpeter and Tartar and beat it to powder. Then take of strong distilled Vinegar four quarts and a half. Put into it of *Sal Armoniack*; of Salt of Tartar likewise eight ounces (I shall teach how to make it at the end of the directions). Digest this to the evaporation of the Vinegar and mingle with the Salts three parts of *Venice Tripoli* and distill the Spirit, which is of a singular nature and property.

Pour this spirit on the pulverized *Regulus* of Antimony and having the Glass well luted let it stand in digestion sixteen days; then distill the Spirit from the matter to a dryness and grind four times the weight of filings of steel with the same. Put it into a Retort, and putting thereto a large Receiver full of water, distill it, forcing at last with a strong fire, and the Mercury comes over in Fumes and is quickened in the Water which is the true Mercury of Antimony.

Take common Spirit of Vitriol, add a little common water to it and put your filings of steel into it. Let it stand till the filings are dissolved, then pour it off clean and put away the feces. Afterwards distill the Spirit in ashes to a thickness and set the Glass in a cold place and there will shoot good Vitriol of Iron, which take, and having first vapored away the phlegm, mingle with it three parts of the powder made of burned potsherds of broken pots, put it into a Retort, draw off the phlegm first, then force the Spirit with a strong fire into a proper Glass, which rectify to the height and there will remain an Oil in the bottom. Pour this Oil upon the Mercury made before and draw off the phlegm in hot ashes, and the tincture of the *Aqua Vitae* remains behind and does precipitate the Mercury into a fair, high-colored powder of very great virtues in curing old, running sores.

The Conjunction of the Three Principles:
Sulphur, Salt and Mercury of Antimony

Take then of the precipitate well edulcorated with common Spirit of Wine, one part; and pour on it of the above mentioned sweet Oil, three parts, in a Phial, so that the Phial be not above half full.

Then seal it Hermetically and place it in a Philosophical Furnace and the precipitate will be dissolved in that continual heat. Open then the Glass and continue a strong fire till the Matter become a fixed Powder and do fix, and then the Stone *Ignis* is prepared of which I have written. This Stone is a particular Tincture in men's bodies as well as in those of Metal. This may be used in many hard and dangerous distempers. Take of this Stone or particular Tincture half an ounce, cast it upon twelve ounces and a half of pure Silver or upon as much Pewter or Lead. Let it flow very well for four and twenty hours; then drive it off clean and quart it, as Tryers and refiners do, and you will find in the Silver two ounces and a half of very good Gold and in the Pewter or Lead one ounce upon the Cuppel.

Another Medicine Made Out of Antimony & Mercury
and of its Effects in Outward Sores

Take Hungarian Antimony and Sublimed Mercury and grind them well together and distill them through an Earthen Retort, forcing them at last with the strongest fire imaginable and you will obtain an Oil, which separate and keep apart. Put away the quick Mercury, if so there be any, and the Cinnabar you will find in the Neck of the Retort. But as for the *Caput Mortuum*, grind it small and put it into a new retort, and having poured on it the Oil, first made warm, distill it again from it. Repeat this so often till the *Caput Mortuum* remain behind like ashes and then your Oil is prepared. After this take so much fresh Antimony as first of all the *Caput Mortuum* did weigh, grind it small and pour on it the Oil, first warmed, and so many times distilled as before till the Oil become over as red as a Ruby and the *Caput Mortuum* likewise remain like ashes in the bottom of the Glass and then the Oil is prepared.

Preparation of the Sublimate for this Work

Take one pound and a half of Hungarian Vitriol, one pound of common Salt, four ounces of Saltpeter; grind this together and put one pound of Quicksilver into the bottom of a Glass body; place it in Sand so that the Sand do not come above the Matter in the Glass; put a Head thereupon and give it a convenient fire and the Sublimate will stick to the sides of the Glass, which is to be used in your work.

Take the above prepared *Aqua Vitae* and add thereto eight ounces of it three ounces of Saltpeter water and distill it out of a coated, Glass Retort and you will have an ounce of the *Aqua Vitae* remain behind fixed. Then put again to the *Aqua Vitae* one ounce of fresh Saltpeter water in a Retort and distill as before and there will stay more behind. This addition of fresh Saltpeter water to the *Aqua Vitae*, as distillation out of a Coated Retort, as has been said before, repeat so often till all remain fixed in the Retort.

The Saltpeter Water is Made Thus and Its Use

Take unburned Potsherds ground small and with three parts of the same grind one part of purified Saltpeter. Put into the Receiver half a pound of water to one pound of Saltpeter and force the Spirits over into it. That which is fixed with this water, put into a Glass body and pour upon it the common *Aqua Vitae Vitrioli* so that it be four fingers high upon it. Then distill it till the matter become dry. Take out this Matter and dry it yet more that the rest of those corrosive Spirits may evaporate, then edulcorate it well with Spirit of Wine and the Medicine is prepared.

Three or four grams of this Medicine being taken in some good Treacle for some days cures the French Pox; there {is} no sore so old and festered but is cured infallibly by it. I have cured with it likewise many spreading, old, running Ulcers, as Fistulas, Cancers, the Wolf and the like. The name of the Lord be praised therefore.

The Preparation of a Medicine Out of Common Sulphur

Take common Sulphur and grind it small, then grind with it three parts of calcined Vitriol, put it together into a high Cucurbit and Sublime it in Sand till nothing will sublime more. Take then these Flowers, {*Flores Sulfuris*, the correct spelling of Sulphur in Latin. It sums to 180 by gematria, equal to the letter spelling of QPh (qoph). It implies the "back of the head" area stimulated by the rising Flowers.} put them into a Glass and pour on them a common *Aqua Vitae Tartari* {167}, which has been dissolved in a Cellar, so that it swim on the top of it a hand's breadth. Place it in a convenient heat and the Sulphur will open itself in a few hours and become transparent red like a Ruby. This being done pour off the extraction into another Glass and put to it very good distilled Vinegar and the Sulphur falls to the bottom with a great stink. Pour off the *Aqua Vitae* and edulcorate well the Sulphur and dry it gently. Put this Sulphur again into another Glass Cucurbit and pour upon it Spirit of Wine, which is prepared with Philosophical Tartar, set it in heat for three days and the Spirit of Wine imbibes again that excellent Tincture of the Sulphur. Then pour off the Extraction and draw off the Spirit of Wine with a pretty strong fire in Sand and there will come over with it a pleasant, sweet smelling *Aqua Vitae*. Having done so, rectify the Oil in *Balneo Mariae* and draw off the Spirit of Wine gently and the *Aqua Vitae Sulphuris* remains in the bottom. {Our original author certainly would have known about the misspelling of Sulphur. *Aqua Vitae Sulphuris* changes the gematria to 201. A Hebrew term, AMTzO (emeza), Middle or Means, hints the Living, Liquid Sulphur is the middle means toward the Stone. That is, Chokmah, Wisdom, Fire, Sulphur or Desire (between Mercury and Salt) is The Path of Means when these Fires are rechanneled.}

The Use of This Medicine

Six or eight drops of this Oil being taken in a spoonful of Wine are good for those that are in a Consumption. It is good likewise for Coughs, opens the breast and Ulcers of the breast, as also Imposthumes; It relieves against whatsoever may occasion any putrefaction in a man's body, if the use of it be continued for some time.

The Preparation of the Tincture of Corals

Take red Corals, break them to pieces, and pour on them a common Spirit of Salt and the Corals will be dissolved. This being done, draw off by distillation the Spirit of Salt, and edulcorate them well. Then take to one Marck {a European unit of weight} of this powder half an ounce of common Sulphur, pulverized, and having mingled it together, reverberate it very gently till all the Sulphur be burned away. Having done so, grind as much Camphor with the Corals and burn the Camphor likewise away. Then edulcorate well the Corals and pour upon them high rectified Spirit of Wine and digest them for eight days, and the Tincture of the Corals will elevate itself and go into the Spirit of Wine. Then pour off that which you have extracted and after that draw off the Spirit of Wine from it and there remains the Tincture of Corals behind in the bottom like a red, fat oil of olives. {Coral, in Latin, is *coralium* = 82; the plural, *coralia* = 53. *Pantarva* = 82, but the number 53 evokes a plethora of imagery; like ABN (Stone); *Magnes*; Liber M; GN (garden). Space inhibits the development of these and more ideas.}

The Use of the Medicine

Six drops of the Tincture given in a spoonful of wine to those that are bereaved of their senses, restores them again. This Tincture comforts likewise the brain and strengthens the memory, dispels sadness and melancholy, makes one light-hearted, breeds good blood and strengthens the heart. It is such a noble Medicine for which we are bound indeed to bless Almighty God.

Of the True Solution of Pearls

Take very good Verdigris, {Gematria = 112, as *prima materia*, *semen solare* and *aes hermetis*.} grind it small and dissolve it in distilled Vinegar; pour off the clear and throw away the feces. Then distill off the Vinegar out of a Glass body to a thickness and put it into a cold place and there will shoot from it a fair Vitriol. Put this Vitriol into another Glass and pour on it a high rectified Spirit of Wine and dissolve therein the Vitriol very well. Separate the feces from it; afterwards distill off likewise the Spirit of Wine to a thickness and set it again in a cold place and the Vitriol shoots again. Put then the Vitriol into a Glass body and draw off by distillation the phlegm in *Balneo Mariae* till the matter become dry. Take it out, put it into a glass Retort and distill once more with a stronger fire in Sand, and you will obtain a pleasant Vinegar. Dissolve in this Vinegar as many Pearls as it will dissolve, for this Vinegar works very well upon them, dissolves the substance but not the shells. The Pearls being dissolved, draw off the Vinegar in *Balneo Mariae* till the Pearls be very dry, then take them out and edulcorate them with Rose-water. Put these Pearls thus prepared into a Glass body and pour some Spirit of Wine upon them and digest them in gentle heat four and twenty hours and there rises a pleasant liquor from the Pearls, which does mount and swims upon the Spirit of Wine like an *Aqua Vitae* made of Cinnamon. Pour it off together with the Spirit of Wine and keep it.

The Use of This Medicine

Take of this Spirit of Wine half a spoonful so that four or five drops of the Oil may go with it. It comforts the heart, gives strength to the very marrow and bones; cures swimmings in the head and whatsoever may be hurtful to the eyes. It dispels Rheums in the head and the noise in the ears, opens the passage to hearing and is, moreover, a most precious treasure in many distempers.

A Certain Cure of the Stone

Recipe of common Saltpeter, well purified, one pound and as much of common white Spirit of Vitriol. Pour the Spirit of Vitriol upon the Saltpeter and the Saltpeter will be dissolved altogether. This being done, distill from them the Spirit of Vitriol in Ashes to a thickness and set it into some cold place and the Saltpeter will shoot again from it. Take two ounces of this Saltpeter and the like quantity of the Salt of Wormwood; pour on them a little of the Oil of Sulphur made *per Campanam*, {Gematria = 89, shares value with GUPh (body); *nummus* (coin); and *fundamenta* (fundaments). All these imply materialization. Campania is a region in Italy south of Latium. The area is known for its fertility and fine bronze work. Alchemically speaking, fertility and bronze hint to influences of Venus (desire and creative imagination). The Oil of Sulphur, then, and any other healing for that matter, is done "through the Imagination".} so that the Salts may be like a poultice. Mix with it likewise one dram of Anniseed Oil and as much of Oil of White Amber, adding thereto a pound of Canary Sugar and mix all these ingredients very well together. Let him that is tormented with the stone take of this powder every day five or six times, every time as much as will lie upon a point of a knife, twice repeated, and this Medicine will work upon the stone and break it and throw it out radically.

Of the Soul, or of the Sulphur of *Lune*,
The Philosophers' Silver

Take common Saltpeter and quick or unslacked Lime, reverberate them together in a wind furnace, with the strongest fire, extract again the Saltpeter with warm rain water and coagulate it to dryness; mingle again with it new quick Lime, reverberate it and extract again; repeat this the third time. This being done take Calx of Silver, being after the dissolution in *Aqua Fortis* prepared, and mix it with the prepared Saltpeter; put it into a Glass Viol, pour on it a common Aqua Fort such as the goldsmiths use, made of Saltpeter and Vitriol, and draw it off by distillation in hot Sand. Pour on it some fresh *Aqua Fort* and having distilled it likewise, repeat it the third time, giving at last very strong fire, that the matter in the Glass may flow very well. Let it cool of itself in the furnace and the Sliver will become transparent blue in one piece. Extract this with Vinegar till you can extract no more. Edulcorate that which is extracted with water that the Salt may be separated from it.

Cohobate Vinegar upon the dry Sulphur till it come over like a Sapphire. Reduce the same Silver into small filings and add to it its weight of *Sal Armoniack* and sublime it in a Glass body and the *Sal Armoniack* carries with it the Sulphur of Lune of a very pleasant sky-color. Put this Sublimate into a dish of glass, edulcorate it well with Rain Water, first distilled, and the *Sal Armoniack* will be separated. Then dry the Sulphur of Lune, put it into a little body and pour on it good, rectified Spirit of Wine and set it twenty-four hours in heat and the Spirit of Wine does imbibe the Sulphur of Lune, fine transparent blue, like a Sapphire or Ultramarine, and leaves some few feces behind, which separate from it.

The Use

Five or six drops of this Tincture being taken in Wine does dispel sad and melancholy thoughts. It prevents unquiet sleep, cures those as use to rise and wander up and down in the night and likewise that are Lunatics, and gives rest to all such as are restless in the night.

The Secret of Quick or Unslacked Lime

Take good, pure chalk, burn it in a potters' Furnace with a very strong fire to bring it to an exact maturity. Then grind it small upon a warm stone and pour on it, in a Glass body, Spirit of Wine made with Philosophical Tartar that the chalk become like a thin poultice.

This being done, distill from then the phlegm to the dryness of the chalk, pour fresh Spirit of Wine on it and distill it off again. Repeat this six times; then grind the Matter small and lay it on a Stone in a Cellar to dissolve and there will flow in few days from it a Liquor, which when you have gathered, put it into a Retort of Glass and distill it in Sand and the Phlegm comes over first, which keep apart. After this there comes a spiritual liquor which is likewise to be kept by itself.

Moreover take Crystal stones, pulverize them and grind their weight of Live or Mineral Sulphur with them. Put then this Matter upon a broad, earthen platter, stirring it continually, and burn away the Sulphur from it. Then Reverberate it in an open flaming fire for three hours. This being done, likewise put the matter into a Glass and pour the liquor upon it. Take likewise Crabs' eyes, put them into another Glass and pour on them of the same liquor; let it stand pretty hot for fourteen days and nights and there will rise from both a moisture, which pour off together very clean into a little body of Glass and rectify it in *Balneo Mariae* and the liquor remains behind. Three grains of which, being taken in Wine, have wrought very great and admirable effects. This Medicine cures likewise radically the stone of the bladder and kidneys, both in men and women.

Take this burned chalk, pour upon it and then draw from it again several times an *Aqua Fort* made of Vitriol and Saltpeter. Dissolve it afterwards in a Cellar. Distill that which is dissolved into an Oil with a strong fire. Digest with this Oil a Calx of Lune, opened with *Aqua Fort*, for a month. Reduce this Calx by melting down with Saltpeter and *Sal Armoniack* and refine it with Saturn; then separate it, and you will have a white, fixed Lune, which lay for a day and night in an *Aqua Fort* and you have good Gold, which endures all trials. *Laus Deo*.

The Preparation of the Great Philosophic Stone

Our Stone is made out of its own proper Essence; for it transmutes other Metals into real and true Gold, which Gold must be prepared and become a better Stone. And though nothing of another Nature must be used in the preparation of our Stone, which might obstruct its Majestic Excellency, yet the preparation of it in

160

the beginning cannot be made without means. But observe that, as you will hear afterwards all corrosives must be washed away again from it and separated, so that our Stone may be severed from all poison and be prepared to be the Great Medicine. {This is the whole Alchemical Art. Nothing more has been written in this entire book than reiteration of this same one point, albeit in different guises. All the seeming, physical descriptions of processes are but coded procedures of one, grand, internal transmutation. Says Roger Bacon in *The Root of the World*: "For the knowledge of this Art consists not in the multiplicity of things, but in unity; our Stone is but one, the matter is one, and the vessel is one; the government is one, and the disposition is one. The whole Art and work thereof is one, begins in one manner and in one manner it is finished." This is not a blind!} Now I will show the Work itself.

Take of the very best Gold you can have, one part; of good Hungarian Antimony, six parts melt this {one thing} together upon a fire and pour it out into such a pot as goldsmiths use; when you have poured it out it becomes a *Regulus*. This same *Regulus* must be melted again that the Antimony may be separated from it.

This being done, add to it Mercury and melt it again, and cleanse it again. Repeat this the third time and the Gold is purged and purified enough for the beginning of the Work. Then beat the Gold very thin as goldsmiths do when they gild and make an *Amalgama* with common Quicksilver, which must be squeezed through a Leather. Let the Quicksilver fume away little by little upon a gentle fire, that nothing of it may remain with the Gold and stir it about continually with a small Iron {A spoon, rod or spatula is irrelevant here}, and the Gold is become subtle so that its water may the better work upon it and open it.

The Preparation of the Water

Take one part of Saltpeter, well purified, and grind with it the like quantity of *Sal Armoniac* and half as much of pebbles very well cleansed and washed; {Pebbles is *lapilli*. These, "very well cleansed and washed," become *Magnesia* (Philosophic Magnet); and DVNG (duneg), Wax. These are names for the First Matter which becomes "attracted" to Iron Sulphur, and receives the matrix "impression" like a wax. *Lapilli*, *Magnesia* and DVNG each sum to 63. The singular, *lapillus* = 90, that of MIM, Waters.} mingle all these ingredients together and put them into an earthen Retort, that the Spirits may not come through; put the same into a distilling furnace. The Retort must have a pipe behind and put as large a receiver as you can get to the Retort. The Receiver must lie in a vessel full of cold water and a wet linen cloth must be put round about it, which you must continually {redo} with another wet cloth. Then again so much matter {is placed} into the Retort, till all is gone into it and then your water is prepared.

Take then of the prepared Calx of Gold one part, put it into a Glass body and pour three parts of the above made water upon it and place it in warm ashes and the Gold will dissolve in it; but if it should not altogether be dissolved, put more fresh water upon it and it will dissolve all. This being done, pour it out into another Glass and let it stand till it become cold and it will let fall same feces, which separate by pouring the water from them into another Glass; set this Glass in Balneum *Mariae* {*sic*} and put a head upon it. Let it stand in heat day and night and more feces will settle, which separate from it as before. Close up your Glass very well after you have put on the head and lute another Glass to the head and let it stand for fourteen days in a gentle heat, that the body may be well opened. This being done, increase the fire and distill off the phlegm to a thickness that it remain in the bottom like an *Aqua Vitae*. That which has been distilled pour again into the body, having first made it warm, and lute again the head to it and let it stand to digest a day and night. Then draw off the water again by distillation and pour it again warm upon it. Repeat this so long till the Gold is come over altogether into a low body with a flat bottom. Put this spiritualized Solution of Gold again into a Glass and pour on it a considerable quantity of Rainwater, putting thereto three parts of live Mercury to one of Gold, but you must squeeze first the Mercury through a Leather, and stir it very well together and you will see many wonderful colors; and if you do, repeat this, stirring several times, there will fall an *Amalgama* to the bottom and the Water will become clear.

This being done, decant the water and dry gently the *Amalgama*, which, having edulcorated very well, put it upon a broad, shallow, earthen platter under a cover. Stir it about continually with an Iron wire till all the Quicksilver be fumed away and there will remain upon the earthen {body} a very fair powder of a purple color.

Afterwards you must prepare your Spirit of Wine with the Philosophical Tartar in the following manner.

First you are to know that the Tartar of the philosophers, whereby the Lock is unlocked, is not like unto common Tartar as many do think; but it is another Salt and springs from one root and this is the only Key to open and to dissolve Metals and is prepared as follows. {This is the second, blatant warning about the Philosophic Tartar and Wine.} Take ashes of a Vine which has borne Grapes that have yielded good Wine; make of them with warm water as strong a Lee as possibly can be made. When you have a considerable quantity of this Lee, boil it away and coagulate it to a dryness and there remains a reddish matter. Put this Matter into a Reverberating Furnace and reverberate it for three days or thereabouts in an open fire, that the flame may play very well upon it and stir it continually till the Matter is become white.

Afterwards dissolve this reverberated Matter in Fountain Water and let it settle, pour off the clear and filter it, that all the feces may be separated and coagulate it in a Glass body and you will have a pure, white Salt of Tartar from which a true Spirit is drawn.

Take now high rectified Spirit of Wine, fully freed from its phlegm; put the same into a Glass phial with as long a neck as possibly you can get. But first of all put into it your Salt of Tartar and then the Spirit to the supereminency of three figures {sic}. Lute a Head to the phial and put there to another Glass, let it stand in a gentle heat, then distill gently off the phlegm and the Spirit of Tartar is opened by the Spirit of Wine and by reason of their reciprocal, wonderful love it comes over with the Spirit of Wine and is united with it. The remaining feces and some phlegm staying behind with them are to be put away.

This is now the right Spirit of Wine, wherewith you may open that which the Lover of Art desires to know, for it is become penetrant by preparation.

Take now the powder of Gold of a purple color and having put it into another phial, pour on it your Spirit of Wine. Put it, very close luted, in a gentle heat and it will extract the Sulphur of Gold within twenty-four hours of a high red color like blood. Having done so, that it does not yield any Tincture more, pour off the extraction very clear into a little Glass body. The remainder is a white Calx. Pour upon this Calx the aforesaid Spirit of Wine and let it stand in putrefaction, having the Glass well stopped for fourteen days and nights; and the Spirit of Wine will become of a white color like milk, which pour off clear and pour upon it fresh Spirit of Wine; let it stand a day and night longer and it will be colored again, but not much. Add this to the first, and what remains do not dry, but leave it in the Glass. Put the white Extraction into a little body and distill the phlegm from it till it be reduced to a small quantity.

This being done, put the Glass in a Cellar and there will shoot from it fair and transparent Crystals, which having taken out, put the remainder again in a Cellar and you will have more Crystals, which put together into a body of Glass; for it is the Salt of the philosophers, and pour half the Extraction of the Sulphur of Gold upon them and they will dissolve immediately and melt like butter in hot water. And then distill it together out of a Glass body in hot ashes and it will come over together in a form of a red Oil, which falls to the bottom and the Spirit of Wine swims upon the top, which separate from it.

This is the true Potable Gold; not reducible into a body, and my Phalaia, whereby I have cured many by the blessing of God, giving but three grains of it in Wine.

The other half of the Extraction must be distilled gently in *Balneo Mariae* to a dryness; the Spirit of Wine may be separated. Pour on it this Oil of Gold or Potable Gold and it takes the powder in a moment and becomes of a much higher color than it was before; and this will dissolve in common Spirit of Wine and other Wine as red as a Ruby, which constantly and wonderfully cures all such distempers of the body as have their original from within.

Then take that other part of Mercury of pure Gold which you have kept, and pour all this, being its own Oil, upon it and distill by an Alembic, but not too strongly; and there comes over some Phlegm and the Oil does precipitate its own Mercury and becomes white again, the greenness being lost and gone.

This work being done likewise, get a Philosophical Egg, which the philosophers call their Heaven and you will find two parts of the Oil in weight to one part of the precipitated Mercury. Put then the Mercury into a Glass and add the Oil of Gold to it, so that one part of the Glass may be filled and three parts remain empty. Seal it well as Hermes teaches and put it into the Three-fold Furnace, so that it stands not hotter than an Egg which is under a hen to be hatched; and the matter will begin to putrefy within a month, and become very black which, when it does appear, it is then certain that the Matter is open by the putrefaction and you may be glad of the happy beginning. Increase now the fire to the second degree and the blackness will vanish away in time and change into many admirable colors. These colors being gone likewise, increase the fire to the third degree and your Glass will look like Silver and the rays will become ponderous. Then, increasing the fire to the fourth degree, the fumes will cease little by little and your Glass will shine, as it were, beset within with Cloth of Gold. Continue this fire and the Rays will disappear likewise and there will be no more Rays to be seen to rise, but you will see your matter lie beneath like a brown Oil, which at length being become dry, does appear like unto a Granite, which is both fixed and liquid like wax, penetrant like Oil and mighty ponderous.

He that has obtained this may render thanks to God his Creator, for poverty has forsaken him, disease will fly from him and Wisdom has taken possession of him.

Having thus prepared your Medicine, if you intend to multiply it, proceed as follows. Take of the prepared powder of Gold of a purple color, as you have done before, three parts. Add to it of the prepared Tincture one part, in a new Heaven or Philosopher's Egg. Seal it again Hermetically and set it into the Furnace as before and the Matter will unite itself and dissolve and be brought to perfection within thirty-one days, which is a month, which otherwise will take up to ten months. Thus you may multiply your Medicine *ad infinitum* so that you may perform things which the World will account incredible.

Lastly you must know that this Medicine is a very spiritual and piercing one, which cures any distempers of the world in all creatures whatsoever. One only grain of it being taken, it penetrates the whole body like a fume, chases out of the body all that is bad and brings that what is good in the room of it; renews the man and makes of him, as it were, a new man, which it preserves without any accidents to his age and the term prefixed by the Most High. *Contra Mortem Remedium Non Est.* {It is not a remedy against death.}

This Medicine being first fermented with other pure Gold does likewise tinge many thousand parts of all other Metals into very good Gold, as I showed in a former process, whereby such Gold likewise becomes such a penetrant Medicine, that one part does tinge and transmute a thousand parts of other Metals, and much more beyond belief into perfect Gold. God be blessed and praised both now and forever more. Amen.

Spirit of Mercury By Itself, or Mercurial Water
(Additional Preparations for a Fuller Declaration of the Same)

Put running Mercury into a Retort, and put to it a Receiver, which must stand in a Glass with water in it. Distill then, and the Spirit will precipitate itself and is resolved into a Water. Pour out this Water and put the Mercury which sticks to the neck of the Retort back again into the Retort. Distill and rectify till you have brought and reduced it to a Water. This Spirit of Mercury cures almost all distempers and does extract the essence out of Minerals and Metals.

A Tincture Both Upon Men and Metals

Take the Spiritual Gold of a purple color, extract its Sulphur with distilled Vinegar separate the Vinegar again from it, that it become a powder. This Powder being dissolved in Spirit of Red Mercury, that is Gold, put thereto Salt of Gold and fix it. This is an Universal Medicine for sick and diseased bodies of men and likewise it is excellent to exalt Metals to the highest degree.

A Tincture Upon White Mercury

Calcine Silver with Salt and Quicklime and extract its blue Sulphur, which elevate and rectify with Spirit of Wine, that it remain a Liquor. Dissolve this in the White Spirit of Vitriol and in the Spirit of Mineral Mercury.

I do not understand here the Red Mercury, but the common, White, Mineral Mercury, or rather that which is extracted out of Vitriol.

Fix it then, and you have an Universal Medicine against all distempers and a Tincture which does tinge Lead, Pewter, Mercury and Copper into Silver.

To Make an Ounce of Gold out of Half an Ounce

Take Spirit of Salt, rectify it with Spirit of Wine that it become sweet. Pour this upon the Spiritual Gold of a purple color and it will extract only the Soul of Sulphur of the Gold, but does not touch the body of Gold. The Sulphur of Gold does graduate Silver into Gold, yet no greater quantity of it than there has been of Gold. The body of Gold must be as white as Silver. Reduce it upon a Cupel with Saturn and a little Copper and the white body of Gold does recover again its color and property and becomes good Gold.

To Make the Mercury of Gold, or The Philosophical Mercury

Take the Gold of a purple color out of which the Sulphur is already extracted, digest it with the following Water for a month, then revive it again by driving it through a Retort in the neck whereof are to be laid thin iron plates. Drive it into a Receiver with some water in it and it runs together and becomes a quick Mercury of Gold. The Water is made as follows:

Take Salt of Urine of a young man who drinks nothing but Wine and likewise Salt of Tartar and Sal Armoniac, ana. Let all this dissolve into a Liquor, which rectify with Spirit of Wine that it become very sweet. This is the Arcanum wherewith the body of Gold is reduced into a running Mercury. {These little paragraphs are loaded with gematria. Since this is literally the most ludicrous, it is worth investigation. First, *urina pueris*, urine of a young man, sums to 137 and is the number of QBLH, Qabalah, and *Spiritus Dei*, the Spirit of God. The Salt of Qabalah is the Literal Qabalah, the study of the Magical Language. Lacking this tool and/or the Spirit of God this entire manuscript remains unintelligible. Salt of Urine is *Sal Urinae*, equal to *ceram sapientae*, Philosopher's Wax, at 118. This Wax is the Universal Substance, which receives all impressions, like a wax mold. Salt of Tartar is *Sal Tartari*. At 107 it is equal to in *Balneo Mariae*, the vapor bath encased by our aura, the Glass Vessel. This is followed by *Sal Armoniac*, equal to VITRIOL and *Sol Pater*, the Father Sun, at 94. This chief ingredient, within the Vessel, bakes the Phoenix embryo. Father Sun, or Tiphareth, is the sole Artist in this Work. After the discovery of the First Matter, we apportion and Hermetically Seal some of the raw substance within our Vessel, where Father Sun maintains the heat of incubation. *Sal Urinae* (118) + *Sal Tartari* (107) + *Sal Armoniac* (94) = 319. This is the number of the Stone in Greek, *Lithos*, the "Water-Stone" or running Mercury. Every page in this text reiterates phases of this point variously by allegory and metaphor.}

To Make the Salt of Gold

Pour Gold three times through Antimony, beat it into thin plates and dissolve them in *Aqua Regis*. Dissolve likewise Salt of Tartar in Spirit of Wine and draw off the phlegm that it remain like an Oil. With this Oil precipitate your Gold and separate again the Salt of Tartar from it by ablutions, then reverberate it fourteen days. Pour upon this Calx of Gold distilled Vinegar; let it boil gently a day and night and the Vinegar does dissolve the Salt of the reverberated Gold. What remains in the bottom undissolved must be reverberated again eight days. Then boil it again in new Vinegar; put this afterwards to the first solution.

If any thing remains yet behind it must be reverberated eight days more till the body is gone into the Vinegar. Then draw off the Vinegar in *Balneo Mariae* and you have the Salt of Gold in a yellowish powder which cures all distempers. *SOLI DEO GLORIA*.

To conclude these Preparations with a brief discovery of the first Tincture, Root and Spirit of Metals and Minerals; how they are conceived, ripened, brought forth, changed and augmented:

Of the First Tincture—The Root of Metal

Observe that the Tincture, which is the Root of all Metals is a Supernatural flying, fiery Spirit {AIN SUPh AUR}. It has its sustenance and natural habitation in the Earth and Water, where it may rest and work. And this Spirit is found in all Metals, and more abundant in other Metals than Gold; for the Gold is very close, solid and compact by reason of its well digested, ripened and fixed body; therefore it can no more enter into the body than the body does need. But other Metals have not such a fixed body, but their pores are open and dispersed, therefore can the tingeing Spirit abundantly more penetrate and possess them. But because the bodies of other Metals are unfixed, the Tincture likewise cannot stay with these unfixed bodies, but must go out of them, and being the Tincture of Gold, does in no other Metal abound more than in Iron and Copper, as Husband and Wife, their bodies are destroyed and the tingeing Spirit from thence expelled, which breeds much blood in the opened, prepared Gold, and by its feeding does make it volatile. Therefore when the volatile Gold is filled by its meat and drink, it takes up its own blood, does dry it up through its own internal fire with help and addition of a moist fire and is again a conquest, which does fix, nay, produces the highest fixedness, so that the Gold becomes a high, fixed Medicine and cannot make a body again by reason of the superabundant blood, except there be added to it a superfluous body into which the abundant fixed blood does disperse itself, which joined metallic body is penetrated by the exceeding great heat of the fixed blood of the Lion, like fire, cleansed from all impurity and immediately ripened to a perfect maturity and fixity. I now pass to the birth and to the generation, how the Archeus does show and pour forth its power and displays it, by which all the metallic and mineral forms are exposed to the view and are made formal, palpable and corporeal through the mineral, incomprehensible, flying, fiery Spirits.

First you are to know that all the Metals and Minerals of the Earth have one only Matter and one only Mother, by which they in general altogether received their conception and perfect bodily birth. And this Matter, which comes from the Center does divide itself in the beginning into three parts to produce some corporeal thing and a certain form of every Metal. These three parts are fed and nourished by the Elements in the Earth out of its body till they become perfect. But the Matter, which has its original from the Center, is framed by the Stars, wrought by the Elements, formed by that which is Terrestrial and is a known Matter and the true Mother of Metals and Minerals; and is such a Matter and Mother out of which Man himself has been conceived, born, nourished and made corporeal, And may be altogether compared to the Middle World; for whatsoever is in the Great World, that is likewise in the Little, and whatsoever is in the Little World, that is likewise in the Great. And thus what is in the Great and Little Worlds together, that is found likewise in the Middle World, which joins the Great and Little Worlds and is a Soul, which does unite and copulate the Spirit with the

Body. {*Anima Mundi* = 89, that of GUPh, Body. God is to Man as Man is to Nature. Man, in this sense, being the Middle World.} This Soul is compared to Water and is indeed a right true Water, yet does it not wet like other water, but it is an Heavenly Water, found dry in a Metallic, Liquid Substance, and a Soul-like Water, which loves all Spirits and does unite them with their bodies and brings them to a perfect life. Therefore it is certain that the Water is a Mother of all Metals, which, being heated by a warm, aerial, temperate fire, as is the Spirit of Sulphur, brings life into the Terrestrial Body through its ripening, wherein the Salt is apparently found, which does preserve from putrefaction, that nothing may be consumed by corruption. In the beginning and in the birth is wrought first of all the Quicksilver, which yet lies open with a subtle coagulation, because there is but little of the Salt communicated to it, whereby it shows more a spiritual than corporeal body. Other Metals, which are all derived from its Essence and have more Salt, which makes them corporeal, do follow after this. I begin with the Spirit of Mercury.

Of the Spirit of Mercury

All visible and palpable things are made out of the Spirit of Mercury, which is beyond all the Terrestrial things of the whole world, and all things are made out of it and have their original from it. For herein is all to be found that can do all what the Artist does desire to enquire into. It is the principle to work Metals, being made a Spiritual Essence, which is a mere Air, and flies to and fro without wings and is a moving Wind, which, after its expulsion out of its habitation by Vulcan, is driven into its Chaos, into which it enters again, and does resolve itself into the Elements, where it is attracted by the Stars after a magnetical manner, out of Love, from whence it went forth and was wrought out before, because it desires to be united again with its like. But when this Spirit of Mercury can be taken and made corporeal, it does then resolve itself into a body and becomes a clear, fair and transparent water, which is a true Spiritual Water and the first Mercurial Root of Minerals and Metals, spiritual, imperceptible, incombustible, without any commixtion of the Terrestrial aquosity. It is that Heavenly Water of which much has been written. For by this Spirit of Mercury all Metals may be, if need requires, dissolved, opened and without any corrosive reduced or resolved into their First Matter. This Spirit renews both man and beast like the Eagle; consumes whatsoever is bad and produces a great age to a long life.

To declare further the Essence, Matter and Form of this Spirit of Mercury, I must tell you that its Essence is Soul-like, its Matter Spiritual and its Form Terrestrial, which yet must be understood by some incomprehensible thing.

Touching the beginning of this Spirit of Mercury, this is needless to know because it is of no benefit, nor can it do you any good. But observe that its beginning is supernaturally from Heaven, the Stars, and Elements, granted in the beginning of the first Creation to enter further into a Terrestrial Being. And because this is needless as I have told you, leave that which is heavenly to the Soul and apprehend it by Faith. That which is of the Stars, let likewise alone, because such impressions of the Stars are invisible and incomprehensible. The Elements have already brought forth this Spirit perfectly into the World, through the nourishment of it. Therefore do not meddle with them either, for no man can make any Element, but the Creator alone; and insist upon your Spirit already produced, which is both formal and not formal, comprehensible and incomprehensible and yet does appear visibly, and you have the First Matter, out of which are grown all Metals and Minerals and is One Only Thing and such a Matter which does unite itself with the Sulphur of Venus or Copper and is coagulated with the Salt of Mars, so that it becomes one body and a perfect Medicine of all Metals, not only to generate in the beginning in the Earth, as in the Great World, {AIN SUPh AUR is also the Alchemical Earth, an Earth in Atziluth, so to speak. The fluid, mineral-like substance is an earthy matter which comprises all that is physical creation. In this Alchemical Earth is Air (Mercury), Fire (Sulphur) and Water (Salt).} but also by help of a moist fire to change and transmute, together with the augmentation, in the Little World. Let this not seem strange to you, because the Most High has thus permitted it and Nature has wrought it.

But how the Archaeus works further by the Spirit of Mercury in the Earth you are to understand that after the spiritual seed is framed from above by the impression of the Stars and fed and nourished through the Elements, this seed is changed into and is become a Mercurial Water; as in the beginning the Great World likewise was made of nothing; for the Spirit moved upon the Water and thus was this cold, waterish and terrestrial Creature revived to life by an heavenly warmth. It was in the Great World, the power of, and the operation of the Light of Heaven; in the Little World likewise the power of God, and the operation by His Divine and Holy Breath to work in the Earth. Furthermore the Almighty did grant and ordain means for the performing of the same that the Creature might get power to work upon another Creature and one might help and promote the other for the performing and perfecting of all the Works of the Lord. Thus was granted to the Earth an influence to generate by the Luminaries of Heaven and likewise an internal heat to warm and to ripen that which was too cold for the Earth by reason of its aquosity. Thus to every Creature a peculiar Genius {resides} according to its kind, that so there is raised a subtle, sulphurous steam by the Starry Heaven, not a common, but another, clarified, clean and pure steam, separated from others, which does unite itself with the Mercurial Substance, by which warm property in a long time the humidity is dried up little by little and then the Soul-like property, being joined with it, which gives the body and balsam of maintenance and works before too upon the earth by a spiritual and starry influence. Thus happens then, a generation of Metals, according to the commixtion of the Three Principles and according as they take in more or less of these three, so the body is formed. If so be the Spirit of Mercury is directed and formed from above upon *Animals*, then is there produced an *Animal* Being, but if it seizes upon Vegetables, a Vegetable work is brought forth. And if it falls upon Minerals, by reason of its infused nature, there will spring thence Minerals and Metals. Nevertheless every one is differently wrought; the *Animals* by another form by themselves, the Vegetables after a manner proper to themselves and the Minerals likewise on another fashion, every one after a singular way. Now I shall faithfully discover how this Spirit of Mercury may be had and obtained, the manner how to prepare it, that it may cure diseases and change and alter all Metals of the ignoble kind, as they are generated in the little world by a transmutation and augmentation of their seed.

Take, in the Name of the Lord, Red Mineral Quicksilver which looks like Cinnebar and the best Mineral Gold that can be gotten. Take an equal quantity of them both and grind them together before they have been in any fire; pour upon them an Oil of Mercury made by itself out of the common, putrefied, and sublimed Quicksilver; digest them for a month, and you will have an Extraction which is more heavenly than terrestrial. Distill gently this Extraction in *Balneo Mariae* and the phlegm comes over and the ponderous Oil remains in the bottom, which takes up into itself all Metals in an moment. Add to this three times the quantity of the Spirit of Wine, circulate it in a Pelican till it becomes blood-red and has recovered an incomparable sweetness. Pour off the Spirit of Wine, and add to it fresh Spirit of Wine. Repeat this so long till the whole matter be dissolved into an exceeding sweet and ruby-color, transparent liquor, which mingle afterwards together. Pour it upon white, calcined Tartar and distill it with a strong fire in Ashes and the Spirit of Wine remains behind with the Tartar, but the Spirit of Mercury comes over. This Spirit of Mercury being mixed with the Spirit of *Sulphur Solis*, together with its Salt, whosoever shall bring them over thus joined and united together, that they may not be separated in infinitum, he will have such a work (if so be it does receive its Ferment in a due measure and prefixed term, with Gold, by a solution, and is brought in its perfect maturity to a *plusquam* {a little more} perfection) to which nothing may be compared for the preventing of diseases and poverty. This Spirit of Mercury cures the dropsy, consumption, gaut, stone, French pox and all other lasting sores. It is the only Key to make the Corporeal Gold Potable. {Alchemically charged physical blood through Art.}

Of the Spirit of Copper

Venus is clothed with a heavenly Sulphur, which does far exceed the splendor of the Sun, because there is found much more Sulphur in her than in Gold. But learn what the matter is of the said Sulphur of Gold, which dwells and reigns abundantly in Venus; is a flying and very hot Spirit, which can search and penetrate all, as also digest, ripen, and bring to maturity, viz., the imperfect Metals into perfection. {This Spirit of Copper is the Desire Nature or Kama Manas of Eastern philosophy.} If you ask how the Spirit of Copper can ripen and bring to perfection other imperfect metals, it being itself, in its body, imperfect and not fixed, I answer that this Spirit cannot have or hold in Copper a fixed body for an habitation; therefore the habitation being burned by fire the Guest goes out of it likewise and must leave his habitation with impatience, for he dwells therein like an hireling. {The Venus Chakra or force center is itself imperfect initially. It must be cleansed and perfected. But when the pure Desire Nature is sublimed, desirous of the Higher Wisdom, it does all the things enumerated above.} But in the fixed body of Gold he has a protection that nothing can drive him out without the Sentence of a peculiar Judge, because he has taken possession of his habitation like an heir and has taken root in that fixed body, that cannot be cast out so easily. {Gold, Tiphareth, the One True Ego now guides the perfected Desire Nature, where before it was separative and selfish. These desires are now under the King on His Throne.} The Tincture which Venus has obtained is likewise to be found in Mars, yea, much more powerful, higher, and more excellent; for Mars is Husband, Venus the Wife. {Universal Sulphur, intrinsic in AIN SUPh AUR and initially activated in Chokmah, is the Tincture in Venus as Desire. In Mars, two spheres higher on the Tree and therefore more excellent, Tincture manifests as Will. The Gold King balances the two as Tiphareth, between Geburah and Netzach.} This Tincture {Sulphur} is likewise found in Verdigris and Vitriol as in a Mineral, of which a volume might be written. And in all these things there is found a Sulphur which does burn and yet another Sulphur which does not burn, which is a wonderful work. The one is white, the other red in the operating birth; but the right and true Sulphur is incombustible, for it is a mere and true Spirit, out of which is prepared an incombustible Oil and is indeed the Sulphur out of which the Sulphur of Gold, out of one and the same root, is made and prepared.

This Sulphur may be very well called and christened the Sulphur of the Wise, because in it is found all wisdom, {Indeed, Chokmah is Wisdom on the Tree.} if you except the Mercurial Spirit, which is to be preferred, and with it, together with the Salt of Mars must be united through a Spiritual Copulation that three may be brought to a correspondency and be exalted into one operation.

This Spiritual Sulphur does likewise and in the same manner derive its original from the upper Region {The Three Supernals}, as the Spirit of Mercury does, but with another form and fashion, whereby the Stars do show a separation in fixed and unfixed, in tinged and not tinged things. The Tincture does consist only in the Spirit of Copper and chiefly of its consort and is a mere steam, stinking and of very ill scent in the beginning. And this must be resolved in a liquid manner, that the stinking, incombustible oil may be prepared out of it. This Oil is easily joined with the Spirit of Mercury and does soon take up all metallic bodies, being first prepared according to the account I formerly declared. Venus has much Sulphur; she has been, together with Mars, digested and ripened sooner than any other Metals; but because they have had but little help from the inconstant Mercury, being he had no room left him to work harder, by reason of the superabundant Sulphur, they could not receive or obtain amelioration of their unfixed bodies.

Now I will discover a Mystery to you, that Gold, Venus and Mars have in them one and the same Sulphur, one Tincture and the same Matter of their Tincture, which matter of the Tincture is a Spirit, a Mist and a Fume, which has penetrated and does penetrate all bodies. If you can bring it into captivity and do actuate it with the Spirit, which is found in the Salt of Mars and then do join with the same the Spirit of Mercury according to their weight, and do separate them from all impurity, that they become sweet and sweet-smelling, without any corrosive, you have then a Medicine to which nothing in the world may be compared. If you ferment this Medicine with the shining Sun you have made an ingress which is penetrant to work and to transmute all Metals. {If we capture Sulphur (our base passions) in all its expressions and cleanse it of Salt tendencies, we have a Sulphur aligned with Mercury, which conjunction is sometimes called Cinnabar. Finally, if our consciousness is "fermented by the Shining Sun," that is, wholly influenced by the One-Ego in Tiphareth, we have successfully experienced Our Medicine turned into the Stone.}

Lastly, take notice, that the root of the Philosophical Sulphur, which is an heavenly Spirit, together with the root of the Spiritual Supernatural Mercury, and the principle of the Supernatural Salt, is in one and is found in one Matter {AIN SUPh AUR or Alchemical Earth}, out of which the Stone, which has been before me, is made, and not in many things; although the Mercury be drawn by itself by all the philosophers and the Sulphur by itself, besides the Salt apart. That, so Mercury is found in one, and the Sulphur in one, and the Salt in one. Notwithstanding all this, I do tell you, that this is to be understood of their superfluity, which is found most in every one, and particularly in many ways may be used profitably and prepared to a Medicine and {to the} transmutation of Metals. But the universal, as the greatest treasure of terrestrial knowledge and wisdom and of all the Three Principles, is one only thing and is found in one only thing and is drawn out of it, which can reduce all Metals into one only thing and is the true Spirit of Mercury and the Soul of Sulphur, joined together with Spiritual Salt, enclosed under one heaven and dwelling in one body; and is the Dragon and the Eagle; it is the King and the Lion; it is the Spirit and the Body, which must tinge the body of Gold to be a Medicine, whereby it gets abundant power to tinge others, its consorts.

Concerning the generation of Copper, observe that the Copper is generated out of much Brimstone, but its Mercury and Salt are equal in the same for there is neither more nor less in quantity of one and the other to be found. {The mysterious Basil Valentine wrote the same at about the time of this original MS. In Vedic terms, the Vishudda Chakra (Venus or the Metal Copper) generates much rajasguna, with lesser, equal quantities of sattvaguna and tamasguna.} Now because the Brimstone does exceed in quantity the Salt and Mercury, there arises from thence a great tingeing redness, which great redness has so possessed the Metal that the Mercury could not perfect its fixedness, that a more fixed body might have been produced out of it. You are further to know that the form of Venus's body is of the same condition that a tree is which has and does yield an abundance of Gum, as is the pine and fir tree, with other sorts of trees, which Gum is the Sulphur of the Tree, which drives out sometimes this Gum at the sides of it by reason of its too great abundance and because it cannot harbor it all. Such a Tree now, that is tinged with so much fatness by Nature and the ripening of the Elements, burns and takes fire immediately; neither is it heavy and is never so durable as Oak and the like hard wood, which is solid and compact and has not his pores so open as that sort of light wood, that the brimstone might abundantly reign in it. But therefore has the Oak wood more Mercury and a better Salt than the pine or fir tree. And such wood is never so much apt to swim upon the Water as the fir tree is, because it is close, solid and compact that the Air in it cannot bear it up. The same is to be understood of Metals, but especially of Gold, which by reason of its much fixed and well ripened Quicksilver, has a most solid, compact, close, fixed and invincible body, to which neither Fire nor Water, neither Air nor any putrefaction of the Earth can do any hurt because its pores are closed up and the corrupting power of the Elements cannot injure it. Which fixedness and solid and compact conjunction do demonstrate its natural ponderosity, which is not to be found or proved in other Metals, which may be discerned not only by weighing it in a pair of scales, but you will find it likewise, if you put but a Scruple of pure Gold upon a hundred pound weight of Quicksilver, it will fall presently to the bottom, whereas all other ponderous Metals laid upon Quicksilver swim upon it and do not sink to the bottom because their pores are more largely extended that the air or wind may pass through them to bear them up.

Concerning the Spirit of Venus or Copper in physics, you are, in fine, to observe that it is found very necessary and wholesome in its virtue and efficacy; not only that Spirit that lies in *Primo Ente*, but that Spirit likewise which is found in the last Matter. Its virtue, power and operation is such that in the rising of the Mother it is to be preferred before any Medicine whatsoever; also against the falling sickness, the dropsy, the stone. If you have a special care of this Spirit of Copper, it will work such wonders both inwardly and outwardly as will be accounted by all incredible and supernatural.

To conclude, the Spirit of Copper is a hot Spirit, penetrant and searching, consuming all the bad humors and phlegm both in men and Metals and may be justly accounted the Crown of physics. It is very fiery and piercing, incombustible, yet spiritual and without form; and therefore, is capable like a Spirit, to further in particular the ignition, digestion and ripening of things without a form. {That is, imagery, which precedes any formation.}

Of the Generation of Mars, Its Spirit and Tincture
Mars and Venus have one and the same Spirit and Tincture as the Gold and

other Metals have; though this Spirit be found in every Metal, in some a greater, in some others a smaller quantity. It is undeniable and confessed of all that there are diverse men and diverse opinions; although men in the beginning are made out of one First Matter and generated and born out of one seed, yet there is a manifold difference of their opinions because the operation of the Stars has occasioned this and not without cause. For the influence of the Great World works the other (namely the difference of opinions) after itself in the Little World, because all the Opinions, Nature, and Thoughts, together with the whole complexion of Man, do derive their original only from the influence of the Stars of Heaven and do show themselves according to the Planets and Stars, where nothing can withstand nor obstruct such an influence because the generation of their perfection is already performed and brought to a period or finished. {Here our author develops the origin and vein of Divine Intent, which is manifest as God's Will-Force. Under this section the Spirit of Mars is understood as this Will working through Man, but not originating therein.} For example, a man is naturally inclined to study, one has a mind for Divinity, another for the study of the Law, the third for Physics, the fourth will be a Philosopher. Besides all this, there are many wits that have a natural inclination for mechanical arts, as one turns a limner, another a goldsmith, this man a shoemaker, that man a tailor, another a carver and so forth. All this happens by the influence of the Stars, whereby the imagination is strengthened and found supernaturally, wherein it resolves to continue {Qabalists call the influence of the Stars, Masloth. If we could but surrender our pseudo, separative and selfish will and desire urges, Masloth would flow through us unobstructed. This is the inheritance of Free Will in the True Man, the Christ Consciousness, the King returned to His Throne. All other ideas of "man's free will" are erroneous doctrines, distorted and self-serving, which keep us in the state of hell we experience in this physical world.}; as we do find, if a man has once taken up a resolution in his mind and laid a foundation upon it, that no man is able to bring or keep him from it, that he should not so obstinately stand upon it, Death only excepted, which at last closes up all. The same is to be understood of Chemists and Alchemists, who, having got once into the Secrets of Nature, do not intend to give them over so easily, except they have more exactly searched Nature, and wholly absorbed and finished the study thereof, which yet is no easy matter. Thus you are likewise to understand of Metals that according as the infusion {Will} and imagination {Imagination} happens from above, so happens the form likewise; although Metals are altogether called Metals and are indeed Metals, yet as you have understood by diverse opinions of men, which are altogether men out of one Matter, there may be manifold and diverse Metals, of which one has got an hot and dry, another a cold and moist, another a mixed complexion and nature. Therefore because the Metal of Mars has before others been ordered by a gross Salt in the greatest quantity in its degree, its body is the hardest, most inflexible, strongest and most coarse which nature has thus appropriated to it. It contains the least part of Mercury, a little more it has of Sulphur, but the greatest part of Salt; and from this mixture is sprung its corporeal being and is thus born into the world with the help of the Elements. Its Spirit is in operation equal to other Spirits but if the true and right Spirit of Iron can be discerned, I assure you one grain of its Spirit or Quintessence, taken and administered in Spirit of Wine, comforts and strengthens a man's heart, mind and courage not to fear his enemies. It stirs up a Lion-like heart within to fight Venus' battles. If the conjunction of Mars and Venus does rightly happen in a certain constellation {Astrologically there might be two optimum conditions, depending on the other aspects. But Mars is exalted in Capricorn, wherein Venus rules the second decanate; or Venus is exalted in Pisces, wherein Mars rules the third decanate. Since this section is treating of Mars the conjunction of the two in the second decan of Capricorn would exalt the Will and temper it with Venus' creative imagination and love.}, they have success and conquest, both in love and sorrow, in fights and peace, and will continue of one mind though the whole world should bear a spleen and enmity against them. This Spirit cures wonderfully all Martial distempers.

This Spirit of Iron, being rightly discerned, has a secret affinity with the Spirit of Copper {Will and Desire}, that they may be so joined together that there rises one only matter from them {Sulphur}, of one and the same operation, form, substance and being, which will cure the same distempers and transmute the particulars ies of metals with profit and honor.

But Iron, together with its virtue, ought properly to be considered in the manner following, that it has a terrestrial body only in its corporeal form, which body may be used to a great many things, to alter the blood, to outward wounds, to a graduation of Silver and inwardly to the constipation of the body, which yet is not always beneficial to use, neither in a man's body inwardly and outwardly, nor yet as concerning Metals, because there is no great advantage to be made per se without the known right means, which do belong to Nature's secret knowledge. Observe one thing more, that the Loadstone and the True Iron are almost of one and the same use in bodily distempers and are almost of one and the same nature, even as it is according to a Divine, Spiritual and Elemental sense betwixt the Body, its Soul and the Chaos out of which the Soul and Spirit are gone; the Body is framed last of all out of that Composition.

Of the Spirit of Gold

If you are desirous to get this Golden Loadstone, your prayers must be rightly made to God, in true knowledge, sorrow, contrition and true humility, for to know and learn the three different worlds, which are subject to human reason {This might imply the three major divisions of the Tree in Assiah (Three Supernals; Sephiroth 4 through 9; and Malkuth), rather than the lower three of the Four Qabalistic Worlds.}; as there is the super-celestial world, wherein the immortal Soul keeps its seat and

175

residence {Neshamah, the Divine Soul in Binah}, besides its first original and is by God's Creation the first moving sensibility or the first moving sensible Soul, which of a supernatural being has wrought a natural life. And this Soul, and this Spirit is the Root and the first fountain and the first Creature existing in the life of anything. And the *Primum Mobile* {Rashith ha Galgalim, Kether Assiah}, which has been so much controverted by learned men. Observe likewise the second Celestial World and take good notice of it for therein do reign the Planets {Masloth, the Sphere of the Zodiac, in Chokmah Assiah} and all the Heavenly Stars have their course, virtue and power in this heaven and do perform therein their service, for which God has placed them there and do work in this their service by their Spirit {upon} both Minerals and Metals.

Out of these two Worlds arises another different World, wherein is found and comprehended what the other two Worlds have wrought and produced. Out of the first super-celestial World is derived the Fountain of Life, and of the Soul {MQVR ChIIM (makor chaim) is Hebrew for Fountain of Life. It Sums to 414, as does AIN SUPh AUR. AZUTh (azoth), the Astral Light, is called "Soul of the World" by Eliphas Levi, J.A.Seibmacher and various sages. AZUTh = 414.}. From the second Celestial World does spring the light of the Spirit and from the third, the Elemental World {Malkuth Assiah}, comes the invincible, heavenly yet sensible fire, by which is digested and ripened that which is comprehensible. These three matters and substances do generate and bring forth the form of Metals, amongst which Gold {Anahata Chakra} has pre-eminency because the Sidereal and Elemental Operation has mellowed and ripened the Mercury in this Metal the more substantially to a sufficient and perfect maturity. And as the Seed of a man does fall into the Womb and touches the *Menstruum* which is its Earth; but the Seed which goes out of the Man into the Woman, is wrought in both by the Stars and Elements; that it may be united and nourished by the Earth to a generation. So you are likewise to understand that the Soul of Metals, which is conceived by an imperceptible, invisible, incomprehensible, abstruse and supernatural, Celestial composition, as out of water and air, which are formed out of the Chaos and then further digested and ripened by that heavenly, Elemental Light and Fire of the Sun, whereby the Stars do move the powers, when its heat in the inward parts of the Earth, as in the Womb, is perceived. For by the warming property of the Stars above, the Earth is unlocked and opened that the infused Spirit of the same may yield food and nourishment and be enabled to generate something as Metals, Herbs, Trees and Beasts, where every one particularly brings with it its Seed for a further multiplication and augmentation. And as the Conception of Man is spiritual and heavenly, whose Soul and Spirit, by nourishment of the Earth in the Mother's Womb, are formally brought up to a perfection, so likewise it is to be observed and understood in every particular of Metals and Minerals. But this is the true secret of Gold, viz; to instruct and teach you by an example and similitude, whereby the possibility of Nature and its mystery is to be found in the manner following. It is probably true that the heavenly light of the Sun is of a fiery property and of a fiery being, which the Most High God, as Creator of Heaven and Earth, has granted to it through an heavenly, constant and fixed Sulphurous Spirit for the preservation of its substance, form and body, which Creature, by reason of its swift motion and course, through its swiftness is inflamed and set on fire by the Air, which inflammation will never be extinguished as long as the motion does last and the whole created, visible world does continue and endure, nor in the least diminishes in its power; because there is no combustible matter extant which might be given to it, whose consumption might cause the decay of that great light of Heaven. So is Gold {the Chakra} by the superior of its Essence thus digested and ripened and is become of such a fixed invincible nature that nothing at all can hurt it, because the upper fixed Stars have penetrated the lower, that the lower fixed Stars {the other six Chakras}, by reason of the infusion and grant of the upper, need not to give place to their equal because the lower has received and obtained such a constant fixedness from the upper.

I will add another similitude according to the manner of philosophers, of the great Light of Heaven and of that small fire, which, being terrestrial, is here kindled every day and is made to burn before our eyes, because that great light has a magnetical likeness and an attractive, loving power with that small fire here upon Earth, which is yet without form and impalpable and found only spiritual, invisible, insensible and incomprehensible. It is remarkable, as it is demonstrated and proved by experience, that that great Light of Heaven has a great Love for and bears an affection and inclination to the little fire, which is terrestrial, by reason of the Spirit whereby both are agitated, and preserved from their utter ruin and destruction. For do but consider that as soon as the Air, through great moisture which it has attracted, conceives any corruption, that so through mists and further coagulation and conjunction clouds are generated, the beams of the Sun are hindered and obstructed that the Sun cannot obtain its reflection, nor have its due penetrating and searching power. So likewise this little terrestrial fire does never burn so clear in dark, rainy weather, neither does it show itself with that gladness in its operation as when the air is fair, pure and clear. The cause is this, for through the obstacle of the moist air the love is hindered that the attractive power, growing sad, cannot exercise its perfect love and operation as it ought to do, for the contrary element, the aquosity, causes this obstruction. As now the Sun, that heavenly great Light, has a special communion and love with the small terrestrial fire to attract after a magnetical manner, so likewise has the Sun and Gold {Chakra} a special correspondency and a peculiar attractive power and love together, because the Sun has wrought the Gold through the Three Principles, which have their Loadstone, and is nearest of all related to the Sun and has attained to the highest degree, so that the Three Principles are found most mighty and powerful in the same. Next to it is Gold in its corporeal form, because it is framed out of the Three Principles, but has its original and beginning from the heavenly and golden

Loadstone. This is now the greatest wisdom of this world. In this golden Loadstone is and lives buried the dissolution and opening of all the Minerals and Metals, their government as also their matter of the first generation and their power as touching health; moreover, the coagulation and fixation of Metals, together with the operation to cure all diseases. Take a special care of this Key, for it is heavenly, sidereal and elemental, out of which the terrestrial is generated. It is supernatural and natural together and is born out of the Spirit of Mercury, heavenly; out of the Spirit of Sulphur, spiritual; but out of the Spirit of Salt, corporeal. Out of this Spiritual Essence and out of this Spiritual Matter, from which the Gold first of all is made corporeal into one body, the ancient and modern Rosicrucian Philosophers do make Potable Gold more substantial than out of Gold itself, which must be made spiritual before the Potable Gold can be prepared out of it. This Spirit cures Leprosy, the French Pox, as being a super fixed Mercurial Essence, dries up and consumes the Dropsy, and all running, open sores, which have affected a long time. It comforts the heart and brain, strengthens the memory and breeds good blood. Thus can the Soul of Gold, reduced into Water, the spiritual Essence of Pearls, and the Sulphur of Corals, united in one, do such things which to nature seem otherwise incredible; but because experience confirms this truth it is deservedly a cordial in this mortal life to be preferred justly before all other cordials by reason of its wonderful effects. The preparation thereof is this. Take Spirit of Salt and with it extract the Sulphur of Gold. Separate the Oil of Salt from it and rectify the Sulphur of Gold with Spirit of Wine that it may become pleasant without corrosiveness. Then take the true Oil of Vitriol, made out of the Vitriol of Verdigris, dissolve in it Iron; make again a Vitriol out of it and dissolve it again into an Oil or Spirit, which rectify likewise as before with Spirit of Wine. Put them together and draw off the Spirit of Wine from thence. Dissolve the Matter which remains dry behind in Spirit of Mercury in a due proportion or weight. Circulate and coagulate it. When it becomes constant and fixed without rising any more, you have then, if you ferment it with prepared Gold, a Medicine to cure diseases and to tinge Metals.

Of the Spirit of Silver

The Tincture and Spirit of Silver is of a sky-color, otherwise it is of a waterish Spirit, cold and moist and not so hot in its degree as the Spirit which is found in Gold, Iron or Copper; therefore is Silver more phlegmatic than fiery, although it has been reduced by fire out of its waterish substance unto a coagulation. In the same manner have the stones likewise received their hardness, fixedness and tincture, as by one and the same influence. In a Diamond is found a fixed and coagulated Mercury, therefore this Stone is harder and more fixed than other stones and is not to be broken as they are. In a Ruby is found the Tincture of Iron or the Sulphur of Iron; in an Emerald the Tincture of Copper; in a Granite the

Soul of Lead; in Pewter the Tincture which is found in the Stone called Topasius {For Topaz our author chose the Latin form. It sums to 112, that of *Prima Materia* and *Gemma Pellucida* (Transparent Jewel), which is a reference to the mature pineal gland. Pewter is a blend of Tin and Lead. It is the benevolent influence from the Solar Plexus (the Jupiter Center) which begins to turn Lead. The Sacral Plexus (Saturn Center) is washed of its hard Salt by expressions of love, compassion and beneficence toward all creation and creatures. It is a sure route toward the Stone, *Topasius*.} Crystal is attributed to Common Mercury and in a Sapphire is found the Tincture and Sulphur of Silver, yet every thing in particular, according to its nature and kind, and in Metals {The force-centers or chakras} likewise according to their form and kind. And when the blue color is separated and taken away from the Sapphire, then is its garment gone and its body is white like a Diamond. Thus when Gold has lost its Soul it yields then a white body and a fixed white body of Gold, which is called *Luna fixa* {Gematria = 77, that of *Vivum*, referring to *Argent Vive*.} by the searching students and novices in this Art.

What has been said as concerning the Stone called Sapphire, for your instruction you may apply to the better knowledge of the nature of Metals, for this blue Spirit is the Sulphur and Soul out of which Silver has its life as well in the Earth as above the Earth by Art, and the white Tincture of Silver upon white always, in a magnetical form of that one thing and Creature, wherein the *Primum Ens Auri* likewise is found. This Spirit of Silver alone contains that which will perfectly cure and dispel the Dropsy, even as the Spirit of Gold and of Mercury can radically cure the consumption so that even the center itself of the said distemper may not be found.

But that Silver is not so provided in its degree with a hot substance and quality in the veins of the Earth, but is subjected to a waterish kind; this fault is to be laid upon the Great Light of Heaven, which by reason of its waterish influence has planted this quality into the Second Creature and into the second Planet of the Earth as into Silver {Ajna Chakra}. And though Silver does carry with it a fixed Mercury or fixed Quicksilver, which is born in it, nevertheless it wants the hot fixed Sulphur, which might have exactly dried up and consumed the phlegm, which is the cause it has not obtained a compact body, except it be done afterwards by Art of the Lesser World. And because the body is not solid and compact, by reason of its waterish substance, hence are its pores not well stopped up nor consolidated, that it might have a due ponderosity and endure a fight with its enemies. Which virtues ought altogether to be found in Gold, if so be it must conquer all its foes and endure all the trials without fault.

You are likewise to understand that the First Matter of Metals must be observed, studied and found out through the discovery of their last matter, which last matter, as there are the absolute and perfect metals, must be divided and separated that it may appear altogether naked to a man's eyes and then there may be learned and known by such a division what the First Matter has been in the beginning, out of which the last is made. Observe diligently this Arcanum. {The "last matter" in the

Earth is us, not minerals, gems or physical metals. The furthest expression from the AIN SUPh AUR is the absolute individualization and full development of Self-Consciousness, which then regains its lost Source to fully cooperate with the Creative Process from the Enlightened Conscious Level.}

Take the sky-colored Sulphur of Silver, which has been extracted out of Silver and rectified by Spirit of Wine. Dissolve it according to its weight in the white Spirit of Vitriol and in the sweet scented Spirit of Mercury and coagulate them together through a fixation of fire and you will get the possession of the White Tincture and its Medicine. But if you know the *Primum Mobile* it is then needless, because you may bring the thing to perfection out of one.

Of the Soul or Tincture of Pewter

The benign Jupiter is almost of a middle nature amongst all the Metals. He is neither too hot nor yet too cold, nor too warm nor too moist. He has not too much of Mercury nor yet of Salt and of Sulphur there is least of all in him. Pewter is found white in its color, yet of these Three Principles one does exceed the other as it has been clearly discovered in its division according to the true inquiry into Nature's secrets. Out of this composition and mixture of the Three Principles is generated and wrought and coagulated into a Metal and brought to a maturity of perfection benevolent Jupiter. The Spirit of Jupiter does preserve and protect from all distempers and diseases incident and hurtful to the liver. Its Spirit is naturally, as for its taste, like unto Honey. Its Mercury being made volatile does get a venomous quality, for it purges vehemently and penetrates with violence. Therefore it is not always good that its unlocked Quicksilver should be thus simply used by itself; but if a correction goes before, it may be very well used with exceeding great usefulness in those diseases and distempers which are immediately subject to his influence, that is to say, when you have taken away from Zadkiel its venomous volatility and it is placed into a better and more fixed state, which does resist poison. To conclude, if you do extract out of the benign Jupiter his Salt and Sulphur and make Saturn flow very well together with them, Saturn does get a fixed body, is purified, and becomes clear by them and is a total change and real transmutation of Lead into good Pewter, as you will find it upon a most accurate trial {Refer again to the commentary on *Topasius* in the preceding section.}. And though this may seem to you not to be true, yet are you to understand that by reason that the Salt of Jupiter is made Corporeal only by its Sulphur, it likewise has received an efficacy and power to penetrate Saturn, as the vilest and most volatile Metal, and to bring it to its own substance by making it better, as you will really find it to be so.

Of the Spirit of Saturn or Tincture of Lead

Saturn, to generate his Metal, which is Lead, is placed in the upper Heaven, above all the Stars. But in the lower parts of the Earth he does keep the lowest degree. {Saturn, attributed to Binah and the Divine Soul, Neshamah, is the Door of the Art. This is *Corvus Niger*, the Black Crow, the thick, constricted darkness from whence all begins. In the Earth, the human body, Saturn is the lowermost Metal or Chakra, located in the spinal column at the level of the Sacral Plexus. On the Road of Return this force center is the first to unfold, releasing the Serpent Power.} As the uppermost Light of Saturn is mounted to the highest altitude of all the Lights of Heaven; so likewise in imitation of the same has Nature given leave and permitted that his Children of the Lower Region have retired themselves by Vulcan to those of their quality according as Saturn has been moved. For the Upper Light is the cause of it and has generated an unfixed body of Lead through which go and are drawn open pores, that the Air can have its passage through this Saturnine body and bear it up. But the fire easily works upon and consumes it because the body is not solid and compact by reason of its unfixedness. This is well to be observed by a serious inquirer into all things because there is a vast difference betwixt fixed and unfixed bodies and then the causes of this fixedness and unfixedness. And though Saturn is of a singular ponderosity before other Metals, yet will you observe that when they are poured out together after their conjunction in the melting of them, the other Metals will always fall to the bottom, as likewise it happens with other Metals by pouring them through Antimony. Whereby it does appear that other Metals have a more solid and compact body then Saturn can raise, because it must give place to other Metals, make room for them and yield the victory; for it vanishes away and is consumed together with these inconstant and unfixed Metals. For there are the three grossest qualities of the Three Principles in Saturn, and by reason that its Salt is altogether fluid in comparison to other Metals and Planets, therefore is likewise its body more fluid, inconstant, unfixed and more volatile than any metallic body.

How Saturn does proceed towards his regeneration, you are to know that as common water, through naturally cold, by the alteration of the Upper Heaven is congealed, so that it becomes a coagulated Ice {It has been noted at the beginning of this MS. that this world is really "frozen mind-matter." The AIN SUPh AUR is congealed into forms by the constricting, Saturnine influence. The First Matter, Universal Mercury, is the Universal Subconscious Mind-Substance. In the Metal Lead or the Saturn Force-Center there is more Mercury than in any other Metal, which is why our author notes the great fluidity of Lead.}. So likewise it is demonstrated that Lead is coagulated and made corporeal by reason of the great cold, which is found in its Salt before any other Salt. The congealed Ice is resolved through warmth and so is the coagulated Lead made fluid by fire. It has most Mercury in it, yet inconstant and volatile; but less of Sulphur and, therefore, according to the small quantity of the same, its cold body cannot be heated; and least of all of Salt, but fluid; otherwise Iron would be more liquid and malleable than Saturn if the Salt alone could impart both the malleableness and fluidity, because Iron does carry with it more Salt than any other Metal. And being there is a difference to be found in these things, you must carefully observe how Metals are to be distinguished.

All the Philosophers, indeed, besides myself have written that the Salt causes the coagulation and the body of every Metal. And this is true, but I shall show by an example how this is to be understood. *Alumen plumosum* {58 + 114 = 172. Literally this translates as "a feathered astringent." It hints or implies a compaction, but rather airy or porous.} is reputed and probably accounted to be a mere Salt, and herein may be compared to Iron, which Salt of the aforesaid *Alumen plumosum* is nevertheless found to be as a matter and not liquid as Iron. On the contrary, Vitriol does show itself like Salt in a small quantity, yet liquid and open, and therefore its Salt cannot cause so hard a coagulation in its appropriated Metal as that other Salt does. {Salt makes a hardness, not just density. While Lead may be considered the most dense it is not hard. Lead is fluid due to its density of Mercury, not Salt. So the Salt in Lead may be considered as a "feathered" or airy astringency.} Although all the Salts of Metals are grown out of one root, and one seed, {AIN SUPh AUR} yet there is a difference of their Three Principles to be observed. As one herb differs from the other, likewise in men and other beasts a difference is found as concerning the original of their qualities and their Three Principles, where one herb has something more of this, another herb more of that kind, which is likewise to be understood of men and beasts. {Ayurvedic Medicine places human personality into three major categories: Mercurial (Airy), Sulphuric (Fiery) and Saltish (Watery).} The Soul of Lead is of a sweet quality, as also the Soul of Jupiter, and yet sweeter, so that as for sweetness there is hardly anything comparable to it, being first highly purified by separation, that the pure being very well severed from the impure there may follow a complete perfection in the operation. Otherwise the Spirit of Lead is naturally cold and dry, therefore I do advise both men and women not to make too much use of it, for it over-cools Human Nature, that their seed cannot perfect or perform its natural operation, nor is it good for the spleen and bladder. It does attract the phlegmatic quality, which breeds melancholy in men. For Saturn is a governor, and such a melancholy one whereby a man is upheld and strengthened in his melancholy. Therefore if its Spirit be used, one melancholy spirit does attract the other, whereby a man's body is freed and released from its infused melancholy. Outwardly is the Soul of Saturn very wholesome in all sores and wounds, whether they be old or green, whether they happen by thrusting or cutting or naturally by means incident, so that hardly any other Metal will do the like. It is a cooling thing in all hot and swelled members, but to eat away and to lay a foundation for healing in all corrupt and putrefied sores, which have their issuing forth from within, there the noble Venus has the pre-eminency, because Copper is hot in its essence to exiccate and dry up, but Lead, on the contrary, is found to be cold in its essence.

That Heavenly Light of the Sun is much hotter than the Light of the Moon, because the Moon is much lesser than the Sun, which does comprehend the Eight

Part of magnitude in the Circle of Measuring and Dividing. And if the Moon should exceed the Sun in this Magnitude of the Eight Part, as the Sun does exceed the Moon, then all the fruit and whatsoever grows upon the Earth would be spoiled, and there would be a continual Winter and no Summer would be found. But the Eternal Creator has herein wisely prescribed a certain Order and Law to His Creatures, that the Sun should give light by day and the Moon by night and thus be serviceable to all creatures.

Those Children which are addicted to the influence of Saturn are melancholy, surly, always murmuring like old covetous misers, which do not good to their own bodies, and are never satisfied. They use their bodies to hard labour, vex and fret themselves with troublesome thoughts and are very seldom so cheerful as to recreate themselves with other people, neither do they care much for natural love of women although handsome.

To sum up all, Saturn is generated out of little Sulphur {Rajasguna}, little Salt {Tamasguna}, and much immature, gross Mercury {Sattvaguna}, which Mercury is to be accounted like scum of froth which swims upon the water in comparison to that Mercury which is found in Gold, being of a much hotter degree. {As Lead generates the most Mercury, fixing the Intellect, Iron contains the most Salt, hardening the Will; and Copper contains the most Sulphur, rendering the Desire Nature hot and intense.} Hence it is that the Mercury of Saturn has not so fresh and so running a life as that which is made out of Gold, because more heat is found in Gold, to which the running life owes its original. Therefore it is likewise to be observed in the inferior world of the little Vulcan {In this case, Man}, in the Augmentation and Transmutation of Metals, what description I have given you of these Three Principles of Saturn concerning their Original, Quality and Complexion.

And every one is to know that no transmutation of any Metal can arise from Saturn by reason of its great cold, except the coagulation of Mercury, because the cold Sulphur of Lead can quench and take away the hot, running Spirit of Quicksilver if the Process be rightly performed; therefore it is rightly observable that the Method be so kept that the Theory may agree with the practice, and concur in a certain measure and concord. Wherefore you must not altogether reject Saturn, not vilify and disparage it, for its nature and virtues are but known to a few. For the Stone of the Philosophers has the first beginning of its heavenly, resplendent Tincture only from this Metal and by the infusion of this Planet is the Key of Fixedness delivered to it through putrefaction; because that out of the yellow there cannot come any red thing except there be first made out of the beginning of the black a white one. {After we have managed to dissolve all of our neuroses or negative habit patterns within our personal consciousness, it is the Saturnine Influence, the "Key of Fixedness," which coagulates Universal Mercury into our personal awareness. When we attain Adeptship and are able to manipulate and transmute physical substance, it is the Saturnine Influence that reintegrates or coagulates the Substance into new forms. This ability lies deep within us at the level of the Divine Soul, Neshamah, which is accessible to us only after all vestiges of petty, separative, selfish desires are but a distant memory within our awareness. For it is not we who employ it, but the King from His Throne.}

{This ends the main body of The Rosicrucian Secrets as presented in Harley Manuscript #6485 from the British Museum Library. What immediately follows this main portion are two letters reputed to have been penned originally by Dr. John Frederick Helvetius. They were not deemed necessary to duplicate here as they have been extant for a number of years under a separate cover titled John Frederick Helvetius' *Golden Calf* (*Which the World Worships and Adores*). Edmonds, WA: Alchemical Press, 1987.}

Gordon James has been a student of the
Western Tradition for over thirty years and
offers lectures and classes in Alchemy
and Qabalah. To arrange a presentation
in your area, forward all inquiries to:

Mr. Gordon James
c/o Holmes Publishing Group
Postal Box 623
Edmonds WA 98020 USA